Rethinking Education and Poverty

RETHINKING EDUCATION AND POVERTY

Edited by
WILLIAM G. TIERNEY

Johns Hopkins University Press
BALTIMORE

© 2015 Johns Hopkins University Press
All rights reserved. Published 2015
Printed in the United States of America on acid-free paper
9 8 7 6 5 4 3 2 1

Johns Hopkins University Press
2715 North Charles Street
Baltimore, Maryland 21218-4363
www.press.jhu.edu

Library of Congress Cataloging-in-Publication Data

Rethinking education and poverty / edited by William G. Tierney.
    pages cm
  Includes bibliographical references and index.
  ISBN 978-1-4214-1767-7 (hardcover : alk. paper) —
ISBN 978-1-4214-1768-4 (pbk. : alk. paper) —
ISBN 978-1-4214-1769-1 (electronic) —
ISBN 1-4214-1767-7 (hardcover : alk. paper) —
ISBN 1-4214-1768-5 (pbk. : alk. paper) —
ISBN 1-4214-1769-3 (electronic)   1. Children with social
disabilities—Education.   2. Poverty.   I. Tierney, William G.
  LC4065.R48 2015
  371.93—dc23   2014047473

A catalog record for this book is available from the British Library.

*Special discounts are available for bulk purchases of this book. For
more information, please contact Special Sales at 410-516-6936 or
specialsales@press.jhu.edu.*

Johns Hopkins University Press uses environmentally friendly book
materials, including recycled text paper that is composed of at least
30 percent post-consumer waste, whenever possible.

Contents

Acknowledgments

I want to thank Lisa D. Garcia, Dorothy Le, Julia Duncheon, and Bryan Rodriguez for meticulously editing evolving versions of the book, and thanks to Monica Raad and Diane Flores for their seemingly effortless administrative support.

Rethinking Education and Poverty

1

Education's Role in the Elimination of Poverty in the Twenty-First Century

WILLIAM G. TIERNEY

The Context of Poverty in the Twenty-First Century

Around the world, children in poverty are much more likely than other children to die before the age of five or to fall seriously ill from communicable or environmental diseases. The poor have a greater likelihood of being poisoned by lead or having worse nutrition and less access to quality health care. They experience higher rates of asthma, heart disease, and mental illness. Low-income communities also have more air pollution and environmental toxicity than middle- and upper-income communities (Carter and Welner 2013; Tierney and Colyar 2009). Children are particularly susceptible; more than sixteen million children live in poverty in the United States (DeNavas-Walt, Proctor, and Smith 2013).

The number of homeless children enrolled in public schools in the United States now exceeds one million. One in forty-five children experiences homelessness in the United States each year. Homeless and foster care youth are among the country's students least likely to attend college, much less graduate from it (Tierney and Hallett 2012). Absence from school can be chronic for homeless youth, and even though schools are supposed to provide services for children who are homeless according to the McKinney-Vento Act, many children let no one know of their status and thus do not receive any benefits. The result is doubly troubling. The lack of attendance at school is a cause for low achievement, and student turnover makes teaching and learning that much more difficult for the school. In this light, housing reform is education reform.

The recession during the first decade of the twenty-first century exacerbated these problems. The Census Bureau (Bishaw 2012) reported in 2010 that forty-six million Americans—nearly one in six—were living below the poverty line of $22,000 for a family of four; this was the greatest number of Americans living in poverty since records were first tallied in 1959. Consider, too, that for a family of four who earn $22,000, their basic needs are twice that amount in over six hundred cities and regions of the United States. Poverty is also increasing in the United States as income disparity continues to rise. The share of elderly single women, for example, living in extreme poverty increased by approximately 20% (2.6% to 3.1%) from 2011 to 2012 (Entmacher et al. 2013). Moreover, inequality in the United States has risen to a level not seen since the 1920s. In the 1960s the income of the richest people was 30% that of the poorest. By the 2000s, this ratio increased to 80% (Gordon 2004).

Children have been particularly impacted by the recession and the concomitant rise in unemployment. According to 2010 Census figures, 6.5 million children under the age of eighteen lived with an unemployed parent (Isaacs 2011). One in five children lived in poverty. In the District of Columbia, Mississippi, and New Mexico, this proportion approached one in three.

These numbers are deeply troubling because each and every number has a face behind it. The problem by the turn of the twenty-first century has been that the United States considers itself exceptional—and we are. Tocqueville (1840) invoked the idea of exceptionalism in his nineteenth-century travels and the idea has stayed with us. He said, "The position of the Americans is therefore quite exceptional" (36). Unfortunately, in the early years of the twenty-first century, we are exceptional in the wrong way. Rather than having more economic mobility, our country has less in comparison to other industrialized countries. True, white middle-class mobility is similar across countries, but the United States "has more low-income persistence and less upward mobility" (Jäntti et al. 2006). Based on analyses that have utilized the National Longitudinal Survey of Youth (U.S. Department of Labor, n.d.), intergenerational mobility is among the lowest for the United States of all of our industrialized counterparts. Moving out of the poorest sector of society has become even harder. If someone is born poor, then the individual has a 40% chance of remaining poor as an adult (Economic Mobility Project 2012).

It is also crucial to understand the impact of concentrated poverty insofar as its impact is especially pernicious with regard to economic mobility, a point that Hogrebe and Tate in their chapter examine in detail. The proportion of high-poverty schools grew by roughly 10% in the first decade of the twenty-first century (Aud et al. 2013). We know that socioeconomic integration matters; some have argued that it trumps extra resources in boosting achievement, and yet we are moving in the opposite direction. As Reardon and colleagues (2012) have noted: "The desegregation of public schools in the 1960s and 1970s was highly visible. [It] led to significant changes in the quality of schooling available to black students" (91). Economic segregation suggested in the 1960s and suggests a half-century later that children in poorer communities will receive an inferior education.

The problem of inadequate education is troubling on many levels. On an individual level, poor children are not afforded equal opportunity. On a societal level, the country needs a better skilled workforce. The best research that exists with regard to the country's future job needs suggests that we need more people moving from high school to college (Carnevale, Jayasundera, and Cheah 2012; Lumina Foundation 2012; Public Policy Institute of California 2013). If the economy is to restart again, more people participating in some form of postsecondary education, even if it is a certificate program, is necessary. More students need to be prepared for high-wage jobs and greater civic engagement.

The United States, however, is losing ground with regard to participation in higher education when we look at comparable countries (Organisation for Economic Cooperation and Development 2009, 2010a, 2010b). Thus, as a country we have lower participation rates and lower economic mobility. A bachelor's degree is likely to earn an individual a significantly larger amount of money than if he or she only has a high school degree (U.S. Census Bureau 2012). As I discuss in chapter 8, not everyone needs a bachelor's degree—but a high school degree is no longer sufficient for the vast majority of our students. And we know from Russell Rumberger's (2011) work on dropouts that those who will fill jobs that only need a high school degree will need better preventive measures that keep them from dropping out. There is a need for better workforce preparation.

We also know that too many students who go on to college are not college-ready. Consider my own state of California. At the California State University (CSU), close to 60% of the students and 26% at the University of California (UC) needed to take a remedial course in writing or math in 2010 (California Legislative Analyst Office 2011; Long and Boatman 2013; National Center for Public Policy and Higher Education 2010). And this is after having taken a college-ready curriculum.

Education's Role in Eliminating Poverty: Substantial or Irrelevant?

Education has long been seen as a way out of poverty, both in the United States and globally. Since Horace Mann's time in the early nineteenth century, the citizens of the United States have assumed that education enhances the economic and social prospects of the individual and improves the larger democratic public sphere. The importance of education has been so critical to the country's well-being that elementary and secondary education has been a free public good, and postsecondary education has been heavily subsidized through grants to public institutions and students. By the late nineteenth century, when a state was admitted to the union it had to demonstrate a commitment to free public education. By the time of the Great Recession, attendance in high school was considered to be commonplace, and by the 1950s the word "dropout" came into the lexicon insofar as high school students were expected to graduate rather than leave (Tierney and Rodriguez 2014).

More recently, others have considered the central importance of education to a democratic nation (Carter and Welner 2013; Tierney 2013). A great deal of research has pointed out how the earnings of individuals and, of consequence, the United States increases when our citizens are able to attend a postsecondary institution (Carnevale, Jayasundera, and Cheah 2012; Tierney and Hentschke 2011), although others have argued that there are too many individuals attending postsecondary institutions (Vedder 2012). Almost no one, however, has sought to roll back the requirement that students attend high school; indeed, states increasingly seek to ensure that all of its students have a high school degree or its equivalent.

Still others have pointed out that education has more than a training function. John Dewey (1902, 1936) is perhaps the country's most well-known spokesperson for the democratic function of education. What Dewey, and Horace Mann before him, argued has been borne out by examinations of participation rates in democracies. Those who go to college are more likely to vote than those who do not, and those who are better educated are more likely to participate in civic association (National Conference on Citizenship 2009). Michele Moses and John Rogers (2013) nicely summarize the democratic purposes of education by stating: "We argue that the democratic purposes of education ought to be centrally invoked in calls for more equitable schooling, and education's role in fostering a more racially integrated, equitable, and democratic society ought to be highlighted in the quest for educational improvement" (214). Thus, the argument has been made on several fronts that insofar as education is "the great equalizer," if one wants greater human capital development and greater civic engagement among the poor, a primary path is through the schoolhouse door.

Some, of course, might suggest that education plays no role in reducing poverty, or that education systems mask inequality and perpetuate cycles of poverty and wealth. These critics will see the failure of schools to move groups out of poverty and to point to a student's success as singular rather than representational. Another interpretation is that meritocracy works—those who work hard will succeed; it is less the educator's efforts and more the individual's success or failure. Others may go further and suggest that the resilience and/or "grit" of the individual, despite inequitable school structures, is what matters. From this vantage point, society is made up of winners and losers, and social structures such as schools are relatively unimportant. Finally, observers of global education might note that education is used as public policy by governments—democratic and authoritarian—in efforts to control, reduce, and manage poverty, but it can also be used as a weapon to marginalize some (i.e., girls, indigenous peoples, rural inhabitants) and privilege others (i.e., boys, the majority racial group, the wealthy).

However, the most pervasive assumption and critique in the twenty-first century is that schools matter and, of related concern, they are failing. Teachers, in particular, have been seen as the culprits. The result has been the charter school movement and efforts such as Teach for America to improve education. The Gates Foundation and President Obama's Secretary of Education, Arne Duncan, have led the reform efforts, but their overall achievements have been limited. Some successes have been accomplished, while a great many goals have not been realized. Richard Rothstein (2013), in a blistering critique of the reform movement, wrote:

> [Duncan] designed and implemented the competitive grant program Race to the Top in which states earned points for expanding the charter school sector, developing data systems to tie teacher performance to student test scores, and making other educational changes. But no points were awarded for providing eyeglasses or food, or for implementing any of the multitude of practical programs that might actually improve disadvantaged youths' school readiness. (69)

The assumption by many is that the criticism of schools and teachers is un-
fair, but nevertheless the movement to end teacher tenure or radically overhaul
teacher education has gained proponents and the support of a great many phi-
lanthropists, foundations, and the government. Furthermore, in 2014 a judge
in California ruled in what came to be known as "the Vergara decision"
(Medina 2014) that many protections for teachers were unconstitutional
because they unduly harmed children in low-income neighborhoods. Such a
critique, of course, assumes that education organizations matter. From this
perspective, if individuals are to be lifted out of poverty then educational opportunity as defined by those who teach must be equal. The assumption is that
a majority of substandard teachers should not be in poor neighborhoods
whereas the wealthier areas only have superior teaching. Teachers should have
to earn tenure over a number of years rather than be granted it upon starting
their jobs, because it protects inferior teachers who overwhelmingly teach in
poor neighborhoods.

An equally compelling argument can be made by those who concur that
equal opportunity is important but deny that all matters revolve around who is
in the classroom teaching the child. Jean Anyon (2014) speaks for many of this
persuasion when she noted: "One of the most important causes of poorly
funded, staffed, and resourced schools is the poverty of the families and neighborhoods in which the schools are located. What is rarely acknowledged, however, is the proactive role of the federal government in maintaining this poverty" (29). From this perspective, education can play a role in creating change,
but macroeconomic policy is what determines whether individuals escape
from poverty. Increasing the minimum wage, creating a full employment
economy, and ending hunger and other such macrosocial policies are examples
of the sorts of issues these critics support. As Berlin (2007) has noted: "There
is a remarkably strong body of research—much of it based on large-scale, well-
implemented, experimental research designs—showing that supplementing
the earnings of parents helps raise families out of poverty and improves the
school performance of young children." Thus, what matters is less the individual teacher in the classroom and more the social and economic structures
of the surrounding neighborhood.

Part of these arguments is a "chicken and egg" scenario. Does less social
poverty create better outcomes for children in schools or do schools create less
social poverty? David Berliner (2013), a longtime critic of the movement to
focus solely on school reforms such as Race to the Top to overcome economic

inequity, has noted: "When the variance in student scores on achievement tests is examined along with the many potential factors that may have contributed to those test scores, school effects account for about 20% of the variation in achievement test scores; teachers are only a part of that constellation of variables associated with 'school'" (5). Out-of-school variables play a much more significant role. These social indicators of poverty intervene in a manner that makes change from the school seem difficult.

At a time when public policy reform seems impossible, the task forward is straightforward, if daunting. On the one hand, as David Grusky (2014) has pointed out, poverty can be eliminated or radically reduced if the government plays a significant role. Thus, a case still needs to be made that the federal government enact policies that move the United States toward full employment, a higher minimum wage, and a resolve that poverty can be eliminated. Such an argument must be made again and again to combat either misinformation and/or pessimism. The country ought to have moved well beyond the idea that either anything we do will not help us lower poverty or that there is a "silver bullet" that if enacted will succeed as no other solution has. That is, many critics, especially those on the right, look back on the country's War on Poverty as a failure, when, in fact, it was not. Hunger was almost eliminated. The desegregation of schools did improve learning outcomes. People were moved out of poverty. To be sure, failures existed and some individuals took advantage of one policy or another as is always to be expected, but the vast majority of efforts worked in a manner that has not been seen since.

Others like to place all of the blame on schools. If schools performed better, then students would learn more and get better jobs, and poverty would be eliminated. And yet we know that children who are hungry perform less well than children who are not; children who have a home do better than children who live on the street; children who have access to mental health services will have higher graduation rates than those who do not. The thought that simply improving teacher quality or any other school-based measure by itself will move everyone out of poverty is as facetious as assuming that nothing is possible.

One further concern is those who reject school reform. The Vergara decision is complex in part because it overlooks the root causes of poverty; and yet, who does not want their child to be taught by a superior teacher? Who believes that it should cost a school district over a quarter of a million dollars to replace an incompetent teacher? Educational organizations can, and must, do better. But rather than rely on one solution, we must try many.

Accordingly, one purpose of this book is not to require a doctrinaire adherence to a single viewpoint. Rather, the intent is to develop a variety of interpretations pertaining to the relationship of education to poverty. Poverty interacts with education through local, national, and international systems of financial markets and the global knowledge economy. The interdependencies embodied in globalization (Tierney 2014) as well as the deep inequities created and maintained by globalization play a substantial role in the lives of marginalized communities and the educational organizations that serve them.

What do we do? How might we attempt to increase the numbers of students going to college? What do we do to ensure that students are college ready?

The Arguments of the Chapters

My intent with this book has been to engage scholars from around the world in considering how research pertaining to education might contribute to alleviating poverty. We seek to understand, for example, how local efforts to alleviate poverty through education interact—or do not—with international assessment efforts (e.g., PISA, TIMMS, IEA). Does geography play a role in determining educational quality? Does the availability of the arts help children improve? Who decides what a child should learn? These are the sorts of questions that the ensuing chapters consider.

The purpose of the book is not to have one point of view on one particular group (e.g., a Marxian analysis of schooling in a low-income neighborhood). Rather, I have sought to present diverse viewpoints that will enable the reader to form his or her own opinion about the interactional effects of education and poverty; these chapters are less in conflict with one another and more orthogonal in order to present a fulsome portrait of what education might accomplish in the reduction of poverty.

In the next chapter, Fernando M. Reimers examines the results of a global movement to expand educational opportunity over the past three decades. He traces the origins of this movement to the creation of the public school, itself a product of another era of globalization, and, more recently, to the creation of the post–World War II global architecture to advance human rights. The results of this movement are paradoxical: while this expansion has been successful in increasing access to basic education and attainment, it has had a relatively limited impact in cultivating the acquisition of skills and dispositions that foster individual autonomy and the capacity for engaged, and critical, citizenship. This paradox contradicts the rationale for the creation of public schools, a byproduct of the philosophical and political movement that invented the idea that people could rule themselves. Reimers discusses various hypotheses for the deficiencies of this global expansion in educational opportunity, examining the implementation challenges faced by education leaders of UNICEF, one of the UN agencies that has most deliberately aligned its education strategy with a human rights approach. Such an examination is particularly pertinent at a time when the world seems smaller due to instantaneous news events of what is happening around the world and movements such as the Arab Spring that first afforded hope that change might come that then turned into despair. Educational opportunity seems to have the potential of playing a dual role. On the one hand, in countries such as Egypt, the hope is that through education a more democratic nation might occur, and on the other, in areas such as the West Bank and Gaza, students might be afforded the same sorts of opportunities that their neighbors have.

In his chapter, Jamal Abedi considers the recent literature on the impact of poverty on student academic achievement, and methodological issues in examining such impact will be discussed. He elaborates on the aforementioned challenges students in poor schools have and then considers possible educational solutions that might be put forward. He also critiques the literature pertaining to these solutions and highlights the challenges with how one studies particular problems and solutions. Among the methodological issues he considers is the need for a comprehensive model for studying the impact of poverty on achievement and a need to establish reliable and valid measures of poverty.

C. Matthew Snipp focuses his work on a specific group that is among the poorest and least educated in the United States—Native Americans. He points out that educational deficits are routinely cited as one of the root causes of the poverty and economic disadvantage endemic to this population. These deficits are, in turn, linked to an argument that asserts that American Indians and Alaska Natives are the victims of a system concerned less with their education and much more with their detribalization. Further, this argument alleges that formal education, as practiced in the United States, is an inherently alien institution that runs deeply against the grain of tribal culture. Snipp acknowledges that there is an element of truth in this argument but argues that it is also true that many American Indian tribes have welcomed and accommodated Euro-American schooling and embraced it as their own. More pointedly, since the late 1960s and early 1970s, American Indian communities have more or less taken control of local schools. The 1976 passage of the American Indian Self-Determination and Educational Assistance Act formalized this control as a matter of public policy. Four decades have passed, and American Indians and Alaska Natives have assumed control of the education of their children, creating colleges and schools for primary and secondary education. Still, Snipp points out, the educational deficits of American Indians and Alaska Natives persist and are as closely connected with poverty and economic disadvantage as they were forty years ago. The chapter concludes by raising some difficult questions that American Indian educators and community leaders need to confront and address.

Zeus Leonardo works from a different perspective in his chapter by addressing three senses of "poverty" in the educational and social science literature. First, there is the common understanding of poverty as having to do with material deprivation. Dilapidated images of inner-city schools or urban centers come to mind. An appropriate perspective that explains this materialist definition of poverty is Marxism. A second perspective on poverty also signifies a deficit perspective, often associated with cultural mindsets and psychological dispositions. Less a materialist explanation, this second definition takes on a cultural content and has found its expression in the "culture of poverty" thesis appropriated from Oscar Lewis, as well as the reactions to it. The third connotation of poverty is ideological and includes "impoverishment." One such example is David Berliner's (2013) use of the term in a *Teachers College Record* article on educators' impoverished views of school reform. This last sense of poverty includes ideologies that have recently been called into question, such as the poverty of whiteness, which, in David Roediger's view, is empty of substance and exists plainly to reinforce racial hierarchy, leading him to pronounce that "whiteness is nothing but false and oppressive."

Mark C. Hogrebe and William F. Tate consider the spatial parameters of poverty by using Missouri as a case analysis. Like other states, Missouri has endeavored to implement an ambitious biotechnology industrial growth plan. Nevertheless, development efforts intended to provide opportunities for indigenous populations are typically uneven. They suggest that the decentralization of blue-collar jobs reduces labor force participation among less-educated individuals. This may be due to limited mobility and high housing costs in suburban areas, which negatively affect low-income workers' pursuit of higher-paying employment opportunities. Although research on this theory has been mixed, it remains relevant, as biotechnology and related industries locate in geographic areas with talented human capital and high-quality educational opportunities.

They then suggest that educators interested in providing young people opportunities within a growing industry such as biotechnology may ask the following question: "How does place influence biology performance in the state?" As Anyon (2014) has noted: "If we were to make a list of the strategies typically called upon to improve education in impoverished urban communities, policies intended to improve curriculum, assessment and pedagogy would all appear. Policies that would place jobs in urban communities would not appear" (92).

Hogrebe and Tate suggest by way of reviewing previous research that one's social location matters in moderating variable relationships in algebra performance. A specific focus of the chapter, then, is to determine if place matters in moderating variable relationships between high school biology performance and educational variables because there are differences on the socioeconomic status (SES) poverty-affluence continuum that shape local contexts. They examined the relationship between variables representing district demographic composition, teaching and financial contexts, student behavior, and biology performance, as measured by a statewide test aggregated at the district level. The investigation explored how these relationships vary across 471 districts within Missouri using spatial mapping. In light of the potential relationship between poverty, place, and academic proficiency, the importance of the proper interpretation of educational indicator systems is argued.

In her chapter, Jeannie Oakes argues that the United States is a society intent on preserving inequality, and victories in the sobering struggle for social equity are mostly partial and fragile. Education is a key site in this struggle. She argues from evidence and decades of efforts to remedy educational inequalities that researchers have crucial, but nontraditional, roles to play in achieving more equitable policy and practice. Her chapter utilizes the following logic: Educational inequality is not going away; at the same time, there are opportunities to make education more equitable. Inequality is kept in place by structures, culture, and individual actions that "effectively maintain inequality," even in the face of workable technical solutions. Inequality is also a moving target. It manifests differently in response to education equity efforts and to changes in the larger ecology of inequality outside of schools.

Education reformers, she argues, are more likely to lessen inequality and make things better if they approach their work with a mix of strong social theory, evidence, and activism. Absent this mix, their efforts will likely be ineffective or, even worse, exacerbate inequality. This equity reform mix requires that equity-minded scholars be public intellectuals and also passionate activists, as well as scrupulous researchers—taking on roles that go far beyond those of scholars working on more technical educational problems. A major challenge is to persuade universities, colleagues, and funders to recognize, reward, and nurture this essential scholarly work.

In my own chapter, I consider what has been defined as "the college readiness agenda." The agenda, I point out, is clear, straightforward, and ambitious. Proponents of college readiness suggest that a "college for all" curriculum needs to be implemented such that all high school students will be able to attend college. Increasingly, the goal is being expanded to suggest that students should not simply be able to enter a college but also graduate from college. Such a goal goes to the heart of a democratic assumption that all individuals are equal.

A conundrum exists, however, in that research shows that a "college for all" high school curriculum increases the likelihood that those who are least academically able will dropout from high school and be mired in poverty. As a result, critics suggest that schools should have a "college and career" readiness agenda where some will go to college and others will be prepared for a career. The problem, of course, is that such an agenda speaks to the idea of tracking, and, if implemented, individuals from a particular race or class will likely be overrepresented in a career track that prevents them from entering the middle class. I analyze these challenges by way of a case study of a school district in California that has implemented "college for all" curricula.

In chapter 9, Lois Weis, Kristin Cipollone, and Amy Stich argue that marked intensification of academic inequalities and outcomes (Reardon 2011) must be understood as linked both to the abandonment of children of poverty and to commensurate intensification of particular kinds of "classwork" among relatively privileged populations. The authors draw upon data from two large-scale, ethnographic investigations: (1) a study of the opportunity structure and linked college application and admissions process in two iconic privileged secondary schools (one private/one public) that serve largely white students and the children of "flexible immigrants" of color, and (2) a comparably conceived study in four urban nonselective secondary schools that evidence over 70%–80% free/reduced-lunch rates and serve a high proportion of African Americans and multigenerational Latinos/as. Data suggests that as the middle-/upper-middle class runs harder and faster, with an eye toward positioning the next generation for class advantage in markedly altered, global economic circumstances (Brown, Lauder, and Ashton 2011), the poor are increasingly left behind. Data will leverage discussion and analysis of "effectively maintained inequality" and linked intensification of poverty and privilege under conditions of educational massification.

Shirley Brice Heath looks at poverty from a different perspective than those who focus on economic inequality. She argues that aside from the fulfillment of basic needs, such as food, shelter, and consistent love, perhaps the greatest absence in the lives of children growing up in poverty is vibrant, fluent, language interaction. Working-poor parents, as well as those living without paid employment, have little time or inclination for talking with children about experiences beyond the here and now of their own worlds. Undertaking an art project at the kitchen table, in the backyard, or in honor of a grandparent—with planning and assessment of the project along the way—takes time, resources, and a spirit of creativity. She suggests that much of what poverty does is suck energy, invention, hope, and a sense of renewal out of children and their parents.

Her chapter draws from data collected in several modern economies to illustrate the following: (1) how public institutions, such as museums and theatres, create ways to engage young people and parents living in poverty in the creative arts and the ongoing contexts of the language of projects and (2) how these institutions are evolving to see themselves as learning environments that have a responsibility to "the public" when this expression means *all the public* and not simply the wealthy. Data suggests that these shifts of focus also bring about a "cultural commons" in which children and young people gain experiences generally associated with the middle-/upper-middle class, such as advanced coursework in the literary, visual, and dramatic arts, as well as the sciences.

In the penultimate chapter, Simon Marginson returns to the international focus that Reimers initiated at the start of the book. He focuses on the role of higher education and science systems as nations evolve out of macropoverty, with specific attention to the miracle of accelerated development in the Sinic societies of East Asia (Japan, South Korea, Singapore, Taiwan, and China). Are education and science conditions or products of accelerated development? Marginson explores factors that mediate relationships between higher education, technological change, productivity, and innovation in East Asia. In doing so, he argues that, in East Asia, the Sinic state tradition and political culture, in addition to Confucian educational cultivation in the home, are key elements, and that this is suggestive for development in other country sites yet sets some limits on the potential for transfer of the post-Confucian model.

For the conclusion, Professors St. John and Bowman return to the issues raised here and argue that increasing inequality is a common pattern across nations promoting educational advancement as a means of stimulating economic development. Although they summarize and analyze the chapters, their primary focus is one of policy—what are the trajectories of policy and how do they mirror political realities in the country as opposed to the research that has been outlined in the preceding chapters? They consider what needs to take place if the authors' arguments are believable. In effect, they are the policy arm of what Oakes suggests: analyses cannot simply be theoretical or methodological, but we also need to think about what might be done if a particular author argues for one position or another.

Our intent for readers by the time they have arrived at the book's conclusion is neither to provoke optimism that the solutions are at hand, as if we have offered a cookbook for reform, nor despair that there is nothing that can be done. Underlying all of the chapters is a sense that education is a social organization embedded in national structures during a period of global upheaval—whether that upheaval occurs because of climate change in Bangladesh, the Arab Spring in Libya, or economic compression in Greece. We reject the assumption that schools, colleges, and universities cannot accomplish any reforms, but we also are decidedly more circumspect than those who assume that one reform or another will fix what ails the country in its goal to reduce poverty. Overriding all of the chapters is the assumption that in a democratic nation, education can provide opportunity if the country has structures that enable it to happen.

REFERENCES

Anyon, Jean. 2014. *Radical Possibilities: Public Policy, Urban Education, and a New Social Movement*. 2nd edition. New York: Routledge.
Aud, Susan, Sidney Wilkinson-Flicker, Paul Kristapovich, Amy Rathbun, Xiaolei Wang, and Jijun Zhang. 2013. *The Condition of Education 2013* (NCES 2013-037). Washington, DC: U.S. Department of Education, Institute of Education Sciences.
Berlin, Gordon. 2007. "Remarks." National Summit on America's Children, May 22. http://www.mdrc.org/publication/investing-parents-invest-children.
Berliner, David C. 2013. "Effects of Inequality and Poverty vs. Teachers and Schooling on America's Youth." *Teachers College Record* 115 (12): 1–26.

Bishaw, Alemayehu. 2012. *Poverty: 2010 and 2011 (American Community Survey Briefs)*. Washington, DC: U.S. Census Bureau.

Brown, Phillip, Hugh Lauder, and David Ashton. 2011. *The Global Auction: The Broken Promises of Education, Jobs, and Incomes*. New York: Oxford University Press.

California Legislative Analyst Office. 2011. *Higher Education: Answers to Frequently Asked Questions. Are Entering Freshmen Prepared for College-Level Work?* Sacramento, CA: Author. http://www.lao.ca.gov/sections/higher_ed/FAQs/Higher_Education_Issue_02.pdf.

Carnevale, Anthony P., Tamara Jayasundera, and Ban Cheah. 2012. *The College Advantage: Weathering the Economic Storm*. Washington, DC: Georgetown Center for Workforce and Economy.

Carter, Prudence L., and Kevin G. Welner, eds. 2013. *Closing the Opportunity Gap: What America Must Do to Give Every Child an Even Chance*. New York: Oxford University Press.

DeNavas-Walt, Carmen, Bernadette D. Proctor, and Jessica C. Smith. 2013. *Income, Poverty, and Health Insurance Coverage in the United States: 2012*. Washington, DC: U.S. Census Bureau.

Dewey, John. 1902. "Academic Freedom." *Educational Review* 23:1–14.

———. 1936. "The Social Significance of Academic Freedom." *Social Frontier* 2:165–67.

Economic Mobility Project. 2012. *Pursuing the American Dream: Economic Mobility among Generations*. Washington, DC: Pew Charitable Trusts, Economic Mobility Project.

Entmacher, Joan, Katherine Gallagher Robbins, Julie Vogtman, and Lauren Frohlich. 2013. *Insecure & Unequal: Poverty and Income among Women and Families, 2000–2012*. Washington, DC: National Women's Law Center.

Gordon, David. 2004. *Eradicating Poverty in the 21st Century: When Will Social Justice Be Done?* Bristol, UK: Townsend Centre for International Poverty Research. http://www.bris.ac.uk/poverty/downloads/childpoverty/Inaugural%20Lecture%20Transcript%2018.10.041.pdf.

Grusky, David. B. 2014. "4 Myths about Poverty." *The Chronicle of Higher Education*, February 24.

Isaacs, Julia B. 2011. *The Recession's Ongoing Impact on America's Children: Indicators of Children's Economic Well-Being through 2011*. Washington, DC: Brookings Institution.

Jäntti, Markus, Bernt Bratsberg, Knut Røed, Oddbjørn Raaum, Robin Naylor, Eva Österbacka, Anders Björklund, and Tor Eriksson. 2006. *American Exceptionalism in a New Light: A Comparison of Intergenerational Earnings Mobility in the Nordic Countries, the United Kingdom, and the United States* (IZA Discussion Paper No. 1938). Bonn, Germany: Institute for the Study of Labor.

Long, Bridget Terry, and Angela Boatman. 2013. "The Role of Remediation and Developmental Courses in Access and Persistence." In *The State of College Access and Completion: Improving College Success for Students from Underrepresented Groups*, edited by Anthony Jones and Laura Perna, 77–95. New York: Routledge Books.

Lumina Foundation. 2012. *A Stronger Nation through Higher Education*. Indianapolis, IN: Author.

Medina, Jennifer. 2014. "Judge Rejects Teacher Tenure for California." *New York Times*, June 10.

Moses, Michele S., and John Rogers. 2013. "Enhancing a Nation's Democracy through Equitable Schools." In *Closing the Opportunity Gap: What America Must Do to Give Every Child an Even Chance*, edited by Prudence L. Carter and Kevin G. Welner, 207–16. New York: Oxford University Press.

National Center for Public Policy and Higher Education. 2010. *Beyond the Rhetoric Improving College Readiness through Coherent State Policy*. San Jose, CA: Author.

National Conference on Citizenship. 2009. *2009 Civic Health Index*. Washington, DC: Author.

Organisation for Economic Co-operation and Development. 2009. "Tertiary Level Educational Attainment for Age Group 25–64." In *OECD Factbook 2009*. Paris: Author. doi:10.1787/20755120-2009-table3.

———. 2010a. "Tertiary Education Entry Rates." In *OECD Factbook 2010*. Paris: Author. doi:10.1787/20755120-2010-table2.

———. 2010b. "Tertiary Education Graduation Rates." In *OECD Factbook 2010*. Paris: Author. doi:10.1787/20755120-2010-table1.

Public Policy Institute of California. 2013. *California 2025: Planning for a Better Future*. San Francisco: Author.

Reardon, Sean F. 2011. "The Widening Academic Achievement Gap between the Rich and the Poor: New Evidence and Possible Explanations." In *Whither Opportunity? Rising Inequality, Schools, and Children's Life Chances*, edited by Greg J. Duncan and Richard J. Murnane, 91–116. New York: Russell Sage Foundation.

Reardon, Sean F., Elena Tej Grewel, Demetra Kalogrides, and Erica Greenberg. 2012. "Brown Fades: The End of Court-Ordered School Desegregation and the Resegregation of American Public Schools." *Journal of Policy Analysis and Management* 31:876–904.

Rothstein, Richard. 2013. "Why Children from Lower Socioeconomic Classes, on Average, Have Lower Academic Achievement Than Middle-Class Children." In *Closing the Opportunity Gap: What America Must Do to Give Every Child an Even Chance*, edited by Prudence L. Carter and Kevin G. Welner, 61–74. New York: Oxford University Press.

Rumberger, Russell W. 2011. *Dropping Out: Why Students Drop Out of High School and What Can Be Done about It*. Cambridge, MA: Harvard University Press.

Tierney, William G. 2013. "2013 AERA Presidential Address—Beyond the Ivory Tower: The Role of the Intellectual in Eliminating Poverty." *Educational Researcher* 42 (6): 295–303.

———. 2014. "The Disruptive Future of Higher Education." In *Postsecondary Play: The Role of Games and Social Media in Higher Education*, edited by William G. Tierney, Zoë B. Corwin, Tracy Fullerton, and Giselle Ragusa, 21–44. Baltimore: Johns Hopkins University Press.

Tierney, William G., and Julia E. Colyar, eds. 2009. *Urban High School Students and the Challenge of Access: Many Routes, Difficult Paths*, revised ed. New York: Peter Lang.

Tierney, William G., and Ronald E. Hallett. 2012. "Homeless Youth and Educational Policy: A Case Study of Urban Youth in a Metropolitan Area." In "Living on the Boundaries: Urban Marginality in National and International Contexts," *Advances in Education in Diverse Communities: Research Policy and Praxis, Vol. 8*, edited by Carol Camp Yeakey, 49–78. Oxford, UK: Emerald Group Publishing Limited.

Tierney, William G., and Guilbert Hentschke, eds. 2011. *Making It Happen: Increasing Access and Attainment in California Higher Education, the Role of Private Postsecondary Providers*. La Jolla, CA: National University System Institute for Policy Research.

Tierney, William G., and Bryan A. Rodriguez, eds. 2014. *The Future of Higher Education in California: Getting In and Getting Through—Problems and Solutions*. Los Angeles: Pullias Center for Higher Education.

Tocqueville, Alexis de. 1840. *Democracy in America*. Translated by Henry Reeve. New York: J. & H. G. Langley.

U.S. Census Bureau. 2012. *Back to School: 2012–2013.* Washington, DC: Author.
http://www.census.gov/newsroom/releases/pdf/cb12ff-15_backtoschool.pdf.
U.S. Department of Labor. n.d. *National Longitudinal Survey of Youth 1997 (NLSY97).*
Washington, DC: Author. http://www.bls.gov/nls/nlsy97.htm.
Vedder, Richard. 2012. *Twelve Inconvenient Truths about American Higher Education.*
Washington, DC: Center for College Affordability and Productivity.

2

Educating the Children of the Poor

A Paradoxical Global Movement

FERNANDO M. REIMERS

In this chapter, I discuss the relationship between education and poverty globally in order to shed light on the nature of the relationship between schools and society and in particular on the question of whether schools can alter social organization and structure or whether they can merely reproduce them. To address this theoretical issue, I examine the relationship between educational opportunity and poverty around the world over recent decades and discuss the role of education policies as they influence that relationship.

From Educating Elites to Education for All

The idea that the "poor," those occupying the most subordinate roles in social hierarchies—the large masses—could have access to formal education is, in historical perspective, relatively recent. For most of human history, the task of providing children with opportunities to develop specialized skills, such as literacy, numeracy, or more advanced knowledge, was reserved for children born into privileged circumstances, who often gained such opportunities from tutors or private schools. Significant milestones in advancing the idea that the poor should be schooled include the notion that educating all persons would reduce conflict, advanced by Jan Amos Comenius, a Moravian minister who lived in the seventeenth century. The ideas of Enlightenment-era philosophers about the fundamental equality of all persons and the power of reason and science to improve society, developments of educational models such as the *Lancasterian system for the education of the poor*, and various efforts of religious orders to educate poor children were also instrumental in the thought and movement toward more accessible education. But it was only with the creation of public education systems committed to educating all children—initially in Prussia, subsequently in some European republics in the 1800s, and later in the United States and other newly independent republics in the Americas—that an institutional infrastructure was created to materialize the idea that the "poor" should be schooled. Certainly, the inclusion of subordinate groups in schools was a process spanning over decades, if not centuries, a result of the work of social activists and other progressive reformers who challenged practices, norms, and, on occasion, legislation when those did not fully support the educational inclusion of all students.

In the United States, for example, such struggles for educational inclusion began with the ideas of Thomas Paine and Thomas Jefferson in the eighteenth century, took force with the creation of the Common School and the advocacy of Horace Mann in Massachusetts in the mid-1800s, and extended throughout most of the 1900s with important contributions by the women's movement and the peace movement by activists such as Jane Addams, who effectively advocated in favor of the inclusion of poor and immigrant children in the early 1900s. Subsequently, the civil rights movement advocated for the educational opportunities of African Americans and other ethnic minorities, successfully impacting a series of court rulings that challenged the institutionalized educational segregation and marginalization that African Americans had endured since being forcibly brought to the American colonies as slaves. In the 1960s, a series of progressive policies from the executive and legislative branches of government, initiated under the administration of Lyndon B. Johnson, continued to advance the expansion of educational opportunity.

Globally, the incorporation of education as one of the human rights included in the Universal Declaration in 1948 provided direction to efforts by the United Nations (UN) to mobilize governments into expanding access to fundamental education to all children, including the poor. Global educational expansion, particularly in the developing world where most children and youth live, is therefore largely the result of efforts beginning in the second half of the twentieth century. During the 1980s, expansion had slowed down considerably as a result of limitations of the approaches used to intensify use of facilities and teachers during the previous decades, such as the creation of double- and triple-shift schools or multigraded schools in rural areas, and also as a result of the economic adjustment programs that were put in place by many governments in the developing world as a result of the debt crisis.

In 1990 many governments around the world and the leading international development institutions convened a global education conference, the Education for All conference, in Jomtien, Thailand, to review the state of educational opportunity and recommit to a program of reforms that would continue to improve access and quality of basic education by the end of the century. A framework for action agreed at this conference included a commitment to reach, by the year 2000, universal access to learning, better education equity, and greater emphasis on learning outcomes and to broaden the means and the scope of basic education, enhancing the environment for learning and emphasis on partnerships as a way to reach these goals. Ten years later, government and international development representatives met again in Dakar, Senegal, at a conference to take stock of the Education for All (EFA) movement. It was obvious that the goals agreed upon in Jomtien had not been achieved, so the Dakar Framework for Action recommitted to these goals, this time identifying measurable objectives. The goals included:

1. Expand early childhood care and education.
2. Provide free and compulsory primary education for all.
3. Promote learning and life skills for young people and adults.
4. Increase adult literacy by 50%.
5. Achieve gender parity by 2005 and gender equality by 2015.
6. Improve the quality of education.

UNESCO (United Nations Educational, Scientific and Cultural Organization), the United Nations's specialized agency to advance the right of education, undertook the responsibility to periodically assess progress toward these goals, developing an Education for All Development Index and producing an annual Monitoring Report. The indicators measured include net enrollment rates in primary education, adult literacy rates, gender parity indexes for primary and secondary enrollment and for adult literacy, and completion of grade 5 for students who begin primary school.

A related global effort to reduce poverty, the Millennium Development Goals (MDGs), which also launched in the year 2000, focuses on eight goals, two of which include specific education goals. The MDGs are to reduce extreme poverty and hunger by half; achieve universal primary education; promote gender equality and empower women; reduce child mortality; improve maternal health; combat HIV/AIDS, malaria, and other diseases; ensure environmental sustainability; and develop a global partnership for development.

At present, the education goals agreed on in the Dakar EFA and the MDG frameworks are the operational definition of the global commitment to educating all children. Note that the goals emphasize access to education, completion of a certain number of years of education, and parity between girls and boys. To the extent that global education has, in recent cases, focused also on quality has meant ensuring greater access to the opportunity to gain basic literacies, essentially to improve the efficiency of schools in attaining their basic goals. These goals do not focus on the content of what should be learned in education, the skills and knowledge that should be gained in school, or how those skills should empower children. In this sense, these goals are devoid of the clear purposes that undergird earlier narratives about educating the poor, a topic I will return to later.

What Can Education Do about Poverty?

The case for educating all children, and therefore also the children of the poor, was predicated on the assumption that the skills and knowledge gained in school might benefit them. The kinds of benefits that education was supposed to provide have been variously conceived over time. For Comenius, the first person on record to make the case for universal education, the misery that education could help overcome was the misery of violence and conflict that resulted from intolerance. He expected that education would empower people with the skills to work out their differences in peaceful ways. During the times of Comenius, this meant principally religious intolerance. This idea is also central to the inclusion of education as a human right in the Universal Declaration. The thirty articles included in the declaration were thought to be instrumental in securing peace and stability in the world, to prevent the return to the violence, destruction, and death of the previous two world wars. These ideas were also central to the creation of UNESCO as reflected in the preamble of UNESCO's constitution: "since wars begin in the minds of men . . . it is in the minds of men that the defences of peace must be built."

The philosophers of the Enlightenment expected broader benefits from education. The Enlightenment, a social project that replaced the aspiration of salvation with the aspiration of reducing human suffering as a result of the work of ordinary people to improve themselves and their societies, placed great hope in the power of human intellect and on reason and knowledge, particularly knowledge based on science. Enlightenment philosophers also postulated that through deliberation in the public sphere ordinary people would find ways to work together toward improvement of their communities. Education was therefore both a means of self-improvement, which would translate into benefits to the individual, as well as a means of collaboration toward collective organization and improvement, translating into benefits to the society. The effects of educational opportunity, as it extended to individuals who had previously been denied it, would be material as well as civic, individual, and collective. It was Adam Smith, the famous figure of the Scottish Enlightenment, who first coined the term "human capital" to characterize the acquired abilities and talents that would return economic benefits to individuals and society in making them more productive, and Jean Jacques Rousseau, a seminal Swiss Enlightenment philosopher, who saw education as central to enabling individuals to accept a social contract. Benjamin Franklin, an American Enlightenment thinker, led the creation of universities because he saw them as part and parcel of preparing the inhabitants of the new political experiment for self-rule. Thomas Jefferson sketched a system of public education for males and saw universities also as indispensable to the new republic.

For almost a century, however, the expansion of the first systems of public education was largely predicated on civic purposes. Horace Mann, the first secretary of education of Massachusetts, advocated for the Common School largely in order to help assimilate immigrants and support the socialization of people from different walks of life into a common language and set of customs to prepare them for citizenship. It was the development of the concept of human capital in the 1950s that expanded the civic and political aims of education to include the expectation that education could also help people improve their material condition in life. In the United States during the 1960s, education was framed in the public imagination as part of the "war on poverty," as a means to help the poor become non-poor. Similar claims were advanced as part of the global efforts coordinated by the United Nations during the three decades of greater educational expansion, following the adoption of education as a human right, in part as a result of the development of the theory of human capital.

Can Education Empower the Children of the Poor?

What does it mean to empower the poor? To the philosophers of the Enlightenment, who were convinced that ordinary people could improve their lives and reduce human suffering aided by their reason and the power of scientific knowledge, autonomy, agency, and skill were the central ingredients of social transformation. To the extent that public education served this project of self-government, the aims of education would be to cultivate human reason, autonomy, and agency. It is no accident that literacy is one of the universal goals of public education. Not only does literacy have instrumental value in providing access to written texts and enabling self-study, it also allows individuals the ability to enter in direct dialogue with texts, including sacred texts, without intermediaries, and to form their own views resulting from such dialogue. Literacy is, in this way, a foundation of autonomous thinking. There are two ways in which education empowers any person, including the poor. The first is that access to knowledge and the development of the habits of mind, skills, and dispositions that result from education are in themselves worthy. Being able to read, write, appreciate a work of art, or create art is humanizing even if these abilities have no further consequence. In addition, because these skills enable communication with others and organization and transactions with others, they have also instrumental value; they are means to other ends. These ends can be private, as when gaining access to knowledge about how to best take care of one's health leads us to adopt habits that indeed improve our health. They can benefit others, as when learning how to negotiate our differences with others in peaceful ways reduces the pain we cause others (i.e., Comenius's aspiration), or they can be communal or social, as when learning the legal framework and processes leads us to live within the rule of law of the social contract (i.e., Rousseau's view of one of the ends of education).

Over time, a robust body of knowledge developed in various disciplines, documenting beneficial effects of education directly to the individuals who are educated and indirectly to those influenced by such individuals (e.g., their children, families, or communities), the productive organizations to which they contribute, or their societies. The latest Global Education Monitoring Report, for example, an annual effort of UNESCO to document the advancements of the Education for All movement, summarizes the effects of education in several dimensions. The report provides ample evidence that people with more education are advantaged in a number of dimensions relative to those with less education. They are less likely to be poor, more likely to earn higher wages ("Globally, one year of school increases earnings by 10%, on average" UNESCO 2014, 13), more likely to be more productive for those working in the informal sector, more likely to start a business, more likely to draw profits from the business, and more likely to have children who are better educated. Countries with greater equality in educational attainment of the population have higher rates of growth (14). Educated people are also healthier, and their children are also more likely to survive and be better nourished and healthier. People with more education understand political processes better and are more likely to participate in politics, support democracy, and be tolerant of differences and less tolerant of corruption (17–18).

The evidence documenting the effects of education is limited in several ways in making casual claims about its impacts on poverty. First, much of this evidence is essentially correlational in nature. Even when statistical controls are used, the basic analytic framework compares groups with different levels of education and assumes that the groups compared are essentially identical in the characteristics that are not observed and included in the analysis. Furthermore, this approach assumes that the benefits of education are invariant across income groups, that is, that the same benefits that, say, middle-class children derive from accessing a particular education level can be expected to accrue also to poor children as they gain access to that level. This approach also assumes that the observed benefits of education are relatively independent of context or time, that is, that the observed differences in earnings, for instance, associated with different education levels in one region or in one particular period of time might be expected in a different region or in the future. There are obvious limitations to such assumptions. People with additional education may be more likely to create their own businesses, but for those who work in contexts where there are barriers to business creation, they may be unable to reap the economic benefits of education. Similarly, people with additional education may be more productive in their jobs, but if there are no jobs available, those benefits will remain unrealized. The same goes for civic and political consequences of education. People with additional education may be more vocal, more supportive of democracy, or even more critical of corrupt governments, but in nations where those behaviors are negatively sanctioned by governments, they may be unable to translate their gained knowledge and understanding into visible change. It is possible that the changes that education produces in individuals may, over time and as a critical mass of individuals experiences those changes, translate into some form of collective action that eventually leads to social change. For instance, as more individuals become more tolerant because of their higher levels of education, they may, collectively, change the cultural and institutional norms to make them more tolerant. There is less evidence available that demonstrates how change at the individual level translates into this kind of aggregate social or cultural change, although some political scientists have speculated that one of the reasons political and economic elites do not favor reforms that more evidently empower the poor is because they fear the social pressures that would result from such empowerment (Tendler 2002).

Furthermore, there is another limitation with these analyses of the benefits of education. Benefits are generally assessed in relative terms, not with respect to a normative criterion. For instance, in comparing the income, health, tolerance, or political participation of those who have achieved a particular level of education with those who have less education, the empirical evidence documents whether there are differences in those outcomes of interest, not whether the benefit attained is sufficient or adequate by some normative criterion. For example, a study of a cross-national survey of political attitudes showed that adults with higher levels of education are more likely to support democracy and to be more tolerant of people of a different race and religion, those who speak a different language, immigrants, homosexuals, and people with AIDS (Chzhen 2013). However, the magnitude of these differences varied greatly by region. This analysis shows that the probability that a person in East Asia will express intolerance toward people of a different race is 0.3 for those with incomplete primary education, compared to 0.2 for those with complete primary education. This difference suggests that those with more education are more tolerant, but is the fact that 20% of the people are racially intolerant adequate or sufficient for life without conflict in a racially diverse democracy? Similarly, the probability that a person with complete primary education will express intolerance toward homosexuals in Latin America is 0.4, compared to 0.25 for those with complete secondary education and 0.2 for those with university education, suggesting that the most educated are more tolerant. But is the fact that 20% of the university graduates discriminate against those who do not share their sexual identity adequate and sufficient to democratic life? To illustrate how these effects of education vary by context, in Europe and Central Asia the probability of expressing intolerance toward homosexuals is 0.8 for those with complete primary education, compared to 0.7 for university graduates, which are much higher levels of intolerance than in Latin America (Chzhen 2013). The evidence on the benefits of education in several dimensions is thus limited to marginal benefits, not to helping individuals reach a minimum or absolute threshold of benefit.

Despite evidence that education can empower people in various ways, and despite the fact that the educational opportunities available to the children of the poor have expanded as a result of the Global Education for All movement over the last six decades, there is much more schools can do to empower the children of the poor. The educational opportunities available to such children are limited not just because some of them do not go to school or learn to read poorly; they are limited because the curriculum offered to them is itself limited and too narrow. It speaks to a conception of human talent that is a very dim reflection of the aspirations of the enlightenment for public education. Their experiences in school are not aligned with the goal of developing skills, autonomy, or agency; on the contrary, some of these experiences are toxic and convey to students messages that diminish their capacity for independent thinking and for the kind of empowerment that would enable them to improve themselves and work with others to improve their communities. We know that children need to learn much more than how to read to take charge of their destinies, and yet many education systems do little more than focus on improving the quality of literacy instruction, and perhaps numeracy. In some systems, the social and emotional climate is toxic, exposing some or all students to abuse and humiliation from peers or teachers.

A recent report of the National Research Council (Pellegrino and Hilton 2012) synthesizing available scientific research on the human qualities that have beneficial consequences to individuals and communities identifies them as belonging in three categories: cognitive, interpersonal, and intrapersonal. Cognitive skills include processing (critical thinking, problem solving, analysis, logical reasoning, interpretation, decision making, and executive functioning), knowledge (literacy and communications, active listening, knowledge of the disciplines, ability to use evidence, and digital literacy), and creativity and innovation. Interpersonal skills include collaborative group skills (communication, collaboration, teamwork, cooperation, coordination, interpersonal skills, empathy, perspective taking, trust, service orientation, conflict resolution, and negotiation) and leadership (responsibility, assertive communication, self-presentation, and social influence). Intrapersonal skills include intellectual openness (flexibility, adaptability, artistic and cultural appreciation, personal and social responsibility, intercultural competency, appreciation for diversity, adaptability, capacity for lifelong learning, and intellectual interest and curiosity), work ethic and responsibility (initiative, self-direction, responsibility, perseverance, productivity, persistence, self-regulation, metacognitive skills, reflexive skills, professionalism, ethics, integrity, citizenship, and work orientation), and self-efficacy (self-regulation, and physical and mental health).

Most education systems are not aligned to help students gain a wide range of those skills. The vast majority emphasize some of the skills included under cognitive skills, largely knowledge and cognitive processing.

To assess the extent to which some of these skills were intended goals of education systems around the world, I surveyed a small group of senior education officers working for UNICEF, a UN agency involved in advancing educational opportunities for the most marginalized children around the world. The results are presented in table 2.1. Consistent with the available global figures, taking into account that these officers focused on the most marginalized children, most of them think that all or most students gain initial access. The percentage who report that students gain initial literacy drops considerably, from 50%, who agree to a great extent that most children have initial access, to 25%, who report that most students gain early literacy. A very large percentage do not think that students gain knowledge in schools, and even less think that students learn to use knowledge to solve problems or be innovative and creative. The majority thinks that schools do not offer students the opportunity to gain self-knowledge, develop character, work with others, or be tolerant of those who are different. Many of them have very negative views of the pedagogical efficacy of teachers or the emotional climate teachers create in classrooms.

To sum up, available evidence, albeit limited, suggests that education can be beneficial in a number of dimensions to individuals and the communities to which they contribute. The theoretical merit for such benefits is easy to see; educated individuals can cultivate qualities that transform them into people with the agency and qualities that the project of the enlightenment posed as necessary for self-rule. Available evidence suggests that it is probably the case that those who are most educated are also those with more agency, knowledge, skills, and health, with all the qualities that allow them to become self-authoring individuals and contributing members of their communities. We have less evidence demonstrating that the education the children of the poor receive actually empowers them in those ways, which leads us to examine what kind of educational opportunities are available to those children.

Poverty and Educational Opportunity

The Global Education for All movement has developed in three distinct stages: (1) the efforts of nation states to educate all children resulting from the creation of the public school, (2) the expansion of those efforts to most of the world resulting from the advocacy of the United Nations based on the recognition of education as a human right in 1946, and (3) the most recent commitment to global education resulting from the Education for All framework

Table 2.1 Views of a sample of UNICEF education officers based in field offices in developing countries

Statement	Not at all (%)	Not much (%)	To some extent (%)	To a great extent (%)	Total
All or most students gain initial access to school	8	18	24	50	38
All or most students gain early literacy in the first grades of school	8	36	31	25	36
All or most students progress through school at the expected rate	8	39	31	22	36
All or most students finish primary school	8	22	35	35	37
All or most students transition to secondary school	3	42	34	21	38
All or most students finish secondary school	11	46	38	5	37
Schools offer students the opportunity to gain knowledge	0	38	50	12	34
Schools offer students the opportunity to learn to use knowledge to solve problems	12	56	32	0	34
Schools offer students the opportunity to learn to innovate and be creative	14	64	22	0	36
Schools offer students the opportunity to gain self-knowledge and develop character	9	66	26	0	35
Schools offer students the opportunity to learn to work with others productively	6	63	31	0	35
Schools offer students the opportunity to learn to be tolerant and accepting of those who are different	6	47	44	3	32
Teachers use effective pedagogies	6	76	18	0	33
Teachers know the subject matter they teach	0	33	61	6	33
Teachers manage classes effectively	6	52	42	0	31
Teachers create a positive emotional climate in classrooms	3	63	33	0	30
Curriculum is relevant to the context where students live	9	43	46	3	35
Girls and boys have similar educational opportunities to receive a quality education	5	19	51	24	37
Disparities in the quality of education are an important barrier to achieve equality of educational opportunity	3	6	25	67	36

Source: Survey administered by the author to UNICEF Education Officers participating in the Education Leadership Development Program at Harvard University.

developed at Jomtien in 1990, perfected in Dakar in 2000, and reflected also in the 2000 Millennium Development Goals efforts, unquestionably transforming the structure of educational opportunity around the world. Indeed this movement is reflected in the creation of an educational architecture and the public school systems by national governments, with support from the international development commitment. Examined from a historical perspective, this movement is one of the most remarkable achievements of humanity. Seventy years ago, before education was recognized as a human right in the Universal Declaration, the vast majority of the world's children did not have the opportunity to set foot in a school, and today they do. Around the world, the fact that most people today have attained greater levels of education than their parents is testament to the ongoing expansion in educational aspirations and opportunity that resulted from this movement and the powerful idea that all persons, including the poor, should be educated.

Resulting from this global educational expansion, the children of the poor today have more opportunity to begin elementary education and in many places to gain knowledge and skills as a result of spending a portion of their lives in schools. In 2011, 137 million children enrolled in the first grade of primary school, representing 98% of the children of the relevant age to begin school in each country. This rate of initial access to school is 99% in the developed countries and 98% in the developing world, a remarkable fact given that the developing world accounts for 89% of the total number of children. On average, those children who begin school in the developing world will spend 11 years in school, compared to 16.4 years in school in the developed world. The figures are very similar for girls and boys. In the developing world, girls have a school life expectancy of 10.8 years, whereas boys can expect to spend 11.3 years in school (UNESCO 2014, 344–49). Of all children of primary school-going age, 90% were enrolled in school in the developing world, compared to 98% in the developed world. In the developing world, net enrollment rates were 89% for girls, compared to 91% for boys (355).

Despite this remarkable progress, there are still many children who are not enrolled in school, including some who never enroll and others who enroll but drop out before they complete a basic education. Disproportionately, those children who do not have access to education or drop out before completing a basic education are the children of the poor and marginalized; they are often children who suffer multiple forms of marginalization. Notwithstanding the large number of children in school, 57 million children are not enrolled in primary school, and 55 million of those children live in the developing world. Of the children not in school, 54% are girls. About half of these children live in conflict-affected regions. Only 75% of those children who enroll in first grade complete primary school. Only half of the countries in the world have achieved universal primary education, but 70% have achieved gender parity, meaning they have equal numbers of boys and girls enrolled in primary education. There are gross disparities in the completion of lower secondary, with 69 million adolescents out of school, a 31% decline from 1999. Of the 69 million adolescents out of school, 67 million live in the developing world.

Just as important, even for many of the children who have gained access to school, there is evidence that many of these children do not learn very much in school. The task of systematically assessing basic literacies among students is relatively recent and not yet a common practice in most countries. It was only in the late 1960s that the concept of educational opportunity in the United States, Sweden, and other countries began to include opportunity to learn and not just to enroll in school. The systematic measurement of student learning is even more recent and focuses on a narrow range of cognitive skills, typically literacy, numeracy, and, on occasion, science. The first international comparative studies, conducted by the International Association for the Evaluation of Educational Achievement, initially included only a few countries dated also from the 1960s. Similar cross-national efforts conducted by the Organisation for Economic Co-operation and Development (OECD) began only in the year 2000. For most of the developing world, regular assessments of student learning are also relatively recent. For the Education for All movement, the latest Global Education Monitoring Report indicates that there is just too limited information globally to determine whether students are learning what is intended in school or what kind of learning achievement gaps exist in various countries. There are still 774 million adults who cannot read, and two-thirds of them are women. At the preschool level, only 50% of children have access to preschool, although this figure is 85% in the developed world and 45% in the developing world (UNESCO 2014, 338).

Indicative of how government efforts matter, however, and also of how international collaboration influences and supports government efforts, between 1999 and 2011, the most recent period of the Global Education for All movement, the number of children out of school was cut in half, and primary net enrollment in the developing world increased from 82% to 90% (UNESCO 2014, 355). In all indicators reflecting the Global Education for All goals, there has been progress. But, again, relative progress is different from reaching targets in an absolute way. The latest UNESCO report on the progress made with the Education for All goals, however, indicates that not a single one of them will be achieved by the intended deadline of 2015 (15).

To sum up, while the Global Movement for Universal Education has fundamentally expanded educational opportunity in ways that give most children the opportunity to enroll in school, this is not to say, by any means, that the educational playing field has been leveled. Despite the efforts to build educational institutions available to all, today the single most important determinant of how many years of school a person will be able to attain, or of how much they will be able to learn, is their social origin, reflected in the education level of their parents. This is, of course, understandable because there is no "education ceiling," so even as the children of the poor attain more years of schooling, in a context where there are clear benefits to being educated, it is to be expected that all parents will do what is within their means to educate their children. Powerful forces transmit educational inequality across generations; some of them operate outside the school in the cognitive, social, and emotional support that parents provide at home, in the access to health and nutrition that results from parental education and income, or in the quality of life in the neighborhoods and communities that are associated with various levels of education. Other forms of transmission of intergenerational educational inequality result from the educational resources that parents with different levels of education can provide their children, through direct purchasing of education services to replace or supplement the services provided by public schools. In addition, the quality of public institutions often varies in ways that mirror the socioeconomic differences of the groups of students they serve. These forces are powerful, and they work against the school's goal of "leveling the playing field," for even as the children of the poor gain skills and knowledge relative to those of their parents, their distance relative to the children of the non-poor may remain the same or even widen, because all parents are passing on their advantages to their children in ways that are proportional to the resources they command. In contexts of social and economic inequality, often widening, some parents just have more resources to give their children.

Education and Inequality

Poverty is both an absolute and a relative concept. As an absolute concept, poverty refers to the absence of some essential conditions that diminish the humanity of the individual as well as to a form of deprivation that challenges the basic rights of the individual. The notion that there is a minimum level of caloric intake a person needs to stay alive, for instance, informs the definition of a "poverty line," a level of income necessary to eat and stay alive. The declaration of human rights is an attempt to define those essential conditions that individuals need to preserve their humanity. In including education as a human right, we can think of education poverty as a form of deprivation of the most basic forms of education, for example, access to literacy, which undermines a person's ability to become fully human. To a great extent, it is with this notion of education poverty that the goals of the Education for All movement are aligned. They aim to ensure a basic level of education for all persons.

Conversely, poverty is also a relative concept, relative not to an absolute minimum standard but to a standard that reflects the conditions of others. This view of poverty is more aligned with the possibility of participation in the institutions of society, with social inclusion rather than with abject deprivation. The Education Millennium Development goal that seeks parity in education for women and men, for instance, is aligned with this view of poverty as inequality. The idea is that in order to have equality in the opportunity to participate in society, women and men need not have a minimum level of education but equal opportunity to achieve various levels of education. It is possible to achieve this goal of parity and not meet the basic goal of universal education, for instance, as long as girls and boys are enrolled at similar rates in various levels of education. Poverty as inequality, therefore, is more concerned with the social distance that such inequalities would foster. One of the paradoxical results of the Global Education for All movement is that it has produced gains in absolute access to basic education, even as there are large levels of educational inequality. This leads us to question whether focusing on the elimination of basic educational deprivation is sufficient to address the goals of Education for All. It is possible that, several centuries ago, those who laid the intellectual foundation of the public school movement could not have anticipated that it would be possible to include all children in school while simultaneously increasing educational inequality, because the idea that people in vast numbers would be interested in education beyond a basic level was inconceivable. Very few people aspired to postprimary education even one hundred years ago; even fewer aspired to postsecondary education. There were few jobs that required such education, and, for the most part, participation in work, community, or civic life did not require more than basic skills and knowledge. As things have changed, and as it has become obvious that there are significant rewards to higher levels of education and to high-quality education, the Global Education for All movement has been accompanied by a parallel movement of more education for all. This means that there is no ceiling in sight to how much education people can aspire to get, and therefore those who can will aim for higher and higher levels of education, expanding the distribution of knowledge and skills even as most people gain access to school or even complete primary school. Such a spread in educational gains would be in itself complicated in a number of ways—for instance, allowing individuals equal participation and deliberation in the public sphere—but it is particularly complicated if the main predictors of such inequality are the social origin of students. When this is the case, the education system becomes not the "balance wheel of the social machinery" that Horace Mann imagined but one of the mechanisms of reproduction of social inequality, part of the superstructure that reproduces the material relations of economic production that Karl Marx described.

Globally, there is evidence of much educational inequality and insufficient evidence that government efforts are closing it. Perhaps this should not be surprising, as reducing educational inequality is rarely an explicit policy objective, and it is not, except for gender inequality, one of the goals of the international development institutions that lead the Global Education for All movement. Educational inequality is interesting not only because it can lead to social exclusion but because it signals that the efforts of the Education for All movement are not keeping up with the efforts of individuals and families to improve their own educational capital.

The fact that reducing gender inequality was one of the objectives of the Education for All movement is useful to test whether making the reduction of inequality a priority matters. Achieving greater gender equality in education has been an explicit priority of the Global Education for All movement, at least since the Jomtien declaration in 1990, and a very clear objective of the MDGs and EFA Dakar Framework for Action of 2000. On all available indicators, it is evident that the gender gap is rapidly closing. For the decade between 1985 and 1994, the percentage of adults who were literate in the developing world was 76% for men compared to 58% for women, a difference that made a man 30% more likely to be literate than a woman. The gap was smaller for those between the ages of fifteen and twenty-four: 85% for men versus 75% for women. Twenty years later, the gap for the young is 92% for men versus 89% for women. Similar reductions in the gender gap are observed in other education indicators. In the developing world, the gross enrollment ratios at the prepri-mary level are 45% for boys and girls; net enrollment rates in primary educa-tion, which were 85% for boys and 78% for girls in 1999, were 91% for boys and 89% for girls in 2011; of the total number of out-of-school children, 58% were girls in 1999, compared to 54% in 2011; the percentage of children who reach the last grade of primary school is 72% for boys and 73% for girls; enrollment in secondary education is 80% for men and 78% for women; and enrollment in upper-secondary education is 55% for men versus 52% for women. Among adolescents who are out of school, 55% were women in 1999, compared to 50% in 2011 (UNESCO 2014).

There are significant gaps in educational opportunity that are associated with socioeconomic status of the family and location of residence. For in-stance, in all countries for which there is data, the percentage of four-year-olds with access to some form of preprimary education is greater for children from wealthier families than for their poorer counterparts (UNESCO 2014). The effects of social disadvantage are cumulative and compound over time; they begin with disadvantage at home, extend into different opportunities to access preschool, and continue with access to different levels of education quality, translating into differential rates of completion of primary school and transi-tion to subsequent levels. Boys from the wealthiest 20% of households will achieve universal completion of primary school by 2030 in fifty-six of seventy-four low- and middle-income countries, but girls from the poorest 20% of families will reach that goal in only seven countries (7). At the lower secondary level, "there are wide inequalities in completion, with rates reaching 61% for the richest households but 14% for the poorest" (3). In forty-four of the seventy-four countries for which there are detailed demographic household surveys, there is "at least a fifty-year gap between when all the richest boys complete lower secondary school and when all the poorest girls do so" (7). Children with disabilities are particularly poorly served by public education systems as many countries lack effective policies and programs of inclusion.

Conclusion

The children of the poor today have more opportunities than ever to be edu-cated. This is true globally, and it is the result of a global movement that has intellectual roots in the Enlightenment and gains momentum with the cre-ation of public education systems as part of efforts of nation building. This movement gains momentum with the inclusion of education as one of the human rights in the Universal Declaration of 1946 and the creation of the United Nations System and is advanced by the specialized agencies that advocate for and support reforms to achieve the right to education. Since 1990, this movement has focused on achieving specific goals, universal primary education, and closing gender gaps, and substantial progress has resulted from such focus. Despite these efforts, however, the basic goals set out in the Education for All movement and the Millennium Development Goals have not been achieved yet.

More complicated, and to some extent paradoxical, is the fact that there is pervasive educational inequality globally, even as more children gain access to basic education. This paradox results from the fact that schools as institutions do not operate in a vacuum; they serve children who live in families, communities, and regions, and who are affected by the powerful forces of the social class of their parents, location of residence, and the barriers and discrimination that face many marginalized groups. Schools can only do so much in serving children, but they cannot alone counter the influences of these other social institutions.

When the children of the poor have access to school, as most do today, schools clearly serve them, if not for other reasons, because what is learned in school has intrinsic value in humanizing students. In this sense, the educational access resulting from the global education expansion that has taken place over the past six decades has contributed to reducing poverty, educational poverty at least. There is also evidence that what is learned in school has potentially valuable consequences for individuals and communities, and contributes therefore to reduce other forms of poverty: poverty of income, poor health, and poor civic health. In this sense, it appears that schools as institutions have enough autonomy from the social structure to distribute benefits in ways that challenge the existing distribution of wealth, status, and privilege. It is not evident, however, that schools do enough to empower the children of the poor. The documented benefits of schools are almost always measured in relative terms and rarely by reference to a normative standard that specifies what kinds of qualities make a person autonomous, efficacious, or competent. Perhaps it is poverty in these standards that we hold schools to that ultimately accounts for why they fail to do more to empower the poor, enough for them to challenge the social norms that keep them in subordinate roles.

Another complicating aspect of the history reviewed in this chapter is the paradoxical relationship between education poverty and educational inequality.

When everyone is trying to get more and better education, it sets a high bar against which to measure the success of governmental interventions to support the education of the poor. So far, in more places than not, educational inequality continues, even as more poor children gain access to education. This is true for inequality of learning outcomes and of educational attainment. So far, reducing educational inequality has not been an explicit objective of the Global Education for All movement.

This poverty of aspirations about how schools could empower the poor translates in the priorities of the Global Education for All movement and the efforts of international institutions and governments to support educational change. This global movement has emphasized, for most of recent history, educational access and attainment, rarely examining curriculum or focusing on what kind of pedagogical experiences have the greatest potential to produce self-authoring individuals. When reform efforts go beyond access and expand the aspirations for the number of years of schooling that should be free and mandatory, they focus on basic literacies and in simple strategies such as developing assessment systems that measure student achievement in those literacies. Absent from these efforts are discussions of what competencies allow a person to develop skills to be autonomous, even though there is an abundant and robust body of scientific knowledge that describes those competencies and the experiences that help develop them. But this knowledge has not yet made its way to large-scale efforts of global educational improvement, and as a result the global education conversation continues to focus on access and financing, to some extent on measuring student achievement, and barely addresses the nature of the pedagogical experiences that empower students in suggesting that teachers are an important determinant of the quality of an education system. What kind of curriculum and pedagogy empower the poor and how to identify and develop the teachers who can create those experiences for students are footnotes to the Global Education for All movement. This is clearly a missed opportunity as there is evidence that when governments and global coalitions set clear goals, they can make great progress toward achieving them, as has been the case in closing gender equity gaps in education access and completion.

Schools undoubtedly matter to the poor. The fact that most children today can set foot in school—when only seventy years ago they could not—is nothing short of remarkable. Those who have gained such access, and whatever skills they may have drawn from it—basic literacy, numeracy, artistic appreciation, a sense of self, the ability to work with others—are better off for it. However, if we are going to make progress in advancing a world that is more just, where all people not only have the opportunity to be spared the most abject forms of educational exclusion but the opportunity to come together with others from different social origins, to have the skills to participate as equals in the public sphere as was imagined by those who created the intellectual foundations of a world ruled by ordinary people and by human reason, and to collaborate in reducing human suffering, then we will have to become more ambitious and overcome the poverty of our own aspirations for the education of the poor. Only with this audacity might we, in time, be seen as those who took the Education for All project, this four-hundred-year history based on Comenius's idea, forward toward a world of greater justice and peace.

REFERENCES

Chzhen, Yekaterina. 2013. "Education and Democratisation: Tolerance of Diversity, Political Engagement, and Understanding of Democracy." Background paper prepared for the Education for All Global Monitoring Report, April 2013.

Pellegrino, James W., and Margaret L. Hilton, eds. 2012. *Education for Life and Work: Developing Transferable Knowledge and Skills in the 21st century*. Washington, DC: National Research Council.

Tendler, Judith. 2002. "The Fear of Education." Background paper for Inequality and the State in Latin America and the Caribbean. Presented at the Fiftieth Anniversary Meetings of the Banco do Nordeste, Fortaleza, July 19, 2002.

UNESCO. 2014. *Teaching and Learning: Achieving Quality For All*. Paris, France: Author.

3

Student Academic Achievement and Poverty

JAMAL ABEDI

Despite many targeted efforts to boost academic achievement for all students, those with low socioeconomic status (SES) continue to perform lower academically, have higher school dropout rates, and are admitted to and graduate from colleges and universities at lower rates. Current research continues to address differences in academic achievement across socioeconomic groups and provide a better understanding of the role of poverty in education in an effort to narrow the achievement gap between students from different socioeconomic classes. However, the relationship between student academic performance and poverty is complex and multidimensional in nature, and the effects of factors are outside the realm of education policy. External factors such as race/ethnicity, parent- and student-levels of aspiration for education, and family structure often outweigh internal factors.

Although the literature strongly points to poverty as one of the major predictors of low academic performance, it will be more productive to think about factors that can help improve students' academic performance given their low-SES. For example, literature demonstrates that the achievement gap due to poverty can be reduced with proper intervention if detected early in a student's academic career (Farkas 2008; Farkas and Durham 2007; Herbers et al. 2012). Therefore, public policy directed at increasing early education opportunities for these students may have a significant impact on decreasing the achievement gap. The purpose of this chapter is to explore current research findings on the impact of poverty on academic achievement, as well as the effects of interventions to help improve performance of students in poverty, and to discuss the current boundaries and limitations of the research on poverty and education. Acknowledging what we know and do not know about poverty's effect on the educational outcomes of students will help pave the way toward better policies to address and resolve the issue in the future. Research has explored differences in academic achievement across socioeconomic groups as well as expanded our current understanding of the role of poverty in children's academic lives. The following brief review of the literature highlights a few of these studies and provides a foundation for this critical need to provide opportunities for all students to succeed academically.

Validation of the Achievement Gap

Current research on poverty and education addresses multiple aspects of this complex issue, including the achievement gap between students of poverty and their more affluent counterparts (Anyon 1981; Burnett 2008; Heyneman 2005), the link between students of color and poverty (Lewis and Paik 2001; Milner 2012), in-school and out-of-school factors affecting educational attainment of students living in poverty (Belot and James 2011; Berliner 2009; Bower 2011; Gamoran and Long 2007; Gordon and Bridglall 2005; Murray et al. 2007; Steele 2010; U.S. Department of Education 1996), improving education outcomes for students living in poverty (Farkas 2009; Murnane 2008), and the relationship between poverty and poor educational outcomes (Raffo et al. 2007; Sordaindo and Feinstein 2006).

Milner (2012) examined poverty and its impact on students' academic outcomes with a focus on students of color. He expanded the discussion of poverty and education to examine why families of color disproportionately live in poverty, what factors outside of school impact students' lives, and how teachers' pedagogical approaches can be responsive inside of school. Milner suggested that factors both inside and outside of school are important to consider in the discussions of poverty and academic achievement. In a longitudinal study of "summer setback" in mathematics, Entwisle and Alexander (1992) found that a family's socioeconomic status is the most important source of variation in math achievement between African American and Caucasian children.

Berliner (2009) stated, "Poverty limits student potential; inputs to schools affect outputs from them" (1). In order to address the issue of poverty, Berliner suggested that the provisions of No Child Left Behind were inadequate in themselves to promote a narrowing of the achievement gap between income levels and racial and ethnic groups. Instead, he outlined seven key areas that he labeled *out-of-school factors* (OSF). When these factors occur at the same time and with regularity, schools that serve high numbers of students in poverty are significantly challenged.

Bower (2011) questioned whether social reform can have a positive impact in narrowing the achievement gap between different races and classes. He asked the question: "Can social policy close the achievement gap?" (1). He focused on four broad categories of social policy: health and health care, housing and neighborhoods, economic well-being, and family. In this study, the Harlem Children's Zone is used as an example of a school that successfully integrated a number of comprehensive services (e.g., delivery of fresh fruits and vegetables, "Baby College" for pregnant mothers, inclusion of all residents in a ninety-seven-square-block area in Harlem) that may contribute to lowering the achievement gap. However, despite the logic that social policy changes can improve the academic outcomes of lower socioeconomic children, Bower indicated that there is little evidence to substantiate this theory.

Analyses of State Assessment Data to Illustrate the Performance Gap Due to Poverty

Results of analyses of data by students' SES based on a large-scale data file by Abedi, Leon, and Mirocha (2003) showed a gap in the performance of students in poverty when compared with their more affluent peers in content areas, particularly those with higher levels of language demand. In this study, student SES was defined by participation in the free/reduced-price lunch program. Based on this variable, students were grouped into two categories: low-SES students were those who received free/reduced-price lunch and high-SES students were those who were not participating in this program. Data from three states were analyzed. Results of analyses from the three sites and different grades were highly consistent and clearly showed that low-SES students (i.e., students who qualified for the free/reduced-price lunch program) underperformed compared to high-SES students. We present a summary of the results of analyses of data from site 2, one of the three sites (for a more detailed discussion and a complete description of the analyses, see Abedi et al. 2003).

Students' test scores in reading, mathematics, and language subscales of the Stanford Achievement Test, Ninth Edition (SAT 9), were analyzed for students in grades 2, 7, and 9. Means, standard deviations, and number of students were reported for each of the three content areas (reading, mathematics, and language) for high- and low-SES students separately. In addition, the gap between students in the high- and low-SES groups are reported in simple score differences and in terms of a disparity index (DI). DI is an index of the performance gap and is defined as a percentage of gap and computed by subtracting the mean score of low-SES students from the mean of high-SES students divided by the mean of low-SES students multiplied by 100.

The data show that grade 2 students in the low-SES group performed substantially lower than students in the high-SES group in all three content areas (reading, mathematics, and language). The mean reading score for low-SES students was 35.4 with a standard deviation (SD) of 17.5 for a group of $N = 106,999$ as compared with a mean of 47.0 (SD = 20.6, $N = 304,092$) for the high-SES students: a difference of 11.6 score points. The DI for these groups of students is 32.8, suggesting that low-SES students performed approximately 32% lower in reading than high-SES students (Abedi, Leon, and Mirocha 2003).

A similar trend can be observed in mathematics and language subject areas. In mathematics, the mean score for low-SES students was 38.8 (SD = 20.1, $N = 121,461$) as compared with a mean of 48.5 (SD = 22.4, $N = 327,409$) for high-SES students, with a difference of 9.7 score points and a DI of 25.0. In the language subscale, the mean for low-SES students was 35.5 (SD = 20.5, $N = 116,202$) as compared with a mean of 48.0 (SD = 24.0, $N = 320,405$) for high-SES students, with a DI of 35.2.

The trend of underperformance of low-SES students over high-SES students can also be seen for grade 7 students. The mean score for grade 7 students in reading was 34.3 (SD = 18.9, $N = 92,302$) as compared with the mean of 48.2 (SD = 21.8, $N = 307,931$) and a DI of 40.5. In mathematics, the mean score for low-SES students in grade 7 was 38.1 (SD = 17.1, $N = 94,054$) as compared with the mean score of 49.4 (SD = 21.6, $N = 310,684$) with a difference of 11.3 score points and a DI of 29.7. In the language subscale, the mean score for low-SES students in grade 7 was 38.9 (SD = 19.8, $N = 92,221$) as compared with the mean of 51.7 (SD = 22.6, $N = 306,176$) with a difference of 12.8 score points and a DI of 32.9.

Similarly, students in the low-SES category in grade 9 performed significantly lower than their more affluent peers. The mean reading score for low-SES students in grade 9 was 32.0 (SD = 16.2, $N = 56,499$) as compared with a mean of 42.6 (SD = 19.7, $N = 338,285$) for high-SES students, with a difference of 19.7 score points. The DI for these groups of students is 33.12, suggesting that low-SES students performed roughly 33% lower than high-SES students in reading.

A similar trend was observed in mathematics and language subject areas for grade 9 students. In mathematics, the mean score for low-SES students was 42.5 (SD = 16.4, N = 57,961) as compared with a mean of 50.7 (SD = 20.1, N = 343,480) for high-SES students, with a difference of 8.2 score points and a DI of 19.3. In the language subscale, the mean for low-SES students was 41.0 (SD = 16.2, N = 56,572) as compared with a mean of 49.2 (SD = 18.9, N = 337,623) for high-SES students.

The data on performance gaps between high- and low-SES students in the three aforementioned content areas are consistent with the data from other states and school districts in the nation (Abedi et al. 2003) and support the following conclusions:

1. Low-SES students perform substantially lower than high-SES students in all content areas particularly those with higher levels of language demands.
2. The differences are all positive in sign, suggesting that low-SES students always score lower than high-SES students.
3. These performance differences are all statistically significant.
4. The performance differences are all substantial as they correspond to large effect sizes (see Kirk 1995).

Why Might Students with Lower SES Perform Lower?

Lower levels of opportunity to learn for students at the lower-SES categories (Abedi and Herman 2010) may provide some clues. Lacour and Tissington (2011) define poverty as the extent to which an individual performs without resources. According to the authors, the resources include financial, mental, emotional, and physical resources. The authors also list other resources such as support systems, relationships, and role models. Despite the efforts by governments and educational organizations around the world, the achievement gap between low-SES students and their higher-SES peers continues to persist (Kennedy 2010; Lacour and Tissington 2011).

Herbers et al. (2012) found that an achievement gap related to poverty can be seen early in students' academic careers and may persist over a long period if prevention measures are not taken. The authors further indicated that the impact of poverty is particularly evident for students who experience homelessness or high residential mobility.

The timing of poverty can also influence students' achievement. Using the National Longitudinal Survey (NLSY) data, Guo (1998) examined the long-term effect of poverty on students' cognitive ability as well as achievement. He found that long-term poverty substantially affects both ability and achievement. Moreover, poverty during childhood is negatively and significantly associated with cognitive ability as measured by the Peabody Picture Vocabulary Test (PPVT) and digit span tasks. In contrast, poverty experienced during adolescence is more damaging to student achievement than that experienced during childhood.

Howley and Bickel (2000) conducted a series of studies using twenty-nine sets of test scores from different grades in four states to examine the relationship between school size, poverty, and student achievement. They found that school size influences the relationship between poverty and achievement. Their findings suggest the larger the school size, the higher the negative impact of poverty on student achievement.

Gardner (2007) discussed the effect of malnutrition due to poverty on students' cognitive abilities, including their academic achievement. He indicated that inadequate nourishment at a time of extensive body and brain growth may have a serious impact on children's developmental process and consequently may affect students' cognitive abilities.

What Type of Gap: Cognitive Ability and/or Achievement?

Achievement and educational outcome differences have been measured in various ways. Some studies examined the number of years students are in school and dropout rates, while others looked at cognitive ability (e.g., attention, reading ability, working memory) or academic performance (e.g., standardized test scores or grade point average). Guo (1998) differentiates between "cognitive ability" and "achievement," believing ability to be a more stable trait whereas achievement is more acquired and a function of ability, motivation, and opportunities (Draper 1974).

In investigating the effects of socioeconomic status on brain or cognitive development, Raizada and Kishiyama (2010) identified a number of experimental studies on language, math, attention, executive function, memory, and stress that show potential differential patterns for students with different SES backgrounds. For example, in adults with dyslexia, readers using compensatory strategies were from higher-SES schools (Shaywitz et al. 2003). In a longitudinal study of children from three to ten years old, Melhuish and colleagues (2008) found SES to be a predictor of math attainment at age ten. Studies using neuroimaging and behavioral measures also showed some differences in attention, working memory, and executive function (cognitive functions highly associated with school achievement) between children from lower-income and higher-income families (see Kishiyama et al. 2009; Stevens, Lauinger, and Neville 2009).

The effects of socioeconomic status or poverty on school achievement—rather than cognitive development—have also been widely examined. For example, Tienken (2012) discussed the impact of poverty on student academic performance and indicated that poverty strongly influences student academic achievement particularly when achievement is measured by the standardized tests that are mandated by states.

Similarly, in Wallenstein's (2012) study, low-SES students in the sample performed significantly lower on standardized achievement tests than their more affluent peers. Just like in Entwisle and Alexander's (1992) study, Wallenstein found the achievement gap to be less influenced by racial and ethnic factors and more by students' socioeconomic status. However, the low-SES students in Wallenstein's study showed positive attitude and interest in learning.

Interventions or Ways to Help Address the Gap Issue

Given the substantial impact of poverty on the achievement gap, researchers from multiple disciplines have attempted to address the issue and design interventions. Some researchers believe that teachers, if trained properly, can be very effective in educating students in poverty to perform at a level similar to their more affluent peers. They believe that training teachers to provide more attention to students in poverty will assist in reducing the performance gap for these students. For example, Hughes (2010) recommended that teacher training programs should prepare teachers to address the needs of children in poverty (see also Freedman and Appleman 2009; Ladson-Billings 2006). In addition, incorporating positive features into schools and classrooms helps students in poverty to perform substantially better. Parrett and Budge (2012) believed that while school alone cannot eliminate the achievement gap due to poverty, this gap can be substantially reduced by some changes and innovations in a school's environment. The authors provide a Framework of Action that they believe will help turn high-poverty/low-performing schools into high-poverty/high-performing (HP/HP) schools. The Framework for Action includes:

1. "values, beliefs, and norms that HP/HP schools exhibit in their leadership practices, school culture, and academic expectations;
2. ways to increase the school's influence on student, family, and community relationships;
3. tips on optimizing time, resources, and personnel; and
4. strategies for eliminating the mindsets, policies, and practices that are barriers to improving achievement in high-poverty schools." (1)

In a study of five high-poverty districts that demonstrated significant improvements in students' academic achievement, Togneri (2003) found that focusing on system-wide strategies such as effective professional development, making data-driven decisions, and redefining leadership roles will help close the achievement gap between students in poverty and their affluent peers.

Interventions designed to address cognitive or metacognitive skills in preschool-aged students also appear to have lasting long-term effects. For example, the Abecedarian and Perry Preschool programs concentrated on low-SES, predominantly ethnic minority children produced significant improvements on student IQ and other test scores. Although these benefits seemed to disappear after the children left the program, more recent follow-up studies showed that those who participated in the programs had higher achievement, such as higher graduation rates and college enrollment, compared with nonenrolled children (Knudsen et al. 2006; Nisbett 2009; Raizada and Kishiyama 2010).

Duncan and Sojourner (2012) analyzed data from the Infant Health and Development Program (IHDP) and found that such a program offered to low-income children reduced the income-based gap in cognitive abilities for children at early ages. The goal of Duncan's and Sojourner's (2012) study was to determine how effective an intensive two-year center-based Abecedarian-type intervention starting at age one would be in closing the gap in cognitive ability and school readiness due to poverty. Duncan's and Sojourner's (2012) analysis suggested "that at age three—at the end of the program—income-based gaps would be essentially eliminated with either a universal or income-based targeted program" (19). They also found that "income-based gaps in age five IQ were also substantially reduced (in the case of a targeted program) or completely eliminated (for a universal program)" (19; see also Farkas 2009; Hillemeier et al. 2011).

Methodological Issues with the Current Research

There are several major areas related to research on the achievement gap and poverty that need more attention. Of primary importance is the need for a comprehensive model for studying the impact of poverty on achievement and a need to establish reliable and valid measures of poverty.

Poverty is usually based on a person's socioeconomic status, but this variable is broadly defined in the literature and is often multidimensional. Some researchers define SES as family income; others define it as parents' level of education and others as school resources, or a combination of these and other variables. This lack of a common definition of SES makes the research findings on the impact of SES on student performance difficult to interpret. Such discrepancies may also suggest that the SES variable is multidimensional and involves many different components. Therefore, studies on the impact of SES on students' academic performance should pay proper attention to the complex nature of this variable. We elaborate on this issue in the following section.

Operational Definition of SES

Family socioeconomic status (SES) has been used as a proxy for student poverty level. Students at the lower level of SES are often classified as students in poverty. However, literature has not clearly identified the concept and definition of SES. This variable has been defined based on many different criteria that are different both in concept and in what they measure. However, in order to provide literature support on the impact of poverty on student performance, researchers should communicate based on a clear definition of SES, a definition that best conveys the concept of poverty. The following is a summary of literature on the operational definition of SES. This summary illustrates the variation in the concept and definition of the SES variable and the urgent need to understand its complex nature and clearly define it.

Fotso and Kuate-Defo (2005a, 2005b) constructed socioeconomic indices that consist of both household and community attributes. The authors preferred this definition of SES since it goes well beyond a purely economic view of the SES variable and defines SES in a multidimensional manner. The authors discussed the different levels of contribution of SES indices based on the data from households versus those at a community level in understanding inequalities in health and survival.

Callahan and Eyberg (2010) defined SES in two ways: (1) using the Hollingshead Four-Factor Index of Social Status (HI) and (2) SES based on a composite of family income, parent education, and parent occupation. The study found that SES defined as income, occupation, and education has higher power (three times more variance) in predicting maternal prosocial talk than the HI alone.

Tonts, Plummer, and Lawrie (2012) presented results of analyses of socioeconomic performance across thirty-three towns in Western Australia and found that the socioeconomic well-being of people in these towns was dependent upon a range of variables such as the particular commodity, company structure, and location of the city. Van Beek, Bowen, and Mills (2012) defined students' SES based on family household income or parent's educational background, but they defined SES in the Michigan Public High School Context and Performance Report Card based on the percentage of a school's students who qualified for the free/reduced-price lunch program (see also Agnew 2011a, 2011b).

Hackman et al. (2014) conducted a comprehensive study examining the relationship between SES and working memory development in children between ages ten and thirteen. The authors indicated that SES can be measured by family income, parental education, and neighborhood characteristics. They defined neighborhood effects based on the information from the 2000 U.S. Census data, which included "percentage of individuals below the poverty line, unemployed and receiving public assistance, the density of children under the age of 18, and female-headed households with no spouse present" (10). They found a substantial shared variance between these variables by conducting a principal components analysis with the first components explaining 79.1% of the variance in these measures. Hackman et al. presented a comprehensive review of literature on the relationship between SES and cognitive abilities including working memory. However, it is not clear from the literature review section how SES was defined in various studies cited in this chapter. Different studies may have defined SES completely different from what the authors of this chapter have defined. As one of the limitations of the study, they indicated the absence of a common measure of SES.

Providing an operational definition of SES seems even more challenging across nations than within a single country. Different countries view the concept of SES differently and have different measures for this variable. For example, Yang and Gustafsson (2004) found different factor structures of SES in different countries.

Summary and Conclusion

The gap between academic achievement of students in poverty and their affluent peers is well documented in the literature. This chapter summarizes research on the link between poverty and academic achievement as well as how
appropriate interventions can be used to reduce the impact of poverty on student academic achievement.

Most of the studies examining the link between academic performance and
poverty have used SES as an index of poverty. However, a common definition
of SES has been missing. In the literature summarized in this chapter, SES has
been operationalized based on a variety of indices, including family level of
income, parent education, school resources, percentage on free/reduced-price
lunch program, neighborhood characteristics, or family structure (e.g., the
density of children under the age of eighteen and female-headed household;
Burnett and Farkas 2009; Hackman et al., 2014). It is clear that such differences in the operational definition of SES cause major discrepancies between
findings from different studies conducted on the link between poverty and
student academic achievement. However, despite such wide differences in the
definition of SES, the outcomes of studies on the impact of poverty (defined by
a variety of SES indices) and educational performance consistently suggest a
negative impact of low SES on student academic progress.

Results of analyses of data from different states confirm disparities between
academic performances of students in the low-SES category as compared with
their peers in the high-SES group. As discussed in this chapter, low-SES students performed lower than high-SES students in reading, mathematics, and
language content areas. The disparity index (DI), or percentage of difference
in the performance of the high- and low-SES groups, averaged over all three
grades analyzed in this study was 35.5 in reading and 24.7 in math, suggesting
that students in the low-SES category performed 35.5% lower in reading than
students in the high-SES category and 24.7% lower in math than students in
high-SES category. These data suggest that while there were substantial performance gaps between high- and low-SES students in different content areas,
these gaps were larger in areas with higher levels of language demand. For
example, there was a difference of 10.8 in DI units between reading and math,
confirming the larger impact of language on the academic performance of
low-SES students. Therefore, the need for intervention with special focus on
language is evident from these findings.

Since it is difficult to modify families' SES status, the question is: what can be done to control for the negative impact of poverty in education, particularly at earlier ages where children might be more vulnerable to the negative impact of poverty on their cognitive development and in their future academic achievement? This chapter discussed several approaches that could reduce or even eliminate the negative impact of poverty on cognitive development (Duncan and Sojourner 2012; Farkas and Durham 2007). While these approaches require special efforts to implement, they present possibilities, potential, and hope in controlling for the negative impact of poverty on students' academic progress.

Finally, there is an urgent need to reevaluate the methodologies used in examining the impact of poverty on education in general and on students' academic performance in particular. First, the definition of SES as an index of poverty based on a single variable (e.g., family income or parent level of education) may not be productive. A multidimensional index (or indices) for measuring poverty that includes major components (e.g., students' home, school, and community resources) should be created and be carefully validated. Second, in order to be capable of handling the multidimensional nature of the poverty measure(s), multivariate and multidimensional statistical techniques should be considered. For example, if research on the operational definition of poverty (as portrayed by SES) yields several correlated variables, then depending on the nature of correlation of these variables (if redundancy is present) a latent variable of the SES components can be created to serve as a composite SES variable. However, if a set of variables is identified, each making a unique contribution in the measurement of SES, then multivariate techniques should be used to examine the impact of the different aspects of SES on education.

In sum, research on the impact of poverty in education has provided mixed results. The majority of studies conducted in this area link low student academic performance with poverty. However, the nature and extent of this impact varies greatly across different studies, depending on how poverty is defined. The lack of a reliable and valid index of poverty and methodological issues in the design of the studies are primary among the contributing factors to such discrepancies.

ACKNOWLEDGMENTS

The author wishes to thank Dr. Nancy Ewers (UC Davis) and Grace Lin (UC Irvine) for their suggestions for revisions as well as their contribution to the literature review section of the chapter. The author also wishes to thank Kimberly Mundhenk (UC Davis) for her useful suggestions and revisions.

REFERENCES

Abedi, Jamal, and Joan Herman. 2010. "Assessing English Language Learners' Opportunity to Learn Mathematics: Issues and Limitations." *Teachers College Record* 112 (3): 723–46.

Abedi, Jamal, Seth Leon, and Jim Mirocha. 2003. *Impact of Students' Language Background on Content-Based Assessment: Analyses of Extant Data* (CSE Tech. Rep. No. 603). Los Angeles: National Center for Research on Evaluation, Standards, and Student Testing.

Agnew, Steve. 2011a. "The Impact of School Socioeconomic Status on Student-Generated Teacher Ratings." *Journal of College Teaching & Learning* 8 (1): 39–46.

———. 2011b. "Has the Academic Performance of Low Socioeconomic Students and Students from Ethnic Minorities Improved in the Subject of Economics over the First Five Years of a Standards-Based Assessment Regime?" *Citizenship, Social and Economics Education* 10 (1): 3–13.

Anyon, Jean. 1981. "Social Class and School Knowledge." *Curriculum Inquiry* 11 (1): 3–42.

Belot, Michèle, and Jonathan James. 2011. "Healthy School Meals and Educational Outcomes." *Journal of Health Economics* 30:489–504.

Berliner, David C. 2009. *Poverty and Potential: Out-of-School Factors and School Success.* Boulder, CO, and Tempe, AZ: Education and the Public Interest Center and Education Policy Research Unit. http://epicpolicy.org/publication/poverty-and-potential.

Bower, Corey B. 2011. "Social Policy and the Achievement Gap: What Do We Know? Where Should We Head?" *Education and Urban Society* 20 (10): 1–34.

Burnett, Kristin, and George Farkas. 2009. "Poverty and Family Structure Effects on Children's Mathematics Achievement: Estimates from Random and Fixed Effects Models." *The Social Science Journal* 46:297–318.

Burnett, Nicholas. 2008. "Education for All: Am Imperative for Reducing Poverty." *Annals of the New York Academy of Sciences* 1136:269–75.

Callahan, Corrisa L., and Sheila M. Eyberg. 2010. "Relations between Parenting Behavior and SES in a Clinical Sample: Validity of SES Measures." *Child & Family Behavior Therapy* 32 (2): 125–38.

Draper, John F. 1974. "Open Discussion on 'The Logic of the Aptitude—Achievement Distinction.' The Aptitude-Achievement Distinction; Proceedings." Edited by Donald Ross Green, 335–44. Monterey, CA: CTB/McGraw-Hill.

Duncan, Greg J., and Aaron J. Sojourner. 2012. *Can Intensive Early Childhood Intervention Programs Eliminate Income-Based Cognitive and Achievement Gaps?* Bonn, Germany: Institute for the Study of Labor. http://ftp.iza.org/dp7087.pdf.

Entwisle, Doris R., and Karl L. Alexander. 1992. "Summer Setback: Race, Poverty, School Composition, and Mathematics Achievement in the First Two Years of School." *American Sociological Review* 57 (1): 72–84.

Farkas, George. 2008. "How Educational Inequality Develops." In *The Colors of Poverty: Why Racial and Ethnic Disparities Persist*, edited by David Harris and Ann Lin, 105–34. New York: Russell Sage Foundation Press.

———. 2009. "Closing Achievement Gaps." In *Handbook of Education Policy Research*, edited by David Plank, Barbara Schneider, and Gary Sykes, 661–70. New York: American Educational Research Association.

Farkas, George, and Rachel Durham. 2007. "The Role of Tutoring in Standards-Based Reform." In *Standards-Based Reform and the Poverty Gap: Lessons for "No Child Left Behind,"* edited by Adam Gamoran, 201–28. Washington, DC: Brookings Institution Press.

Fotso, Jean C., and Barthelemy Kuate-Defo. 2005a. "Measuring Socioeconomic Status in Health Research in Developing Countries: Should We Be Focusing on Household, Communities or Both?" *Social Indicators Research* 72:189–237.

———. 2005b. "Socioeconomic Inequalities in Early Childhood Malnutrition and Morbidity: Modification of the Household-Level Effects by the Community SES." *Health Place* 11 (3): 205–25.

Freedman, Sarah, and Deborah Appleman. 2009. "'In It for the Long Haul': How Teacher Education Can Contribute to Teacher Retention in High-Poverty, Urban Schools." *Journal of Teacher Education* 60:323–37.

Gardner, David. 2007. "Confronting the Achievement Gap." *Phi Delta Kappan* 88 (7): 542–46.

Gamoran, Adam, and Daniel A. Long. 2007. *Equality of Education Opportunity: A 40-Year Retrospective* (WCER Working Paper No. 2006-9). Madison: University of Wisconsin–Madison, Wisconsin Center for Education Research.

Gordon, Edmund W., and Beatrice Bridglall. 2005. "The Challenge, Context, and Preconditions of Academic Development at High Levels." In *Supplementary Education: The Hidden Curriculum of High Academic Achievement*, edited by Edmund W. Gordon, Beatrice L. Bridglall, and Audra S. Meroe, 10–34. Lanham, MD: Rowman & Littlefield Publishers, Inc.

Guo, Guang. 1998. "The Timing of the Influences of Cumulative Poverty on Children's Cognitive Ability and Achievement." *Social Forces* 77 (1): 257–87.

Hackman, Daniel A., Laura M. Betancourt, Robert Gallop, Daniel Romer, Nancy L. Brodsky, Hallam Hurt, and Martha J. Farah. 2014. "Mapping the Trajectory of Socioeconomic Disparity in Working Memory: Parental and Neighborhood Factors." *Child Development*, 85 (4): 1433–45.

Herbers, Janette E., J. J. Cutuli, Laura M. Supkoff, David Heistad, Chi-Keung Chan, Elizabeth Hinz, Ann S. Masten. 2012. "Early Reading Skills and Academic Achievement Trajectories of Students Facing Poverty, Homelessness, and High Residential Mobility." *Educational Researcher* 41 (9): 366–74.

Heyneman, Stephen P. 2005. "Student Background and Student Achievement: What Is the Right Question?" *American Journal of Education* 112 (1): 1–9.

Hillemeier, Marianne, Paul Morgan, George Farkas, and Steven Maczuga. 2011. "Perinatal and Socioeconomic Risk Factors for Variable and Persistent Cognitive Delay at 24 and 48 Months in a National Sample." *Maternal and Child Health Journal* 15 (7): 1001–10.

Howley, Craig B., and Robert Bickel. 2000. *When It Comes to Schooling . . . Small Works: School Size, Poverty, and Student Achievement*. Randolph, VT: Rural School and Community Trust Policy Program.

Hughes, Joan E. 2010. "What Teacher Preparation Programs Can Do to Better Prepare Teachers to Meet the Challenges of Educating Students Living in Poverty." *Action in Teacher Education* 32 (1): 54–64.

Kennedy, Eithne. 2010. "Improving Literacy Achievement in a High-Poverty School: Empowering Classroom Teachers through Professional Development." *Reading Research Quarterly* 45 (4): 384–87.

Kirk, Roger E. 1995. *Experimental Design: Procedures for the Behavioral Sciences.* Pacific Grove, CA: Brooks/Cole.

Kishiyama, Mark M., W. Thomas Boyce, Amy M. Jimenez, Lee M. Perry, and Robert T. Knight. 2009. "Socioeconomic Disparities Affect Prefrontal Function in Children." *Journal of Cognitive Neuroscience* 21:1106–15.

Knudsen, Eric I., James J. Heckman., Judy L. Cameron, and Jack P. Shonkoff. 2006. "Economic, Neurobiological, and Behavioral Perspectives on Building America's Future Workforce." *Proceedings of the National Academy of Science of the United States of America* 103 (7): 10155–62.

Lacour, Misty, and Laura D. Tissington. 2011. "The Effects of Poverty on Academic Achievement." *Educational Research and Reviews* 6 (7): 522–27.

Ladson-Billings, Gloria. 2006. "It's Not the Culture of Poverty, It's the Poverty of Culture: The Problem with Teacher Education." *Anthropology and Education Quarterly* 37 (2): 104–9.

Lewis, Anne, and Sandra Paik. 2001. *Add It Up: Using Research to Improve Education for Low-Income and Minority Students.* Washington, DC: The Poverty & Race Research Action Council.

Melhuish, Edward C., Kathy Sylva, Pam Sammons, Iram Siraj-Blatchford, Brenda Taggart, Mai B. Phan, and Antero Malin. 2008. "The Early Years: Preschool Influences on Mathematics Achievement." *Science* 321:1161–62.

Milner, H. Richard. 2012. "Analyzing Poverty, Learning, and Teachers through a Critical Race Theory Lens." *Review of Research in Education* 37:1–53.

Murnane, Richard J. 2008. *Educating Urban Children* (Working Paper No. 13791). Cambridge, MA: National Bureau of Economic Research.

Murray, Nancy G., Barbara J. Low, Christine Hollis, Alan W. Cross, and Sally M. Davis. 2007. "Coordinated School Health Programs and Academic Achievement: A Systematic Review of the Literature." *Journal of School Health* 77:589–600.

Nisbett, Richard E. 2009. *Intelligence and How to Get It: Why Schools and Cultures Count.* New York: W. W. Norton & Co.

Parrett, William H., and Kathleen Budge. 2012. *Turning High-Poverty Schools into High-Performing Schools.* Alexandria, VA: ASCD.

Raffo, Carlo, Alan Dyson, Helen Gunter, Dave Hall, Lisa Homes, and Afroditi Kalambouka. 2007. *Education and Poverty: A Critical Review of Theory, Policy and Practice.* University of Manchester: The Joseph Rowntree Foundation.

Raizada, Rajeev D. S., and Mark M. Kishiyama. 2010. "Effects of Socioeconomic Status on Brain Development, and How Cognitive Neuroscience May Contribute to Leveling the Playing Field." *Frontiers in Human Neuroscience* 4 (3): 1–11.

Shaywitz, Sally E., Bennett A. Shaywitz, Robert K. Fulbright, Pawel Skudlarski, W. Einar Mencl, R. Todd Constable, Kenneth R. Pugh, et al. 2003. "Neural Systems for Compensation and Persistence: Young Adult Outcome of Childhood Reading Disability." *Biological Psychiatry* 54:25–33.

Sordaindo, Annik, and Leon Feinstein. 2006. *What is the Relationship between Child Nutrition and School Outcomes.* London: Centre for Research on the Wider Benefits of Learning.

Steele, Paul. 2010. "Rotten Outcomes: How Impoverished Neighborhoods Influence the Life Trajectories of Children in the United States." *Forum on Public Policy: A Journal of the Oxford Round Table* 4:1–15.

Stevens, Courtney, Brittni Lauinger, and Helen Neville. 2009. "Differences in the Neural Mechanisms of Selective Attention in Children from Different Socio-economic Backgrounds: An Event-Related Brain Potential Study." *Developmental Science* 12:634–46.

Tienken, Christopher H. 2012. "The Influence of Poverty on Achievement." *Kappa Delta Pi Record* 48 (3): 105–7.

Togneri, Wendy. 2003. "What Districts Can Do to Improve Instruction and Achievement in All Schools." *State Education Standard* 4 (2): 10–15.

Tonts, Matthew, Paul Plummer, and Misty Lawrie. 2012. "Socio-economic Well-Being in Australian Mining Towns: A Comparative Analysis." *Journal of Rural Studies* 28 (3): 288–301.

U.S. Department of Education, National Center for Education Statistics. 1996. *Urban School: The Challenge of Location and Poverty* (NCES 96-184). Washington, DC.

Van Beek, Michael, Daniel Bowen, and Jonathan Mills. 2012. *The Michigan Public High School Context and Performance Report Card*. Midland, MI: The Mackinac Center for Public Policy. http://www.mackinac.org/archives/2012/HSReportCardWeb.pdf.

Wallenstein, Roger. 2012. "Educating Students of Poverty: One School's Story." *Schools: Studies in Education* 9 (2): 160–75.

Yang, Yang, and Jan-Eric Gustafsson. 2004. "Measuring Socioeconomic Status at Individual and Collective Levels." *Educational Research and Evaluation* 10 (3): 259–88.

4

American Indian Education and Poverty

A Historical Overview and Current Assessment

C. MATTHEW SNIPP

> We know you highly esteem the kind of learning taught in these colleges. And the maintenance of our young men, while with you, would be very expensive to you. We're convinced, therefore, that you mean to do us good by your proposal, and we thank you heartily. But you who are so wise must know that different nations have different conceptions of things. And you will not, therefore, take it amiss if our ideas of this kind of education happens not to be the same with yours.
>
> We have had some experience of it. Several of our young people were formerly brought up in the colleges of the northern province. They were instructed in all your sciences. But when they came back to us, they were bad runners, ignorant of every means of living in the woods, unable to bear either cold or hunger, knew neither how to build a cabin, take a deer, or kill an enemy, spoke our language imperfectly, and therefore were neither fit for hunters, warriors, nor councilors. They were totally good for nothing.
>
> We are, however, not the less obliged for your kind offer, though we decline accepting. To show our grateful sense of it, if the gentlemen of Virginia shall send us a dozen of their sons, we would take great care in their education, instruct them in all we know, and make men of them.
>
> —CHIEF CANASSATEGO (ONONDAGA 1744, QUOTED IN BOYD 1938)

That American Indians are one of the least educated and poorest groups in American society should hardly surprise anyone. The connection between low levels of educational attainment and poverty is self-evident regardless of race. Still, this begs the question of why American Indians remain one of the least educated and poorest groups in American society. Unlike African Americans, American Indians were never systematically denied access to schooling. However, as Chief Canassatego explained in the eighteenth century, American Indians have indeed had a longstanding ambivalence about what schooling has to offer.

This ambivalence is deeply rooted in the conflicts between American Indians and Europeans, especially with the British and later the Americans, over possession of land and sovereignty. However, in the late twentieth century, American Indians acceded to the importance of education, and through political action and statutes took control of their educational destiny. But nearly forty years after the passage of the 1975 American Indian Self-Determination and Educational Assistance Act (P.L. 93-638), American Indians remain poorly educated and mired in poverty.

To understand the persistence of educational disadvantages among American Indians, this chapter begins with a brief overview of the historical experience of American Indians with Anglo-American attempts to educate them and the ways American Indians, including Alaska Natives, have taken control of the education of their children. This is followed by some observations about the educational standing of American Indians and Alaska Natives in the post-self-determination era, especially in relation to income and poverty. It ends with a deceptively simple challenge to present to future leaders of American Indians and Alaska Natives: why have we done so poorly, and how can we do better?

Historical Overview
Colonial Schooling

The history behind the education of American Indians begins naturally enough with the colonial projects of the European nation-states struggling to possess North America, namely Spain, France, and England. Before the arrival of Europeans, knowledge was handed down informally from one generation to another through storytelling and the everyday practice of the skills required for daily living. However, Europeans brought with them an approach to education that was entirely different from that of the indigenous societies they encountered (Szasz 1988).[1]

Although Spain, France, and England differed greatly in their colonial strategies, they did have some features in common (Abernethy 2002). First and foremost, they were seeking to claim North America for the wealth it possessed. Second, they were seeking the souls of converts for the greater glory of the Christian church. How these souls were to be redeemed from among the heathen societies they encountered is relevant to understanding the American Indian experience with formal education.

France and Spain were both Catholic nations with an avowed loyalty to the Holy Roman Church. Spanish and French colonial expeditions to the New World included Catholic priests intent on bringing new souls into the church. However, conversion to the Catholic Church did not rest on the converts' ability to read and understand the Bible. The knowledge required to join the faithful could be passed down orally. In stark contrast, the English colonists were largely Protestants, owing to the history of King Henry XIII and his split with the pope. In some cases, they were radical Protestants being expelled from England for their beliefs (e.g., Puritans). Regardless of their beliefs, the Protestant missionaries did have in common a belief that being able to read the Bible and communicate directly with God was essential for a successful conversion.

As a result of these theological differences, there was a stark difference in how these colonial powers went about educating the Native population and the emphasis they placed on this activity. Among the Spanish and French colonists, an educated indigenous population was merely a by-product of contact with Catholic missionaries. There were few systematic efforts by these early missionaries to construct schools and educate the Native peoples they were seeking to convert. Conversely, acquainting American Indians with the written word of the Bible was an essential feature of the conversion process for the various Protestant sects. Not surprisingly, Protestant missionaries built the first schools in North America. Similarly, in 1663 the first book printed in North America was the "Eliot Bible," which was a translation of the scripture in the Algonquian language. Colleges—notably Harvard, Dartmouth, and William and Mary—included language about the education of American Indians in their charters. The first American Indian author, Samson Occam, published his work in English and also was a Presbyterian minister (Salisbury 1984; Salisbury and Calloway 2004; Szasz 1988).

American Indian Education and the United States

Throughout the seventeenth and eighteenth centuries, school construction and the education of American Indians was virtually the exclusive franchise of English missionaries and their benefactors. American independence from Britain did little to change this in the early years of the nation's history. However, Americans did note that among the Native people who converted to Christianity and spoke English, their habits made them appear more civilized and palatable than their unconverted brethren. George Washington laid out a plan to bring the "blessings of civilization" to American Indians, which relied heavily on the use of missionary organizations. In 1819 Congress passed the Civilization Fund Act that, among other things, supported missionary organizations engaged in the education of American Indians (Prucha 1984; Szasz 1988).

Prior to the Civil War, the federal government relied heavily on missionaries to promote the civilization of American Indians by teaching basic literacy and preaching Christian conversion. After the Civil War, industrialization profoundly changed American society and so too did its strategy for the education and civilization of American Indians. The transformation of the federal government's involvement in American Indian education owes much to the work of a single man: Richard Henry Pratt.

Pratt's interest in American Indian education stemmed from experiences he had while serving as an Army officer. He was responsible for supervising a group of Cheyenne prisoners who were being held at Fort Marion in St. Augustine, Florida. Over time, he came to believe that education was the single most effective method for bringing about the "civilization" (i.e., assimilation) of American Indians. For Pratt, schooling would be the device to "kill the Indian and save the man." Despite his avowed commitment to ethnocide, Pratt was remarkably progressive for his time. Believing that American Indians could be educated drew critics who believed instead that American Indians were impossible to educate and that the most efficient solution to the "Indian problem" was the outright extermination of Native people.

Pratt vigorously pursued a plan that eventually led to the establishment of dozens of boarding schools. American Indian youths were systematically separated from their communities and subjected to a series of measures designed to eradicate their knowledge and practice of tribal culture. For example, students were dressed in military-style uniforms, forbidden to speak their Native language, and attended classes that offered instruction in Anglo American culture (Child 2000; Lomawaima 1994).

The boarding school era peaked in the years before the Great Depression. In 1900 there were nearly 22,000 American Indian students in boarding schools, and in the same year, Congress allocated about $2.94 million to support these schools (Adams 1995). Pratt remained a staunch advocate for the schools' repressive curriculum until his death in 1924. The election of Franklin Roosevelt to the presidency ushered in a new era of federal policies toward American Indians. The Indian New Deal eventually lifted the most repressive measures in the boarding schools, and the passage of the Johnson-O'Malley Act meant that more American Indian children could attend public schools in areas where they were available. The Bureau of Indian Affairs (BIA) also began opening day schools on reservations, allowing school-age students to remain with their families (Prucha 1984).

American Indian Education in the Postwar Era

World War II effectively ended the Indian New Deal, as the United States became immersed in the war. The war profoundly affected American Indians and American Indian communities no less than the rest of the nation. Approximately 25,000 American Indians, mostly men, served in the armed forces. Thousands more went to work in civilian industries supporting the war effort (Bernstein 1991). The war affected American Indian education in several ways. Most immediate was the fact that the GI Bill[2] encouraged American Indian veterans to seek a college education. Where financial resources once prevented Indian youths from attending college, this barrier no longer existed for veterans after the war. This generation of American Indians attended college in unprecedented numbers and went on to become the best-educated generation of American Indians to ever live, including the present generations of American Indians (Snipp 1989).

The war experience also exposed American Indians to life outside Indian country, including amenities absent in many tribal communities—running water, electricity, and paved roadways, to name a few. More significantly, for American Indians with marketable skills and/or a college education, the world outside Indian country offered something mostly missing at home: jobs opportunities and a higher standard of living. For a sizable number of American Indians, this appealed sufficiently to bring an unprecedented number of American Indians into urban areas and offset the costs of leaving behind family, friends, and a familiar way of life in tribal culture.

The postwar years also marked the introduction to a new set of federal policies for American Indians: the era of termination and relocation. This policy initiative was designed to end the federal government's obligations to American Indians by unilaterally dissolving American Indian reservations and relocating American Indians to a preselected set of urban destinations (Fixico 1986). This new policy initiative was met with resistance immediately upon its introduction. Nevertheless, over 110,000 American Indians participated in the urban relocation programs from when they were launched in the early 1950s until the time they were phased out in the mid-1970s (Snipp 1989; Sorkin 1978).

Resistance to the termination and relocation policies in tandem with the spread of the Civil Rights movement sparked a parallel political movement among American Indians. Instead of calling for an end to segregation and discrimination, as Civil Rights leaders demanded, American Indian leaders demanded the right of self-determination for the future of their people. The right to self-determination would end the federal government's role as the final arbiter of well-being for American Indians and return control of tribal communities back to the people who lived in them. The struggle for self-determination began in the 1950s and was initially realized in a special message to Congress by President Richard Nixon in 1970. In this message, Nixon called for the end of termination-era federal policies and the recognition of American Indians' right to self-government. Five years later, Congress responded to this message by passing the Indian Self-Determination and Education Assistance Act (P.L. 93-638) in 1975.

American Indian Education in the Era of Self-Determination

The self-determination movement and the passage of the 1975 act were of immense importance for American Indian education. Quite simply, the doctrine of self-determination meant that American Indians would take control of their educational futures. It meant that American Indian communities, whether on reservations or in urban locations, would take charge of the schooling of their children. The assumption of educational self-determination unfolded in several ways.

Prior to the passage of the 1975 self-determination act, tribal communities and other groups sought to take charge of their children's education by forming their own schools without the benefit of a legal mandate. For example, in 1966 the Navajo tribe opened the Rough Rock Demonstration School. Four years later, three women started a K–8 school in Milwaukee, Wisconsin, that included an emphasis on Native culture (Krouse 2003). Throughout the 1970s, schools appeared in numerous cities with substantial numbers of American Indians. Similarly, a number of tribes established their own schools as alternatives to schools operated by the BIA or religious organizations. These schools often met steep opposition from local officials (Krouse 2003). Nonetheless, a number have survived into the present, including the Rough Rock Community School (formerly named the Rough Rock Demonstration School), the first BIA school to be directly operated by American Indians. Similarly, with support from the Potawatomi tribe, the Indian Community School in Milwaukee broke ground in 2003 for a new multimillion-dollar facility.

The passage of the 1975 self-determination act accelerated school takeovers by the tribes. The act mandated the BIA to contract with tribal governments to provide services that were once the responsibility of the agency. Consequently, BIA schools, particularly day schools operating on reservations, became tribal schools with BIA funding.

In the realm of higher education, the 1970s were also years when tribal colleges first opened their doors. Prior to 1968, the only colleges dedicated to American Indians were the Haskell Institute (later Haskell Indian Junior College, now Haskell Indian Nations University) in Haskell, Kansas, and Bacone College in Muskogee, Oklahoma. Haskell was originally established as a federal boarding school, while Bacone was founded with the support of a missionary organization.

The first tribally controlled college was the Navajo Community College, which opened in 1968. It first operated in the buildings of the Rough Rock Demonstration School and a year later moved to its present location in Tsaile, Arizona. It now operates under the name of Diné College. In the fall of 1970, a group of American Indian students occupied an abandoned military base outside of Davis, California. A group representing itself as the board of trustees of D–Q University began negotiations with federal authorities and in 1971 D–Q opened to serve an American Indian and Latino student body. D–Q University was beset with financial and legal problems for most of its thirty-five-year history until it lost accreditation in 2005 and closed in 2006.

Nonetheless, the example of Navajo Community College and D–Q University sparked a dramatic increase in the number of tribal colleges opening in the 1970s and 1980s. The U.S. Congress, with the passage of the Tribally Controlled Community College Assistance Act in 1978, first provided funding for these institutions. In 1994 tribal colleges were added to the U.S. Department of Agriculture's land grant system, joining state universities and historically black colleges and universities (HBCUs). Belonging to the land grant system brought additional resources and support for these colleges. Today, there are currently thirty-seven tribal colleges located across the country (figure 4.1).

Finally, support and advocacy for American Indian education has been provided by two important auxiliary organizations, both products of the struggle for self-determination in the early 1970s. The National Indian Education

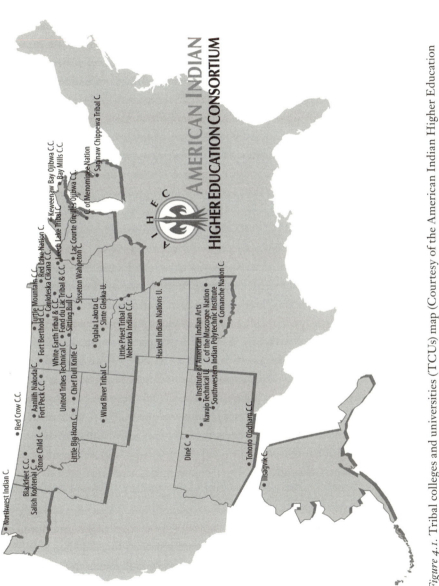

Figure 4.1. Tribal colleges and universities (TCUs) map (Courtesy of the American Indian Higher Education Consortium)

Association (NIEA) was formed in 1970. This organization is mainly dedicated to issues affecting primary and secondary schooling (K–12). It hosts an annual conference for its members, advocates for policies and laws it deems favorable to American Indian education, opposes unfavorable ones, and provides a variety of resources for teachers and others involved in the education of American Indian students. The corresponding organization dealing with higher education, particularly tribal colleges, is the American Indian Higher Education Consortium (AIHEC). Founded in 1972, like the NIEA the AIHEC is primarily an advocacy organization supporting the interests of tribal colleges and universities. However, it also provides information and resources for administrators and students. For students in particular, it provides information about scholarships and financial aid as well as internships and research opportunities.

An Assessment of American Indian Education

For most of this nation's history, education for American Indians amounted to little more than imparting the basic literacy necessary to read the Bible and profess allegiance to the Christian church. It later became the centerpiece of a strategy to bring about mass ethnocide in the late nineteenth and early twentieth centuries. The successful struggle for self-determination has meant that American Indian people are largely, and often exclusively, responsible for the education of their children. Nearly two generations have passed since the induction of the Indian Self-Determination and Education Assistance Act. With American Indians in charge of their own schools, are they becoming better educated? The remainder of this chapter reviews empirical data for two purposes: (1) to assess how American Indians are faring with respect to several measures of educational success and (2) to look at how education accounts for the persistent poverty that afflicts Native communities across the nation.

Enrollment

Although enrollment captures the prevalence of American Indians attending school, it is not a direct measure of educational success. However, it is a self-evident precondition for educational attainment. The data shown in figure 4.2 represent historic trends in American Indian school enrollments from 1900 to 2010 (Carter et al. 2006). These data are taken from Census Bureau reports and, of course, bear all of the flaws associated with the historic enumeration of American Indians. That is, American Indians were most likely grossly under-

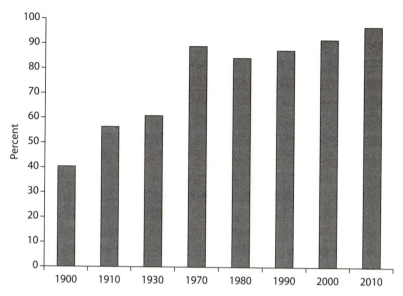

Figure 4.2. Percentage of school-age American Indians enrolled in school, K–12 (Source: Carter et al. 2006)

counted in the early twentieth century.[3] Assuming that American Indians were least likely to be counted due to their location in isolated and inaccessible areas and also least likely to be attending school implies that the percentages of school-age children attending school were most likely overstated in the early part of the century. As the century progressed, the counting of American Indians improved and might be considered reasonably accurate in the decades later in the century.

Enumeration errors notwithstanding, the data in figure 4.2 show that at the beginning of the twentieth century, most school-age American Indians were not enrolled in school. Only about 40% of American Indian school-age youths attended school in 1900. The percentage of American Indians enrolled in school rose rapidly in each subsequent decade. By 1970, nearly nine out of ten school-age American Indians and Alaska Natives were attending school. This rapid growth slowed in subsequent decades, marked even by a small decline in 1980, but since then the percentage of students enrolled in school has gradually increased.

By 2010, school attendance was nearly a universal experience for school-age American Indians and Alaska Natives. In this year, 97% of these youths were

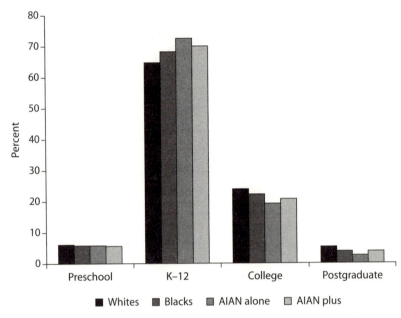

Figure 4.3. Percentage of enrollments of Whites, Blacks, and American Indians age three and older (Source: U.S. Census Bureau, n.d.)

enrolled. At this level of attendance, it seems unlikely that school enrollments will become much higher, and this number may represent an upper bound beyond which there is little room for improvement. The remaining 3% not attending school most likely includes some number of children being home-schooled by their family or unable to attend school due to medical problems.

Figure 4.3 is based on data from the U.S. Census Bureau's American Community Survey. This figure also focuses on school enrollment but from a comparative perspective, showing the enrollment status of American Indians and Alaska Natives age three and older relative to African Americans (Blacks) and Whites. The purpose of this comparison is to show how American Indians and Alaska Natives fare in comparison to the two groups most often regarded as representing the most disadvantaged and most privileged segments of American society.

Figure 4.3 also contains two different groups of American Indians and Alaska Natives. One group is identified as "American Indian and Alaska Native (AIAN) Alone." This group includes only persons identified by a single race. That is, when asked to report their race in the American Community Survey, they responded with no other race but American Indian or Alaska Native. The second group, identified as "AIAN plus," are persons who reported their race as American Indian or Alaska Native plus other races. That is, this is a group of multiracial persons who, in most instances, identified themselves as Black, and/or White, and/or other races as well as American Indian or Alaska Native. This group tends to be more heavily concentrated in urban areas than persons who identify only as American Indian or Alaska Native.

There are several interesting features that can be seen in figure 4.3. Beginning on the left-hand side of this figure, there are four bars showing the percentage of persons who are age three and older and enrolled in some sort of preschool program. This could be a Head Start Program, a Montessori school, or some other program for children too young to attend kindergarten. What this clearly shows is that there are relatively few racial and ethnic disparities with respect to preschool attendance. The numeric range starts with a low of 5.6% for mixed-race American Indians and Alaska Natives to a high of 6.1% for Whites—barely one-half of a percentage point difference in absolute terms. Or it also would be correct to say that the latter is about 9% higher relative to the former.[4] In any case, there are no large differences among these groups with respect to preschool attendance. Undoubtedly, this reflects the important role that Head Start plays in providing access to preschool education for economically disadvantaged groups such as African Americans and American Indians.

The next two sets of bars display a clearer pattern of racial and ethnic disparities in school enrollment. Readers might find this figure a bit surprising insofar as it shows that greater percentages of Blacks, American Indians, and Alaska Natives are enrolled in grades K–12 than Whites. This should be less surprising if one considers that the White population is an older one, with a smaller share of this population being school age. Recalling that school enrollment is nearly universal for American Indians and Alaska Natives, the fact that they have a larger share of their population who are school-age children explains why they have higher percentages enrolled in school than Whites. However, this pattern is reversed for enrollment in college.

For all of these groups, much smaller percentages are attending college than grades K–12. This is mostly due to the fact that there are only four years of college-age persons and thirteen years of K–12 school-age persons. Despite the fact that the White population is relatively older than the other groups represented in this graph, Whites attend college in significantly high numbers that a much greater share of this population is enrolled in college. African Americans have a smaller share than Whites of their population enrolled in college, and American Indians, regardless of how they are identified, have the smallest percentages. However, persons identifying only as American Indian or Alaska Native have the lowest levels of college attendance.

Educational Attainment

Enrollment data are useful for understanding the extent of exposure that American Indians and Alaska Natives, among other groups, have to educational opportunities. However, enrollments do not offer a complete picture of the relative success they have in terms of how much education they are able to obtain. The next figures are more telling with respect to the human capital resources within the American Indian population. Figure 4.4 shows the educational attainment of Whites, African Americans, American Indians, and Alaska Natives who identify with only one race and the total American Indian and Alaska Native population, including persons who identify with two or more races. This figure is restricted to the population age twenty-five and over, an age at which most persons have completed their schooling and entered the labor force.

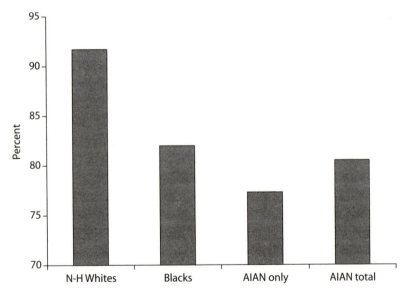

Figure 4.4. Percentage of persons age twenty-five and older with high school diploma/ equivalent or higher (Source: U.S. Census Bureau, n.d.)

Figure 4.4 clearly shows the educational disparities that exist for American Indians and Alaska Natives. Starting with the White population age twenty-five and over, having twelve years or more of schooling is a near universal experience for this population. About 92% of the non-Hispanic White population has attained this level of education. African Americans have considerably less education than non-Hispanic Whites, with 82% of Blacks having twelve or more years of schooling. Yet African Americans are still ahead of American Indians and Alaska Natives with respect to educational attainment. Among persons who identify themselves only as American Indian or Alaska Native, 77% have twelve or more years of schooling. Persons who identify themselves as American Indian or Alaska Native along with one or more additional races are better educated than persons who identify only as American Indian or Alaska Native. It is not possible to say exactly how much they are better educated. However, adding this group to the American Indian– and Alaska Native–only population raises the educational attainment of American Indians and Alaska Natives to 81% for the total population.

A high school diploma or equivalent is a minimum for virtually any sort of job apart from the most menial labor. For work that is well paid, secure, and includes benefits such as health insurance and vacation leave, a college degree is almost without exception a minimum requirement. This has become increasingly the case as unionized jobs have become less common in the American labor market. Figure 4.5 shows the percentage of non-Hispanic Whites, African Americans, and American Indians and Alaska Natives with a baccalaureate degree or higher.

Predictably, non-Hispanic Whites have a sizable advantage over African Americans and American Indians and Alaska Natives.[5] About 32%, nearly one-third of all non-Hispanic Whites over the age of twenty-five, have four years or more of postsecondary education. African Americans complete high school at lower levels than non-Hispanic Whites, and they complete college in even smaller numbers. The evidence for this statement is reflected in the even larger gap for the percentage of African Americans with a bachelor's degree or higher, which is about fourteen percentage points lower than the non-Hispanic White population. Less than one in five African Americans over the age of twenty-five possesses a college-level education.

As dismal as this may seem, the educational attainment for American Indians is even worse. For persons over age twenty-five who identify only as American Indian or Alaska Native, only about 13% have a college education.

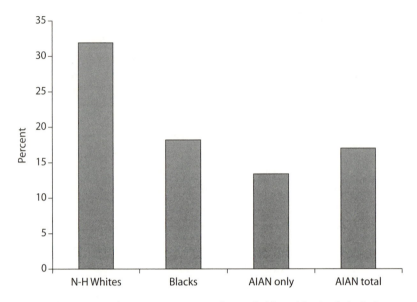

Figure 4.5. Percentage of persons age twenty-five and older with a bachelor's degree or higher (Source: U.S. Census Bureau, n.d.)

In relative terms, the non-Hispanic White population completes four years or more of college at a rate that is about 250% higher than the American Indian and Alaska Native (alone) population. African Americans are about 40% more likely to complete four or more years of college than American Indians. Including the population of persons who identify with one or more races in addition to American Indian or Alaska Native improves these numbers but only modestly, raising the percentage completing four years or more of college from 13% to 17%, more or less reaching parity with African Americans.

Economic Status

Unemployment

To close this brief and necessarily limited assessment of where American Indians and Alaska Natives stand with respect to educational success, it is worth an even briefer look at their economic standing. Inheritance notwithstanding, there is perhaps no other resource more valuable for assuring economic success and a materially comfortable life than the schooling one receives. Lack of schooling bestows a raft of disadvantages that play out in the labor market and

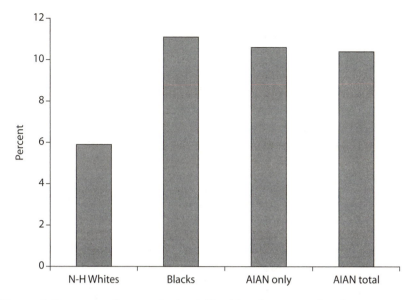

Figure 4.6. Percentage of persons in the civilian labor force unemployed, 2010 (Source: U.S. Census Bureau, n.d.)

elsewhere. The cumulative effect of these disadvantages is most visible in labor force participation and financial income.

Figure 4.6 shows the unemployment rate in 2010 for non-Hispanic Whites, African Americans, and American Indians and Alaska Natives. Readers should keep in mind the usual qualifications connected with this statistic. Most important is that to be counted as unemployed, a person must be jobless *and* actively seeking work. It does not include the long-term unemployed who have abandoned their job search. Another point to keep in mind is that in 2010, the United States economy was deeply mired in the Great Recession. One of the features of this recession was that it disproportionately impacted low-skill, low-wage workers in manual occupations.

Figure 4.6 is a very simple graph and one that is easy to interpret. The unemployment rate for non-Hispanic Whites in 2010 was approximately 6%. Historically, this is a very high unemployment figure for this group. However, the percentage of unemployed African Americans and American Indians and Alaska Natives was nearly double this figure. Specifically, 11.1% of African Americans were unemployed, and for American Indians and Alaska Natives it was 10.6% for the single-race group and 10.4% for the total population, including those identified multiracially. Recall that in the previous figures, adding multiracial American Indians in the total population seemed to elevate the educational attainment of this group, suggesting that they are a better-educated population than those who identify with only a single race. In contrast, unemployment for the total population of American Indians is virtually identical to those who are monoracially identified, suggesting that while multiracial American Indians and Alaska Natives may be better educated, their additional schooling offered them little protection from being jobless.

Family Income

Figure 4.7 shows the median family incomes for non-Hispanic Whites, African Americans, American Indians and Alaska Natives who identify with one race only, and the total American Indian and Alaska Native population, including persons who identify with two or more races. Most American families, regardless of their race, depend on income from employment more than any other source, followed by income from public assistance or unemployment insurance. The differences shown in figure 4.7 could be anticipated from the previous graphs describing the education and labor force experience of these groups.

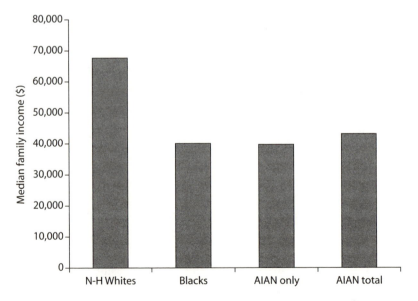

Figure 4.7. Median family income, 2009 (Source: U.S. Census Bureau, n.d.)

African Americans and American Indians and Alaska Natives have very similar incomes, differing by only a few hundred dollars for the single-race American Indian and Alaska Native families. Adding multiracial American Indians and Alaska Natives raises the median family income of the total population by about $3,000. Non-Hispanic White families are clearly more affluent than African Americans or American Indians and Alaska Natives. These families had a median annual income of about $68,000 in 2009. Put another way, non-Hispanic White families have a median income that is nearly 70% higher than the other groups represented in this graph.

Poverty

The federal government's official measure of poverty varies by the size of the household and the number of children living in the household. In 2010 the official poverty threshold for the proverbial nuclear family, two adults and two children, was $22,113. Figure 4.8 shows the percentage of all families with incomes below the poverty threshold. However, it is well known that families headed by a single mother are at far greater risk of falling into poverty, espe-

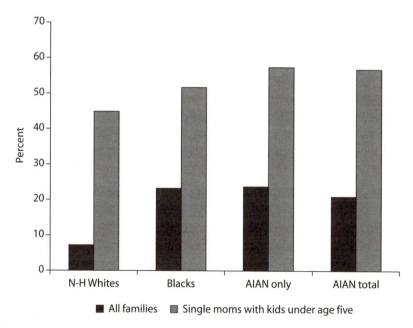

Figure 4.8. Percentage of families with incomes below poverty (Source: U.S. Census Bureau, n.d.)

cially those mothers raising young children. For this reason, the percentage of families headed by a single mother with children age five years and under with family incomes below poverty is also displayed in figure 4.8.

It should be no surprise that the percentage of non-Hispanic White families with incomes below poverty is relatively small—only 7.2%. For African American and American Indian and Alaska Native families, the percentage is over three times as large, hovering around 23%, and is slightly lower for the total American Indian population at 21%. Among families headed by single mothers with young children, the percentages below poverty are staggering. Even among non-Hispanic Whites, 45% of these families are living in poverty. The poverty rate is highest among American Indian or Alaska Native families at 57%, with a negligible difference between the groups represented in the graph. African American families headed by single women with young children fall between these two groups, with 52% living in poverty.

Inequality in Indian Country

To close this review of the economic fortunes (or lack thereof) of American Indians and Alaska Natives, the final graph (figure 4.9) in this chapter shows median family income for a selected group of reservations. The growth of eco-

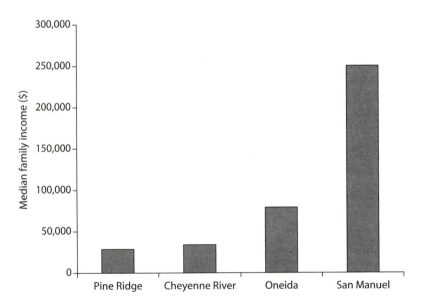

Figure 4.9. Median family income, 2010 (Source: U.S. Census Bureau, n.d.)

nomic inequality in American society is a topic of concern among politicians, journalists, political commentators, and social scientists. Paralleling this development has been a profound increase in inequality across American Indian communities. Inequality in the national economy entails a variety of complicated developments. However, among reservations the rise in inequality has a simpler explanation.

In the late 1970s, many reservations began efforts to stimulate reservation economies. Some tried farming, others recruited manufacturing plants, a few opened small businesses in construction and retail stores (notably tobacco), and still others sought to exploit natural resources such as fisheries, oil, gas, and timber. However, by far the most successful (and controversial) were initiatives that launched tribally owned casinos and related facilities such as hotels, restaurants, and conference sites.

However, not every tribe was able to take advantage of the market for gambling. Some reservations are too remote and isolated to attract large numbers of patrons. Other reservations opened casinos with mixed and mediocre results—again often due to the distance of the reservation from a large population center. However, a handful of reservations are located in or nearby major metropolitan areas and easily accessible by an interstate highway, and these reservations have been extraordinarily successful.[6]

The reservations represented in figure 4.9 include two of the poorest reservations in the nation—Pine Ridge and Cheyenne River. Both are occupied by bands of Sioux and located in South and North Dakota, respectively. The median family income for the Pine Ridge reservation was about $29,000 in 2010 and $34,000 for Cheyenne River. The Oneida reservation is located in northern Wisconsin, just outside the city of Green Bay. The Oneida tribe has a successful casino and conference facility, and they have diversified their earnings in a variety of investments. The median family income of this reservation is about $79,000, well above the federal poverty threshold. Finally, at the upper end of the tribal income distribution, there is the San Manuel reservation in Southern California. The San Manuel community has a very successful casino and has acquired other properties. It is also a very small tribe, numbering 112 persons in the 2010 census. With a small number of tribal members and a lucrative business operation, the members of the San Manuel tribe are best described as wealthy. The reported median family income of the reservation is $250,000 but is likely higher because this is the highest amount that the Census Bureau will publicly disclose for family income.

Conclusion: Education and Poverty:
Why Aren't We Doing Better?

Education for American Indians historically was a strategy devised for "civilizing" them. In the early years of contact, Protestant missionaries established schools mostly for the purpose of teaching basic literacy. In the early nineteenth century, the federal government promoted this practice with financial support. Over the course of the nineteenth century, education became an increasingly important tool for eradicating tribal culture. Boarding schools in particular explicitly incorporated measures designed to indoctrinate American Indian children against the ways of their people. These practices abated in the mid-twentieth century. For the past forty years, American Indians have increasingly taken control of the means by which they educate their children.

There is a close connection between education and material well-being. Unfortunately, educational success has eluded many American Indians, and predictably much of the American Indian population remains mired in poverty. In this regard, American Indians and Alaska Natives share a place with African Americans in the lowest reaches of the American socioeconomic hierarchy.

It was not supposed to be this way. That is, in the push for self-determination, the fundamental postulate asserted that only American Indians could know what is best for their people and their communities. By the same token, only American Indians knew best what kinds of schools and what kinds of education best suited their people, and once they were in charge of the schooling of their children, their children thrived and flourished. The absence of an oppressive presence hostile to tribal culture and traditions enabled American Indian children to succeed in ways they never could in the past.

Yet nearly four decades have passed since the 1976 Indian Self-Determination and Education Assistance Act became the law of the land. Nearly two full generations of American Indian youth have passed through schools largely governed by their own people, excluding, of course, most urban Indian children. Yet the educational progress anticipated in the early 1970s has yet to materialize in any significant way. There is a temptation to demonize the lasting impact of the BIA school system as the source of these failures. To be sure, the long reach of history may still be at work. But over time, this is, and will be, an argument with diminishing credibility.

American Indian leaders and especially educators need to look within themselves and take stock of what is required to assure the academic success of their children and the students they teach. Simply being in charge of their schools may not be sufficient to bring about the kinds of lasting change that the self-determination movement envisioned. Nonetheless, self-determination does bring a responsibility to do better than others have done in the past. As American Indian educators, we bear a responsibility to bring the skills and knowledge that will ensure the survival and well-being of our people long beyond the fore-seeable future. Canassatego understood well what skills were important for the youths of his tribe to learn and how best to learn them. It is time for American Indian leaders and especially educators to follow his example.

NOTES

1. Of course, other nations established colonies in North America, Russia, and the Netherlands, for example, but their presence and influence was relatively short-lived.

2. The Servicemen's Readjustment Act of 1944 (commonly known as the GI Bill) provides a range of benefits, including low-cost mortgages, tuition and living allowances to attend a postsecondary institution, low-interest loans, and unemployment compensation to veterans who had been on activity duty for a requisite amount of time and who had not been dishonorably discharged (U.S. Department of Veterans Affairs, 2015, http://www.benefits.va.gov/gibill/history.asp).

3. The U.S. Census Bureau did not begin measuring coverage errors until the 1950 Census. Since 1950, the Census Bureau has underenumerated American Indians and other racial and ethnic minorities in every subsequent decennial census, including 2010. If the Census Bureau was not able to fully enumerate the American Indian population in 2010, it stands to reason that census takers before 1950, lacking sophisticated technology, accessible roads, and accurate maps, had an even more difficult task. These challenges almost certainly led to less than a full enumeration and, indeed, plausibly the source of large coverage errors.

4. The calculation is 6.1 divided by 5.6 equals 1.089. The numerator is 8.9% larger than the denominator.

5. Asians have even higher rates of educational attainment.

6. Even a desirable location and access to transportation is no guarantee of success. The Foxwoods Casino in western Connecticut was once the largest and most lucrative tribally owned casino in the United States. However, a series of poor business decisions and a downturn in the U.S. economy nearly forced its closure in 2012. The tribe has since restructured its debt and worked with its creditors to keep the casino operating.

REFERENCES

Abernethy, David B. 2002. *The Dynamics of Global Dominance: European Overseas Empires, 1415–1980*. New Haven, CT: Yale University Press.

Adams, David Wallace. 1995. *Education for Extinction: American Indians and the Boarding School Experience, 1875–1926*. Lawrence: University Press of Kansas.

Bernstein, Alison R. 1991. *American Indians and World War II: Toward a New Era in Indian Affairs.* Norman: University of Oklahoma Press.

Boyd, Julian P., ed. 1938. Indian Treaties Printed by Benjamin Franklin, 1736–1762. Philadelphia: Historical Society of Pennsylvania.

Carter, S. B., S. S. Gartner, M. R. Haines, A. L. Olmstead, R. Sutch, and G. Wright. 2006. *Historical Statistics of the United States: Millennial Edition.* New York: Cambridge University Press.

Child, Brenda. 2000. *Boarding School Seasons: American Indian Families, 1900–1940.* Lincoln: University of Nebraska Press.

Fixico, Donald L. 1986. *Termination and Relocation: Federal Indian Policy 1945–1960.* Albuquerque: University of New Mexico Press.

Krouse, Susan Applegate. 2003. "What Came Out of the Takeovers: Women's Activism and the Indian Community School of Milwaukee." *American Indian Quarterly* 27:533–47.

Lomawaima, Tsianina K. 1994. *They Called It Prairie Light: The Story of Chilocco Indian School.* Lincoln: University of Nebraska Press.

Nixon, Richard M. 1970. *Special Message to the Congress on Indian Affairs.* Santa Barbara, CA: The American Presidency Project. http://www.presidency.ucsb.edu/ws/?pid =2573.

Prucha, Francis P. 1984. *The Great Father: The United States Government and the American Indians.* Lincoln: University of Nebraska Press.

Salisbury, Neal. 1984. *Manitou and Providence: Indians, Europeans, and the Making of New England, 1500–1643.* New York: Oxford University Press.

Salisbury, Neal, and Colin G. Calloway. 2004. *Reinterpreting New England Indians and the Colonial Experience.* Boston: Colonial Society of Massachusetts.

Snipp, C. Matthew. 1989. *American Indians: The First of This Land.* New York: Russell Sage Foundation.

Sorkin, Alan L. 1978. *The Urban American Indian.* Lexington, MA: Lexington Books.

Szasz, Margaret Connell. 1988. *Indian Education in the American Colonies, 1607–1783.* Albuquerque: University of New Mexico Press.

U.S. Census Bureau. n.d. *American Community Survey Data Custom Reports.* Washington, DC: Author. www.census.gov/acs/www/.

5

Poverty in Education and the Social Sciences

Three Definitions

ZEUS LEONARDO

The enduring problem of poverty in social life affects just about every facet of educational life. Poverty in education forms one of the central dilemmas in both education research and reform since at least the 1966 "Coleman Report."[1] There are three definitions of "poverty" in the education and social science literature, which this chapter takes up. First, a common understanding of poverty is related to material deprivation. Dilapidated images of inner-city schools or urban centers come to mind. Although rural families and schools form one experience of material poverty, education and social science researchers have been more concerned with understanding urban settings as places where poverty is all but out of control (Leonardo and Hunter 2007). A critical perspective that explains the materialist definition of poverty is Marxism, a paradigm that has thrived since Bowles and Gintis's 1976 publication of *Schooling in Capitalist America*.

In the second and longer section of the chapter, we discuss how poverty signifies a deficit perspective often associated with cultural mindsets and psychological dispositions associated with working-class families in general and communities of color in particular. Less a materialist explanation, this second definition takes on a cultural content and has found its expression in the "culture of poverty" thesis appropriated from Oscar Lewis (1968), as well as reactions to it (Rodrìguez, Olmedo, and Reyes-Cruz 2004). Education scholarship focuses more centrally on this aspect of poverty, partly because it is the element that more educators feel they have some control over when compared with the political economy.

The third connotation of poverty is ideological and includes elements of "impoverishment," such as one finds in David Berliner's (2006) use of the term in a *Teachers College Record* article on educators' impoverished views of school reform. This last sense of poverty includes ideologies that have been recently called into question, such as the poverty of whiteness, which in David Roediger's (1994) view is empty of substance and exists plainly to reinforce racial hierarchy. The chapter ends with a brief consideration of the white abolition movement and its understanding of poverty at the level of race theory. Overall, the chapter introduces and explicates the three definitions of poverty as material, cultural, and ideological.

The Limit Situation of Material Poverty

In the late Jean Anyon's (1997) bestselling book *Ghetto Schooling*, the celebrated social scientist of urban education takes us through a decade's worth of political and economic decisions that made Newark, New Jersey, what it is today. Anyon argues that urban cities like Newark are best understood as historical sites where a combination of political corruption and economic neglect have led to their logical consequences—a city under ruins and a school system equally crippled to ameliorate high rates of attrition and general failure. We might add, as critical pedagogists have insisted, that this failure is predictable as part of the "successful" reproduction of the labor force in schools and fulfills the imperatives found within capitalism. Anyon's meticulous research of district archives; classroom participant-observation; interviews with parents, teachers, and students; and primary and secondary research documents on Newark reveals the multipronged process for *producing* poverty at the city and school levels. The result is neither unavoidable (since it is a product of social policies) nor surprising (since it is a logical outcome of human decisions). Indeed, Newark's current situation is betrayed by decades of prosperity that the city experienced during the early 1900s before the Great Migration of Black influx into the city and the slow but strident economic restructuring of the 1960s and on. Anyon's point is that while material poverty is deplored by any educational reformer with a modicum of empathy or ethics, it is a logical result of the political economic system known as capitalism.

As Bowles and Gintis (1976) and Bowles and Levin (1968), almost ten years before, observed, no number of good intentions or reforming schools within the system that makes them places for social stratification challenges the fundamental pattern of reproducing the division of labor that was put in motion since the creation of the common school. School reform that does not take into account the structures external to the institution of education but gives it form will prove frustrating at best or complicit at worst (see Gottesman 2013).

This does not preclude reforms that are more or less progressive but makes "anti-reformist reforms" (Fraser 1997) or those sweeping changes that fundamentally alter the instrumentalist value orientation of the social system difficult, if not impossible. Although education Marxists who identify with that moniker differ in their degree of commitment to historical materialism, such as the question of "culture" as a possible site of transformation (e.g., Apple 2004; Freire 1993; Giroux 1981; McLaren 1998), they share the conviction that capitalism's evolution represents the culprit for education's devolution from a place of learning to one of social control. To wit, Apple's (2004) distinction between social control that is necessary as part of the organization of society and social control that represents precisely its engineering is prescient. Poverty within capitalism is a species of the second form, which turns schools as apparatuses for social control into a science. This makes poverty an inherent part of the social edifice rather than the failure of families, let alone the failure of schools. To the extent that schools function to reproduce this arrangement, the unequal distribution of wealth is secured. Likewise, its opposite is true: the naturalization of social suffering. Rather than a deviation from the democratic norm, the persistence of poverty becomes the rule.

Locating the source of material deprivation in the structures that produce it does not make light of people's personal limitations. People who are poor may add to their own marginalization by disqualifying themselves from the credential race (see Willis 1977), exacerbate their sense of powerlessness through the acceptance of common sense (see Gramsci 1971), or mystify the processes responsible for their own oppression (see Freire 1993). But as Marx once insisted, people make decisions in conditions they did not, on the whole, create. In fact, one could lay the same argument for the bad choices that capitalists make. Lukács (1971) notes that from the point of view of an individual capitalist (or today's investment banker), decisions that lead to people's exploitation appear rational. It is only when a scientific explanation gives a nod to the "totality" of social relations (e.g., the outer limit of capitalism) that decisions at the personal or local level descend to their irrational form. At this level, they are not justifiable, and the concept of "cognitive dissonance" fails to capture the contradictions that are at the social, rather than personal, level. Affirming structural analysis argues that educators behave in ways that are consistent with the conditions that make their actions possible. Although we would do well to mitigate against Bowles and Gintis's (1976) overestimation of the process of reproduction as seamless, this criticism does not make their correspondence theory seem less powerful. It does not dismiss the possibility that educators are complex beings, some of whom recognize a situation that produces poverty and act against it. Many do. But many more conduct themselves daily within the expectations of capitalism because it is either convenient to do so or they find it difficult to change a system they did not create. More than likely, they accept the social system that produced them and in which they partake as a matter of daily living.

The face of material poverty should not be underestimated. Although the middle and upper classes may interact with poverty in an indirect way through casual relationships or the service economy, or have more direct ties with it through extended family members, the sheer fact of poverty is sometimes difficult to fathom. People who do not live through it daily as an *embodied experience* may find Kozol's (1991) descriptions in *Savage Inequalities* rather surreal. Especially in a mediatized, first-world nation like the United States, the fact that some people live in abject poverty may achieve the quality of a movie on the big screen. When we take into consideration intense class- and race-based segregation, the plight of the poor is out of sight and out of mind for the middle class, and the realism found in the television series *The Wire* becomes a substitute for a real connection with the conditions of the poor. This does not suggest that Americans do not treat poverty as a serious social issue but that some people's opulent lifestyles (recall reports of the 1% during the Occupy movements after 2007) amid others' inability to eke out a dignified, basic existence does not sit well with the average onlooker who may feel surplus powerlessness to alleviate the widening gap between the rich and poor. It is "someone else's problem," and one is fortunate enough to avoid it. After all, the United States represents the apex of western civilization, so images of utter destitution confound Americans' self-image of progress and fairness. Some poignant reminders might help.

In many U.S. urban centers and the municipalities surrounding them, Gunnar Myrdal's (1944) well-worn description of the American dilemma is palpable. To take but one example, circa 1990 Newark, New Jersey, became the fourteenth most segregated neighborhood of the largest one hundred U.S. cities. This was a sign of its racialized poverty, with 78% of students qualifying for free/reduced-price lunches. In Anyon's (1997) school site for her research, Marcy Elementary School, 71% of the students were Black and 27% were Hispanic, 45% of the census tract population lived below the poverty line. Dilapidated buildings and outdated textbooks made up the school's material resources, which made learning higher-order skills difficult, even if desired. It does not take a Marxist to note that educational inputs such as curriculum and teaching may not necessarily trump students' family backgrounds (e.g., Coleman 1966) but neither do studies like the Coleman Report succeed in pairing the structural causes with their educational symptoms. As such, comparing some schools' material conditions with the devastation akin to a war zone would not be an exaggeration. With respect to the curriculum, there is an overreliance on standardized tests and basic skills, leading students down a path of unskilled labor if they are the fortunate ones who graduate. In all, students may find an escape route from the strictures of material poverty by succeeding and continuing with higher education, but it remains to say that they are exceptions to the rule. And here, Marxists and Coleman agree that class status all but determines students' educational outcome.

Because poverty usually comes with a set of social challenges, cities like Newark spend a higher percentage of their budget on social services, such as the police and fire departments, which cut into school resources (cf. Kozol 1991). Although Anyon finds that Newark once experienced better conditions before the 1930s, by 1970 it boasted the highest rate of new cases of tuberculosis, the second highest rate of infant mortality, and the highest rate of maternal mortality. Young children do not fare much better, as the lack or absence of prenatal care makes them vulnerable to neurological and physiological damage, some problems of which the schools inherit in the form of learning disabilities, further sapping their resources. Infant deaths per one thousand live births were high at forty-seven in Newark's ghetto core and thirty-nine in the broader city compared with New Jersey state rates at 23.3 and a national rate of 24.8. This paints a more complete picture wherein, from wealth to health, the working poor, a disproportionate number being of color, suffers setbacks that only a structural understanding that connects material poverty with life chances writ broadly is able to apprehend. These are the same processes that produced the condition that Kozol (1991) documented in other cities within New Jersey, such as Camden, and across the United States in places like East St. Louis, Missouri. Consequently, while Anyon's Newark differs in historical specificity from Kozol's East St. Louis, they share the same chilling portrait of intergenerational poverty. Same story, different cities.

The Culture of Poverty

As one might expect, the material condition of poverty produces cultural practices, social dispositions, and ways of being. Strictly speaking, poverty produces culture, or at least comes with a concomitant set of repertoires: a culture of poverty. Its existence is rather simple to accept if we keep in mind its correlate in the culture of the wealthy, something with which Americans are no doubt familiar and was made popular by the 1980s television series *Lifestyles of the Rich and Famous*, hosted by Robin Leach. Somehow, its equivalent in the form of "lives on the boundary," to use Mike Rose's (2005) phrase, would not translate so well onto the screen. Social suffering does not carry the same cache despite multitudinous representations of ghetto life on television and in music. From an analytical standpoint, poor- or working-class people embody or possess a culture. This seems to be a reasonable, if not uncontroversial, assertion. How educational scholars might proceed with characterizing it is another issue altogether.

In 1968 one such description was attempted by Oscar Lewis. Initially studying poor neighborhoods in urban Mexico and Puerto Rico, he argued that the material condition of poverty created coping strategies in the poor and working class. Because poverty is by definition a life of external limits placed on its targets, poor people navigate daily living in a way that corresponds with these limitations. Among other strategies, they deal with the hand they are dealt through an informal exchange wherein an alternative economy, some of which may be criminal in nature, fulfills financial needs but in no way prepares their participants for the skills required by the formal job market. Because hopelessness may pervade their lifeworld, a bleak future orients them to the present as opposed to the delayed gratification exhorted by official WASP (White Anglo-Saxon Protestant) culture. Because employment prospects are low and stress is high, cultivation of family life suffers, including higher proportions of single-parent homes. No doubt this fact is exacerbated by the high percentages of imprisonment of Black and Latino men living in poverty. As a result, the value of educational credentials is eclipsed by life's exigencies, wherein one statistic indicates that over 80% of prison inmates failed to graduate high school (Anyon 1997). Health disparities are reinforced when dietary information is reduced to the lowest common denominator of cost in both food preparation and raw materials or ingredients. Regarding specific racial populations, Black men are constructed as morally irresponsible and sexually promiscuous, whereas Black women are inappropriately domineering and emasculating of their men (for a history of writings on Black men, see Brown 2011). All in all, poverty creates a cultural architecture that is born from disadvantage and in a cruel irony further reinforces said disadvantages. A rather pathological image of the poor comes out of the other end, whose culture is precisely blameworthy in popular receptions of Lewis's work.

Lewis sparked a concern with cultural arguments, which still haunts social science and education research today. Taken up in both academic arguments (Banfield 1970; Wilson 1987) and policy recommendations (Glazer and Moynihan 1970), the culture of poverty lens becomes the dominant reference point for understanding the problems of the poor. One senses a shift from a study of the conditions of poverty to the people themselves, from the structures that put them in their social place to their idiosyncratic habits. For example, in sociology the "culture question" has been so contested since the height of William Julius Wilson's (1978, 1987) and Elijah Anderson's (1990, 2000) work that the discipline took a virtual hiatus from studying culture until its return during the first decade of the new millennium. Other than the uptake of cultural materialism within postmodern strains in sociology (e.g., see Lemert 2004) or culture without its overt ties with race, or race as only one among many ways to understand culture (Glassner 2000), Small, Harding, and Lamont (2010) cited a return to research that gingerly treads on culture after the domination of the culture of poverty thesis. The recent citations of culture put it back onto the research agenda, but one senses the trepidation in cultural research after Oscar Lewis (1968), Daniel Patrick Moynihan (Glazer and Moynihan 1970), and what Stephen Steinberg (1998) calls the former senator's academic reincarnation in William Julius Wilson.

There have been several reactions to the culture of the poverty line of thought. Several studies in the 1970s argue that rather than exhibiting pathological behavior, urban Black men create adaptive subcultural behaviors to deal with their strictures (see Brown 2011). Not the least of these strategies includes soulful linguistic repertoires to exceed their material limitations through creative cultural practices rather than be constrained by them. In more recent decades, this may include the field and cultural industry popularly known as hip hop (Chang 2005). That is, materially poor does not equate with being culturally poor, as the culture of poverty frame is inclined to promulgate. Culture is redefined precisely as the practice that maintains relative autonomy from economic deprivation, a way to exceed, without escaping, it. An unmistakably clear rejection of the culture of poverty argument is launched by Robin D. G. Kelley (1998) in *Yo' Mama's Disfunktional! Fighting the Culture Wars in Urban America*, which faults the center of gravity found within the social and human sciences for historically framing Black communities as the source of their own demise. Citing scholarship that takes "playing dozens" to new heights, this time without the sense of playfulness, an era of insulting depictions of Blacks becomes policy. Indicting the ideology of whiteness (about which I will have more say in the final section), Kelley prefigures the problematic graduation of perceptions to reality. It should not come as a surprise when, with the arrival of No Child Left Behind in the early years of the new millennium, the culture problem in education is arguably conceived as a Black problem.

The revaluation of working-class culture is introduced into education as a counter to the Lewis-Moynihan-Wilson triumvirate. Across the Atlantic, Paul Willis's (1977) classic study of the "lads" in the United Kingdom puts forth a nuanced portrait of adolescent boys' coping with their class reality through cultural forms. Creating what Hebdige (1979) would call a "subculture," Willis's lads work against the rhythm of bureaucratic school life by carving out a sociality guided by amiable time, a temporal arrangement that functions by use value despite the fact that its exchange value in the labor market is limited. As a case in point, the lads take every opportunity to achieve a "laff," which is a defiant attitude toward educational authority. Their subculture is characterized by informal criteria that increase homosocial behavior among the lads against their female counterparts, the "birds," and their racial others, the "Pakis" and West Indian boys. Although the lads are not free from their own contradictions, such as their nonconformism's ability to disqualify them from the credentials race and thereby fulfill the reproduction of their working-class position, Willis's point is the lack of inevitability and determinism, mixed with some "good sense," in the culture of poverty. They are further shown to cope with their class injury through their race and gender privileges, preventing them from a more complete analysis of their social contradictions. That said, education research gains an appreciation of working-class culture's generativeness in the face of structural limitations (see MacLeod 1987 for comparable results in the U.S. context).

By the late 1970s, the reconsideration of the culture of poverty is in full swing. New studies of poverty and culture are armed with both new theories gained from recent engagements in cultural Marxism (e.g., Gramsci 1971), subjectivity (Giroux 1983), cultural mediation (Apple 2004), and culture's transformative potential (Freire 1993), and aided by a new set of methodological tools gained from the New Sociology of Education with an eye toward micro-cultural processes (Gottesman 2012; McGrew 2011; Whitty 1985; Young 1971). Culture is portrayed as precisely productive, having its sense of autonomy and creativity. The turn to culture counters the disparagement of proletarian outlook already extant, without falling prey to a workerist romanticization of it (Sparks 1996; Williams 1977). No longer reduced to an impoverished choice, working-class culture from all racial groups is reconsidered as part of the overall transformation of education and the analytical frameworks used to understand it.

The cultural content of schooling is arguably the powerful lens that education scholars favor to make sense of what Althusser (1971) once called the ideological state apparatuses. Apple (2004), Giroux (1983), and Willis's (1977) theory of *cultural production* comes at the heels of a more favored theory of cultural reproduction. In the former, the focus, not unlike Gramsci decades before, falls on ideology and consciousness, both of which gesture toward an analysis of culture as a productive force. In the latter, a prominent scholar of cultural and social reproduction in education hails from France by way of Bourdieu (1977). Enjoying general success in sociology (see Lareau 2000, 2003), and imported into education as a way to explain the "distinction" afforded to middle-class culture in general (aristocratic culture specifically in France, see Bourdieu 1984), concepts like "cultural capital," defined as middle-class dispositions and skills afforded status in education despite their "arbitrariness," have become a veritable academic industry. Flanked by "habitus" on one side, or the embodiment of objective structures through subjective or self-understandings, and "fields" on the other, or particular domains of power with their rules for engagement and contestation, Bourdieu's oeuvre is decisive in showcasing the process whereby school rituals and institutional form favor the middle class. On one level, this is hardly a secret, and schools are institutions that pride themselves on promoting working-class children into middle-class mobility (Lareau 2003). However, even as the equalizing force it is touted to be, education consists of class processes that are not justified but make up part of its normative structure (Bernstein 1977a, 1977b), a "cultural arbitrary" (Bourdieu and Passeron 1977) that disguises its specificity in the cloak of universality.

With respect to the targets of cultural reproduction, the culture of poverty does not escape its former status as a disparaged outlook. Although it would be difficult to suggest that Bourdieu justifies the class reproduction he describes (Leonardo 2012, 2013), to some U.S. education scholars his theory does not go far enough to reframe the contestation to account for the valuation of culture in the eyes of the working class or people of color (Yosso 2005). In other words, Bourdieu's understanding, indeed his theory, does not break free of the dominant class or master race's imaginary to suggest an alternative view of marginalized culture, which still receives short shrift in terms of being perceived as a deficit or fundamental lack. Again, it is worth noting that Bourdieu is concerned with power relations as they function and not as he would like them to work, vitiating an otherwise totalizing critique of his theory as hopelessly caught up in deficit thinking.

Lareau (2003) offers her own ethnographic examples of working-class parenting through "natural growth" compared with middle-class "concerted cultivation," the first a Rousseau-guided principle (1979) of child-centered development, the second an overstructured, overcommitted daily life for the child. Lareau's policy recommendations include the reorientation to natural growth as a form of accomplishment and schools' accommodation of this cultural way of being. One could fault her for failing to question the material system that necessitates this class-based parenting difference, but her attempt to invert the normal/normed expectations does not go unnoticed. The revaluation of the culture of poverty considers the use of concepts as somehow colluding with the structures of inequality, in this case, how disparaging discourses lead to further marginalization.

In terms of race power, Yosso (2006) questions whether a framework that conceives of Latino culture in particular, or people of color in general, as impoverished has the ability to reframe the public discourse around educational reform. In addition, here we should note that Bourdieu's cultural sociology takes on a racial turn within a U.S. understanding. When culture is defined from either a bourgeois perspective or whiteness as the point of emanation, it becomes difficult to value the culture of the working class or of color on its own terms. This does not deny that a culture of poverty in its strict sense exists insofar as material poverty creates cultural adaptations as a function of necessity. Although swinging the pendulum to the other side may have its own set of difficulties, not the least of which is the haste to romanticize or uncritically celebrate diversity (see Lubienski 2003), a vigorous push to value lives of color (e.g., their "endarkened epistemologies"; Dillard 2000; Wright 2003) would go a long way to fight against the tilted campaign against them. At stake is a way of conceiving of culture dialectically as bound up with problems *and* possibilities.

As a form of capital, formerly marginalized culture assumes value when viewed from within its own standards rather than from an external and arbitrary value system. From "there," the culture of poverty represents what needs reforming at best or purging at worst. From "here," Latino culture, for example, boasts forms of capital unseen from a majoritarian perspective. Recast as forms of "community cultural wealth," marginalized groups' resilience, resourcefulness, and resistance point to their "richness" (Pérez Huber 2009; Yosso 2006). Valenzuela (1999, 2002) found earlier that education would do well to pay attention to Mexican values of educación as a community-based ethos to counter the naturalized orientation to education as an individual accomplishment. In her ethnography in Texas, Mexican American respondents expressed their concern for the schools' ability to care for them when their experience is "subtractive," or takes away from their cultural orientation. In this instance, the deficit is an educational system that robs Latinos of the ability to learn with their cultural framework intact. In other words, institutional life for Latinos damages their sense of identity, connection with family and community life, and, in the end, affiliation with schooling (see also Portes and Rumbaut 2001). Compare this to Ladson-Billings's (2007) appeal for a shift from the deficit perspective to one of "educational debt" that is owed to African Americans in a nation that owes them a check that has not been cashed.

Another species of the argument questioning the culture of poverty perspective is Moll's use of the anthropological concept of "funds of knowledge." Conceived as a model of cultural exchange, funds of knowledge describes practices used by people in order to meet their daily needs within material constraints (Moll and Gonzalez 2004; Moll and Greenberg 1990). Transcending these daily structures means that maximum resourcefulness between and within households involved in informal exchange mitigates the otherwise limited institutional spaces offered to students from either the class or racial margins. For example, to meet material needs, such as auto repairs, a family may exchange one form of labor for another, such as house improvements for engine upkeep. Children in these families are reared in a social milieu where this form of cultural economy is common practice. As a result, they learn that knowledge is a social relation that becomes a source of human connection rather than a commodity for market-based consumption.

Yosso's (2006) use of community cultural wealth shares an affinity with Moll's funds of knowledge approach. The former differs in inspiration via Oliver and Shapiro's (1997) sociological shift from a focus on income disparities that show a slowing gap between White and Black income since the 1970s to an emphasis on wealth disparities, which are more encompassing and durable by including debt, housing equity, and stock options. The shift to wealth disparities shows a stubborn pattern of two material realities that remain separate: one

Black and the other White. Yosso's (2006) appropriation of Oliver and Shapiro's more or less materialist analysis of race inequality comes in two forms: (1) her cultural understanding of wealth and (2) her inversion of Oliver and Shapiro's thesis to argue for the strength of Latino cultural wealth. From these and other intellectual developments, education scholars, with some help from the disciplines, have shifted the gaze on impoverishment from working-class families or communities of color to the social system that insists on defining them through derision or reduction. An emic view of culture reveals that blaming victims for their own victimization is not only a misplaced understanding of the disparity but underestimates the ability of a people to thrive within conditions that most people would consider inhospitable.

Impoverishment at the Level of Ideology

Berliner (2006) once argued that education scholars possess an impoverished view of reform. By this, he argues that we as scholars are ideologically poor in our understanding of the nature of the problem, that we have strong propensities and inclinations to change schools from within when they and the children who attend them are nested in extra-school relations, such as their families, the economy, and race relations. A central part of his argument calls attention to the universal problem of wealth disparity in U.S. society, which school reform ignores only at its own risk. Equally interesting is his use of impoverishment as a commentary about education researchers' limited perspectives on the problem and therefore solutions to it. This admission does not debilitate educators from changing their specific sites but points out that their understanding of the problem says something about their ideologies about change and stasis. Said another way, in addition to material and cultural poverty, the third level of poverty is ideological, as in an impoverished perspective on social problems.

Although there are many culprits who may fit such a description, from capitalists for Marxists or men for feminism, lately some attention has been devoted to understanding the poverty of whiteness (the early works include Frankenberg 1993; Ignatiev and Garvey 1996; Lipsitz 1998; McIntosh 1992; Roediger 1991, 1994). In education, the "turn to whiteness" indicates a preoccupation with what Lugones (2007) calls the lighter side of the modern/colonial/gender system or what Du Bois (1999) refers to as the "souls of white folk" (see Allen 2005; Cabrera 2012; DiAngelo 2012; Giroux 1997; Howard 1999; Kincheloe and Steinberg 1998; Leonardo 2009; Matias 2013; McIntyre 1997; Sleeter 2011). The turn to whiteness as an impoverished orientation to social and educational life is different from the well-grooved and established focus on white racism (e.g., see Bonilla-Silva 2001; Du Bois [1904] 1989; Feagin 2014; Mills 1997). In neo-race theory, whiteness is less an identity and more an ideology responsible for the conceptual creation of white people and its corollary in people of color as well as the perpetuation of raciology, or a racialized worldview generally speaking. In this last section, I end the chapter with an explication of whiteness as an impoverished perspective on education.

When education turns its gaze on whiteness as the locus of the problem, it accomplishes this on the basis of elevating the study of ideology. The focus on ideology has a long history in Marxism (see Eagleton 1991), and in education it has found a home in curriculum theory (Apple 2004; Giroux 1981; McLaren 1989). The turn to ideology in race theory breaks away from the tradition of referring to race as a set of identities and toward the ideological system that conceptually transforms human bodies into racialized ones. Thus, when Roediger (1994) says that "whiteness is not just false and oppressive it is *nothing but* false and oppressive" (13; emphasis original), he is talking about the ideology of whiteness rather than of Whites as is customary in these matters. In the abolitionist strain of race theory, whereas the first has no redemptive quality, the second could be redeemed, albeit as something else besides white. In Whites, education finds examples wherein particular Whites act against racism, such as "race traitors" (Ignatiev and Garvey 1996) or abolitionists like Brown or Garrison, whereas whiteness has no future and only an oppressive past. Calling for the abolition of whiteness is tantamount to calling it bankrupt as a way of understanding the world. As a knowledge system, it is an epistemology of ignorance, for it is built around the idea of forgetting what has been done in one's name (Leonardo 2013; Mills 1997). It is defined by its ability to withhold from others what the white race monopolizes for itself. From the question of who is human (Mills 1997) to who is able to learn (Leonardo and Grubb 2013), whiteness occupies the normative center.

As an ideology, whiteness becomes accessible to people of color who may answer its call and do its deeds. Thus, whiteness is not absolutely coupled only with Whites and enters even bodies of color. In both instances, it is an impoverished ideology, leading the master race to assume its superiority and the subordinate races to suffer their presumed inferiority (see Fanon [1952] 1967). Fanon provides evidence for *negrophobogenesis*, or the origins of an anti-black world. With whiteness studies, we can trace what I would call *blancophiliagenesis*, or the birth of adoration for anything white. People of color exercise the ability to put on the white mask, but the fact of their blackness, brownness, redness, or yellowness betrays them. As Fanon argues, the Black person's destiny may be whiteness, but his or her origin is blackness. In education, students of color may assimilate white linguistic codes or "act White" (see Fordham and Ogbu 1986), but this is a temporary fix for a structural problem, and one with lived ironies and haunting contradictions. At best, it is a coping mechanism in order to shield oneself from the violence of whiteness (Leonardo and Porter 2010). The solution put forth is then to abolish the ideology that makes racialized outcomes possible and impoverishes all racial groups to the extent that Whites and people of color live in constant insecurity: the first because of fear that the myth of their merit will be discovered and the second because of white surveillance and discipline. In education, the reach of the ideology of whiteness is difficult to underestimate.

A moment to discuss the discursive use of "impoverishment" is required before I approach the conclusion of this chapter. It is possible that using the signifier "poverty" to describe whiteness is unwittingly parasitic on the poor. This is a lesson I learned when on a panel at the Disability Studies in Education annual conference; I argued that whiteness is a form of racial dyslexia because like the *camera obscura* that Marx (1993) once reserved for capitalism or idealist thinking, whiteness leads Whites (and people of color susceptible to it) to read race backward or upside down (see Dwyer and Jones 2000). As long as Whites remain under the sway of the ideology of whiteness, they exhibit a form of racial learning disability when it concerns racial matters. It does not take long to notice that this portrayal adds to the marginalization of people with real or perceived disabilities, White or otherwise, through the ableist tropes of theory. The lesson is even more poignant if we recall the insistence of critical disability scholars that "ability" is a theoretical construct in its own right, which engenders the ability to speak to race and other social relations, such as the assumed disability of people of color, women, and other disparaged people (Annamma, Connor, and Ferri 2013; Baker 2002; Broderick 2010; Erevelles 1996, 2002; Kliewer and Fitzgerald 2001; Ware 2001). My understanding was that although many students of color are constructed as having a learning disability beyond the actual medical condition (itself not free of normative considerations), Whites' racial disability was actually "real," an obstruction to an otherwise accurate understanding of race relations (see also Mills 1997). Against my own intentions, the discourse I used to describe whiteness as a form of disability happened on the backs of conceptually disfigured people and props up the fictive "normate" (Garland-Thomson 1996). This recuperative logic comes with the danger of undoing our progressive work as contradictions are contained within the medium of language.

Here again, a cautionary tale would mitigate against too expansive an appropriation of loaded concepts, such as "wealth" or "poverty." This creates a condition of being politically correct while being discursively compromised, and the search for a less recuperative logic continues (cf. Giroux and Simon 1989 on being politically correct and pedagogically wrong). With the new abolitionists, I agree that the poverty-of-whiteness thesis is sound at the political level and correct as a way of conceiving the problem. Against the reconstruction of whiteness (see Giroux 1997; Kincheloe and Steinberg 1998), abolishing the ideology of whiteness acknowledges that while Whites are transformable, whiteness is not. Or as Dumas (2008) puts it, one may learn to love particular Whites, but whiteness is not to be trusted. But to indict whiteness for its poverty comes with collateral victims such that the trope, fundamentally disparaging at the primary level, implicates poor people as second-hand victims at the secondary level. In other words, being poor, even at the level of ideology, is to be of little worth. It also comes with the concomitant result of valorizing the state of being ideologically "rich," as it were. Again, poverty is understood as a deficit or fundamental lack, and wealth wins out.

Perhaps this limitation is about the "impoverished" language we use to bear on the very issue of poverty in education. Imbricated with capitalist and racist meanings, our public language is shot through with tropes that recall the structures that make them legible. The minute educators enter that language and make sense of poverty in education, we run the risk of reifying the race and class system that interpellates our subjectivity. Poverty in education does not stand separately from the language that is available for our apprehension of it, whose meaning maintains an organic relationship with material life (see Volosinov 2006). Furthermore, because race and class structures contain contradictions, these double binds appear in the language that transforms nature into culture, as Freire (1993) always insisted. This transformation through the critical potential of language also works in the opposite direction and inheres the possibility that language not only covers up social relations but unmasks and demystifies it.

NOTES

1. In 1966 James Coleman and others at Johns Hopkins University were commissioned by U.S. Commissioner of Education Harold Howe to conduct a major study of the best ways to equalize educational opportunities for poor minority students. The authors found that what mattered most in determining the academic success of students was their family background.

REFERENCES

Allen, Ricky Lee. 2005. "Whiteness and Critical Pedagogy." In *Critical Pedagogy and Race*, edited by Zeus Leonardo, 53–68. Malden, MA: Blackwell.
Althusser, Louis. 1971. *Lenin and Philosophy*. Translated by Ben Brewster. New York: Monthly Review Press.
Anderson, Elijah. 1990. *Streetwise: Race, Class, and Change in an Urban Community*. Chicago: University of Chicago Press.
———. 2000. *Code of the Street: Decency, Violence, and the Moral Life of the Inner City*. New York: W. W. Norton & Co.
Annamma, Subini Ancy, David Connor, and Beth Ferri. 2013. "Dis/ability Critical Race Studies (DisCrit): Theorizing at the Intersections of Race and Dis/ability." *Race Ethnicity & Education* 16 (1): 1–31.
Anyon, Jean. 1997. *Ghetto Schooling: A Political Economy of Urban Educational Reform*. New York: Teachers College Press.
Apple, Michael W. 2004. *Ideology and Curriculum*. 3rd edition. New York: RoutledgeFalmer.
Baker, Bernadette. 2002. "The Hunt for Disability: The New Eugenics and the Normalization of School Children." *Teachers College Record* 104 (4): 663–703.
Banfield, Edward C. 1970. "Schooling versus Education." In *The Unheavenly City: The Nature and Future of Our Urban Crisis*, edited by Edward C. Banfield, 132–57. Boston: Little, Brown and Company.
Berliner David C. 2006. "Our Impoverished View of Educational Reform." *Teachers College Record* 108 (6): 949–95.
Bernstein, Basil. 1977a. "Class Pedagogies: Visible and Invisible." In *Power and Ideology in Education*, edited by Jerome Karabel and Albert Henry Halsey, 511–34. Oxford: Oxford University Press.
———. 1977b. "Social Class, Language and Socialization." In *Power and Ideology in Education*, edited by Jerome Karabel and Albert Henry Halsey, 473–86. Oxford: Oxford University Press.
Bonilla-Silva, Eduardo. 2001. *White Supremacy and Racism in the Post-Civil Rights Era*. Boulder, CO: Lynne Rienner Publishers.
Bourdieu, Pierre. 1977. *Outline of a Theory of Practice*. Cambridge: Cambridge University Press.
———. 1984. *Distinction: A Social Critique of the Judgment of Taste*. Cambridge, MA: Harvard University Press.
Bourdieu, Pierre, and Jean-Claude Passeron. 1977. *Reproduction in Education, Society, and Culture*. Thousand Oaks, CA: SAGE.
Bowles, Samuel, and Herbert Gintis. 1976. *Schooling in Capitalist America*. New York: Basic Books.

Bowles, Samuel, and Herbert Levin. 1968. "The Determinants of Scholastic Achievement: An Appraisal of Some Recent Evidence." *Journal of Human Resources* 3:3–24.

Broderick, Alicia A. 2010. "Autism as Enemy: Metaphor and Cultural Politics." In *Handbook of Cultural Politics and Education*, edited by Zeus Leonardo, 237–68. Rotterdam, The Netherlands: Sense Publishers.

Brown, Anthony L. 2011. " 'Same Old Stories': The Black Male in Social Science and Educational Literature, 1930s to the Present." *Teachers College Record* 113 (9): 2047–79.

Cabrera, Nolan Leon. 2012. "Exposing Whiteness in Higher Education: White Male College Students Minimizing Racism, Claiming Victimization, and Recreating White Supremacy." *Race Ethnicity & Education* 17 (1): 30–55.

Chang, Jeff. 2005. *Can't Stop Won't Stop.* New York: Picador.

Coleman, James. 1966. *Equality of Educational Opportunity.* Washington, DC: U.S. Department of Health, Education, and Welfare.

DiAngelo, Robin. 2012. *What Does It Mean to Be White?* New York: Peter Lang.

Dillard, Cynthia B. 2000. "The Substance of Things Hoped For, the Evidence of Things Not Seen: Examining an Endarkened Epistemology in Educational Research and Leadership." *Qualitative Studies in Education* 13 (6): 661–81.

Du Bois, W. E. B. (1904). 1989. *The Souls of Black Folk.* New York: Penguin Books.

———. 1999. *Darkwater: Voices from within the Veil.* Mineola, NY: Dover Publications, Inc.

Dumas, Michael J. 2008. "Theorizing Redistribution and Recognition in Urban Education Research: 'How Do We Get Dictionaries at Cleveland?' " In *Theory and Educational Research*, edited by Jean Anyon, 81–108. New York: London.

Dwyer, Owen J., and John Paul Jones III. 2000. "White Socio-spatial Epistemology." *Social & Cultural Geography* 1 (2): 209–22.

Eagleton, Terry. 1991. *Ideology.* London: Verso.

Erevelles, Nirmala. 1996. "Disability and the Dialectics of Difference." *Disability & Society* 11 (4): 519–37.

———. 2002. "(Im)material Citizens: Cognitive Disability, Race, and the Politics of Citizenship." *Disability, Culture and Education* 1 (1): 5–25.

Fanon, Frantz. (1952) 1967. *Black Skin White Masks.* Translated by C. Markmann. New York: Grove Press.

Feagin, Joe R. 2014. *Racist America.* 3rd edition. New York: Routledge.

Fordham, Signithia, and John Ogbu. 1986. "Black Students' School Success: Coping with the "Burden of 'Acting White.' " *Urban Review* 18 (3): 176–206.

Frankenberg, Ruth. 1993. *White Women, Race Matters: The Social Construction of Whiteness.* Minneapolis: University of Minnesota Press.

Fraser, Nancy. 1997. *Justice Interruptus.* New York: Routledge.

Freire, Paulo. 1993. *Pedagogy of the Oppressed.* Translated by M. Ramos. New York: Continuum.

Garland-Thomson, Rosemarie. 1996. *Extraordinary Bodies: Figuring Physical Disability in American Culture and Literature.* New York: Columbia University Press.

Giroux, Henry A. 1981. *Ideology, Culture, and the Process of Schooling.* Philadelphia: Temple University Press.

———. 1983. *Theory and Resistance: A Pedagogy for the Opposition.* Westport, CT: Bergin & Garvey.

———. 1997. "Rewriting the Discourse of Racial Identity: Towards a Pedagogy and Politics of Whiteness." *Harvard Educational Review* 67 (2): 285–320.

Giroux, Henry A., and Roger Simon. 1989. "Popular Culture as a Pedagogy of Pleasure and Meaning." In *Popular Culture, Schooling and Everyday Life*, edited by Henry A. Giroux and Roger Simon, 1–29. Westport, CT: Bergin & Garvey.

Glassner, Barry. 2000. *Culture of Fear*. New York: Basic Books.

Glazer, Nathan, and Daniel P. Moynihan. 1970. *Beyond the Melting Pot*. 2nd edition. Cambridge, MA: MIT Press.

Gottesman, Isaac. 2012. "From Gouldner to Gramsci: The Making of Michael Apple's Ideology and Curriculum." *Curriculum Inquiry* 42 (5): 571–96.

———. 2013. "Socialist Revolution: Samuel Bowles, Herbert Gintis, and the Emergence of Marxist Thought in the Field of Education." *Educational Studies* 49 (1): 5–31.

Gramsci, Antonio. 1971. *Selections from Prison Notebooks*. Edited and translated by Quintin Hoare and Geoffrey Nowell Smith. New York: International Publishers.

Hebdige, Dick. 1979. *Subculture: The Meaning of Style*. London: Routledge.

Howard, Gary R. 1999. *We Can't Teach What We Don't Know: White Teachers, Multiracial Schools*. New York: Teachers College Press.

Ignatiev, Noel, and John Garvey. 1996. "Abolish the White Race: By Any Means Necessary." In *Race Traitor*, edited by Noel Ignatiev and John Garvey, 9–14. New York: Routledge.

Kelley, Robin D. G. 1998. *Yo' Mama's Disfunktional! Fighting the Culture Wars in Urban America*. Boston: Beacon Press.

Kincheloe, Joe L., and Shirley R. Steinberg. 1998. "Addressing the Crisis of Whiteness: Reconfiguring White Identity in a Pedagogy of Whiteness." In *White Reign*, edited by Joe L. Kincheloe, Shirley R. Steinberg, Nelson M. Rodriguez, and Ronald E. Chennault, 3–29. New York: St. Martin's Griffin.

Kliewer, Christopher, and Linda May Fitzgerald. 2001. "Disability, Schooling, and the Artifacts of Colonialism." *Teachers College Record* 103 (3): 450–70.

Kozol, Jonathan. 1991. *Savage Inequalities*. New York: Harper Perennial.

Ladson-Billings, Gloria. 2007. "From the Achievement Gap to the Education Debt: Understanding Achievement in U.S. Schools." *Educational Researcher* 35 (7): 3–12.

Lareau, Annette. 2000. *Home Advantage*. Lanham, MD: Rowman & Littlefield.

———. 2003. *Unequal Childhoods*. Berkeley: University of California Press.

Lemert, Charles. 2004. *Sociology after the Crisis*. 2nd edition. Boulder, CO: Paradigm Publishers.

Leonardo, Zeus. 2009. *Race, Whiteness, and Education*. New York: Routledge.

———. 2012. "The 2011 R. Freeman Butts Lecture. The Race for Class: Reflections on a Critical Race Class Theory of Education." *Educational Studies* 48 (5): 427–49. doi: 10.1080/00131946.2012.715831.

———. 2013. *Race Frameworks: A Multidimensional Theory of Racism and Education*. New York: Teachers College Press.

Leonardo, Zeus, and W. Norton Grubb. 2013. *Education and Racism: A Primer on Issues and Dilemmas*. New York: Routledge.

Leonardo, Zeus, and Margaret Hunter. 2007. "Imagining the Urban: The Politics of Race, Class, and Schooling." In *International Handbook of Urban Education*, edited by William Pink and George W. Noblit, 779–802. Dordrecht, The Netherlands: Springer.

Leonardo, Zeus, and Ronald K. Porter. 2010. "Pedagogy of Fear: Toward a Fanonian Theory of 'Safety' in Race Dialogue." *Race Ethnicity & Education* 13 (2): 139–57.

Lewis, Oscar. 1968. "The Culture of Poverty." In *On Understanding Poverty: Perspectives from the Social Sciences*, edited by Daniel Patrick Moynihan, 187–220. New York: Basic Books.

Lipsitz, George. 1998. *The Possessive Investment in Whiteness*. Philadelphia: Temple University Press.

Lubienski, Sarah Theule. 2003. "Celebrating Diversity and Denying Disparities: A Critical Assessment." *Educational Researcher* 32 (8): 30–38.

Lugones, Maria. 2007. "Heterosexualism and the Colonial/Modern Gender System." *Hypatia* 22 (1): 186–209.

Lukács, Georg. 1971. *History and Class Consciousness*. Translated by Rodney Livingstone. Cambridge, MA: MIT Press.

MacLeod, Jay. 1987. *Ain't No Makin' It*. Boulder, CO: Westview Press.

Marx, Karl. 1993. "Camera Obscura." In *Social Theory: The Multicultural and Classic Readings*, edited by Charles Lemert, 43. Boulder, CO: Westview Press.

Matias, Cheryl E. 2013. "Tears Worth Telling: Urban Teaching and the Possibilities of Racial Justice." *Multicultural Perspectives* 15 (4): 187–93.

McGrew, Ken. 2011. "A Review of Class-Based Theories of Student Resistance in Education: Mapping the Origins and Influence of Learning to Labor by Paul Willis." *Review of Educational Research* 81 (2): 234–66.

McIntosh, Peggy. 1992. "White Privilege and Male Privilege: A Personal Account of Coming to See Correspondences through Work in Women's Studies." In *Race, Class, and Gender: An Anthology*, edited by Margaret L. Andersen and Patricia Hill Collins, 70–81. Belmont, CA: Wadsworth Publishing.

McIntyre, Alice. 1997. *Making Meaning of Whiteness*. Albany: State University of New York Press.

McLaren, Peter. 1989. "On Ideology and Education." In *Critical Pedagogy, the State, and Cultural Struggle*, edited by Henry Giroux and Peter McLaren, 174–202. Albany: State University of New York Press.

———. 1998. *Life in Schools*. New York: Longman.

Mills, Charles. 1997. *The Racial Contract*. Ithaca, NY: Cornell University Press.

Moll, Luis C., and Norma Gonzalez. 2004. "Engaging Life: A Funds-of-Knowledge Approach to Multicultural Education." In *Handbook of Research on Multicultural Education*, edited by James Banks and Cherry Banks, 699–715. San Francisco: Jossey-Bass.

Moll, Luis C., and James B. Greenberg. 1990. "Creating Zones of Possibilities: Combining Social Contexts for Instruction." In *Vygotsky and Education*, edited by Luis C. Moll, 319–48. Cambridge: Cambridge University Press.

Myrdal, Gunner. 1944. *An American Dilemma*. New York: Harper and Brothers.

Oliver, Melvin L., and Thomas M. Shapiro. 1997. *Black Wealth, White Wealth: A New Perspective on Racial Inequality*. New York: Routledge.

Pérez Huber, Lindsay. 2009. "Challenging Racist Nativist Framing: Acknowledging the Community Cultural Wealth of Undocumented Chicana College Students to Reframe the Immigration Debate." *Harvard Educational Review* 79 (4): 704–29.

Portes, Alejandro, and Ruben G. Rumbaut. 2001. *Legacies*. Berkeley: University of California Press.

Rodrìguez, Clara E., Irma M. Olmedo, and Mariolga Reyes-Cruz. 2004. "Deconstructing and Contextualizing the Historical and Social Science Literature on Puerto Ricans." In *Handbook of Research on Multicultural Education*, edited by James A. Banks and Cherry A. Banks, 288–314. San Francisco: John Wiley & Sons.

Roediger, David R. 1991. *The Wages of Whiteness*. New York: Verso.

———. 1994. *Toward the Abolition of Whiteness*. New York: Verso.

Rose, Mike. 2005. *Lives on the Boundary*. New York: Penguin Books.

Rousseau, Jean-Jacques. 1979. *Emile: Or On Education*. Translated by A. Bloom. New York: Basic Books.

Sleeter, Christine E. 2011. "Becoming White: Reinterpreting a Family Story by Putting Race Back into the Picture." *Race Ethnicity & Education* 14 (4): 421–33.

Small, Mario Luis, David J. Harding, and Michele Lamont. 2010. "Introduction: Reconsidering Culture and Poverty." *The Annals of the American Academy of Political and Social Science* 629 (1): 6–27.

Sparks, Colin. 1996. "Stuart Hall, Cultural Studies and Marxism." In *Stuart Hall*, edited by David Morley and Kuan-Hsing Chen, 71–101. London: Routledge.

Steinberg, Stephen. 1998. "The Liberal Retreat from Race during the Post-Civil Rights Era." In *The House That Race Built*, edited by Wahneema Lubian, 13–47. New York: Vintage Books.

Valenzuela, Angela. 1999. *Subtractive Schooling: U.S.-Mexican Youth and the Politics of Caring*. Albany: State University of New York Press.

———. 2002. "Reflections on the Subtractive Underpinnings of Education Research and Policy." *Journal of Teacher Education* 53 (3): 235–41.

Volosinov, Valentin. 2006. *Marxism and the Philosophy of Language*. Cambridge, MA: Harvard University Press.

Ware, Linda. 2001. "Writing, Identity, and the Other: Dare We Do Disability Studies?" *Journal of Teacher Education* 52 (2): 107–123.

Whitty, Geoff. 1985. *Sociology and School Knowledge*. London: Methuen.

Williams, Raymond. 1977. *Marxism and Literature*. Oxford: Oxford University Press.

Willis, Paul. 1977. *Learning to Labor*. New York: Columbia University Press.

Wilson, William Julius. 1978. *The Declining Significance of Race: Blacks and Changing American Institutions*. Chicago: University of Chicago Press.

———. 1987. *The Truly Disadvantaged*. Chicago: University of Chicago Press.

Wright, Handel. 2003. "An Endarkened Feminist Epistemology? Identity, Difference and the Politics of Representation in Educational Research." *Qualitative Studies in Education* 16 (2): 197–214.

Yosso, Tara. 2005. "Whose Culture has Capital? A Critical Race Theory Discussion of Community Cultural Wealth." *Race Ethnicity & Education* 8 (1): 69–91.

———. 2006. *Critical Race Counterstories along the Chicana/Chicano Educational Pipeline*. New York: Routledge.

Young, Michael, ed. 1971. *Knowledge and Control: New Directions for the Sociology of Education*. London: Collier Macmillan.

6

Poverty, Place, and Biological Proficiency

A Comparative Statewide Analysis

MARK C. HOGREBE AND WILLIAM F. TATE IV

Like other states, Missouri has endeavored to implement an ambitious biotechnology industrial growth plan. Nevertheless, development efforts intended to provide opportunities for indigenous populations are typically uneven. Kain (1968) and Wilson (2012), for instance, have argued that the decentralization of blue-collar jobs reduces labor force participation among less educated individuals. This may be due to limited mobility and high housing costs in suburban areas that negatively affect low-income workers' pursuit of higher-paying employment opportunities. Although research on this theory has been mixed, it remains relevant as biotechnology and related industries relocate in geographic areas with talented human capital and high-quality educational opportunities. For traditionally underserved groups that are indigenous to an emerging biotechnology hub, it partly shifts the focus from fewer professional opportunities to concerns about skills mismatch. The latter is directly related to school quality.

Educators interested in providing young people with opportunities within this growing industry may ask the following question: "How does place influence biology performance in the state?" Past research has indicated that place matters in moderating variable relationships in algebra performance (Hogrebe and Tate 2012). Therefore, a specific focus of this chapter is to determine if place matters in moderating variable relationships between high school biology performance and educational variables because differences on the socioeconomic status (SES) poverty-affluence continuum shape local contexts. Our study will examine the relationship between variables representing district demographic composition, teaching and financial contexts, and biology performance, as measured by a statewide test aggregated at the district level. The investigation explores how these relationships vary across 518 districts within Missouri using spatial mapping. Local R^2 values from geographically weighted regressions (GWR) are mapped to show variation in relationships across districts. This analysis determines the need for region-specific policy and programming in support of students living in poverty. In light of the potential relationship between poverty, place, and academic proficiency, we will discuss the importance of proper interpretation of educational indicator systems.

New Biology, Poverty, and Learning

Categorized by metaphors and models drawn from physics, the industrial age was linked to linear, deterministic, and energy-intensive advances in science and its applications (Naisbitt and Adurdene 1990). For centuries, research in the sciences focused on systems that were either intrinsically simple or capable of being analyzed into simple segments, while overlooking more complex systems incapable of being analyzed one factor at a time (Hurd 1997). In contrast, the problems faced in modern biology defy traditional methods of inquiry. The problem spaces tend to require more holistic thinking, more synthesis, and attention to more complexity. The National Research Council's (2009) *A New Biology for the 21st Century* stated:

> Just as the Internet, combined with powerful search engines, makes vast amounts of information accessible, the core commonalities of biology, combined with increasingly sophisticated ways to compare, predict, and manipulate their characteristics, can make the resources of biology accessible for a wide range of applications. . . . The life sciences have reached a point where a new level of inquiry is possible, a level that builds on the strengths of the traditional research establishment but provides a framework to draw on those strengths and focus them on large questions whose answers would provide many practical benefits. We call this new level of inquiry the New Biology and believe that it has the potential to take on more ambitious challenges than ever before. . . . Many of the solutions the life sciences can offer are common to all living systems. Achieving understanding at this systemic level is the promise of the New Biology. (13)

Examples of the New Biology and related disciplines include bioinformatics, mathematical biology, genetic engineering, and neuroscience. New Biology is characterized in metaphoric terms as: information-intensive, micro, adaptive, holistic, and inner-directed. The New Biology has changed the way educators conceptualize the school science curriculum. Biology has become increasingly important to school science and the development of transferable knowledge and skills for life and work (National Research Council 2012). The National Research Council (NRC) recommended that more attention be paid to the role of assessment, accountability, and teachers as supports in the process of students' acquisition of transferable competencies. While calling for the systemic development, implementation, and evaluation of educational interventions targeting transferable competencies, the NRC report is silent on poverty and the importance of local context. Instead, the report is focused on propensity factors used in theoretical models of individual cognition rather than environmental models at the school district level or geospatial context factors. Yet, research indicates that student poverty influences science teaching, learning, and performance outcomes (Hogrebe and Tate 2010; Wiseman 2012). Poverty as a geospatial condition is receiving more attention in the science education literature (Tate 2008; Tate et al. 2012). However, the relationship between poverty, place, and biology performance represents an area in need of additional research.

This study investigates how the relationships between biology end-of-course (EOC) performance and education variables associated with neighborhood SES differ across school districts in various local contexts. Typically, social science research, including educational research, has sought to determine variable relationships in samples that represent "true" relationships in the overall population. However, due to the complexity and varied nature of local contexts in terms of educational, social, cultural, political, and built infrastructure, it is challenging to specify adequately a model for variable relationships that is applicable across the SES poverty-affluence continuum.

Local Context Importance

School district demographic composition, teacher context, financial context, and student behavior in relation to educational outcomes have been widely examined (Gregory, Skiba, and Noguera 2010; Hogrebe and Tate 2010; Wayne and Youngs 2003; Wood et al. 2006). Study results have not been consistent. The lack of consistency can be traced to dissimilarities in research designs using different types of schools, grade levels, assessment instruments, and measurement techniques. In addition to these examples of factors that affect outcomes and conclusions, variation due to location and spatial clustering is rarely accounted for in educational research. Even when many potential influences are controlled, relationships across local contexts might still vary. The present analysis is designed to determine if variable relationships differ across the local contexts of school districts within an entire state.

The importance of local context is manifested as a function of specific location values that tend to be similar. This similarity of variable values creates a clustering effect or within-group correlation that researchers must take into account. Factors unique to a local context or group influence members in a similar fashion and produce correlation within the groups. Statistical methods that assume observations are independent tend to underestimate standard errors when correlation exists among group members leading to an increase in type-I errors. Today, many research studies that have data from group clusters use multilevel models (MLM) to account for the within-group correlation (O'Connell and McCoach 2008; Raudenbush and Bryk 2002; Snijders and Bosker 2012).

According to Tobler's (1970) first law of geography, "everything is related to everything else, but near things are more related than distant things." In the case of neighboring school districts, there is clustering created by spatial proximity that produces unique local contexts and concomitant within-group correlation. In many instances, families and students within school districts tend to be somewhat similar on factors such as education, income, and housing. The built environment within districts is often fairly consistent and plays a significant role in providing identity to the local context. But this similarity in social and economic characteristics as well as the built environment does not start and stop abruptly at district boundary lines. The argument is that similarity based on spatial proximity is more accurately framed as a continuum, which does not begin and end at socially constructed demarcations such as district boundaries. Similarity to dissimilarity across local contexts functions as a spatial continuum in geographic space. Therefore, while unique local contexts certainly exist and the correlation of factors within them must be accounted for, analysis techniques that do not consider the spatial continuum may be inappropriate for spatially clustered data such as school districts within a region or state. For example, standard multilevel modeling techniques control for within-group correlation but do not account for similarity among adjacent geographic entities (Chaix, Merlo, and Chauvin 2005; Fotheringham 2009; Fotheringham, Brunsdon, and Charlton 2002).

In order to account for the regional clustering of districts, the present study uses geographically weighted regression (GWR) that is designed to incorporate the underlying spatial continuum. GWR allows relationships to vary across groups and clusters (districts in this study), as does MLM, but also does not ignore the similarity among neighboring districts. Since districts are located in geographic space, GIS mapping can be used to show where variable relationships differ across regions and throughout the state.

In line with the poverty and education theme of the book, the purpose of this research is to examine the relationships of financial indicators for students, teachers, and districts with biology end-of-course (EOC) scores aggregated to the district level. The intention is to see how student, teacher, and district measures associated with the poverty-financial strength continuum relate to biology proficiency for the 518 districts across the state of Missouri. Previous research found that relationships at the district level vary by geographic region and local context is an important determinant of this spatial variation (Hogrebe and Tate 2012). The following two research questions guide this study:

1. Is the biology proficiency of students lower in districts that have greater student poverty, higher minority enrollment, fewer teacher assets, and less district spending per student with reduced community financial support?
2. Are the relationships among these variables consistent across the state, or do they vary spatially by geographic region?

Data Source and Variables

Data for this study were from 518 school districts in the state of Missouri in 2011–2012. Of these, 445 were unified districts that contained both elementary and secondary schools and 73 were elementary-only districts. The source of district data was the Missouri Department of Elementary and Secondary Education (DESE) (Missouri DESE 2013).

Each district is assumed to represent a relatively homogeneous local context in terms of students and community, as well as for district policies and operation. In treating districts as the unit of analysis, district average values were used for each variable. The spatial procedures employed in the following analyses allow variable relationships to change as a function of location and to operate over an underlying geographic continuum that is not restrained by district boundaries. The independent variables form four conceptual groups: education outcomes, student composition, teacher assets, and district financial resources:

- Education Outcomes
  - *Biology I MAP Scale Score*: End-of-course scale scores were derived from an end-of-course exam given to all Biology I course participants

and averaged at the district level. The exam was developed by the Missouri Department of Elementary and Secondary Education (DESE) under its Missouri Assessment Program (MAP).

- Student Composition
  - *Free/Reduced-Price Lunch Percentage (FRL)*: The percentage of the district enrollment receiving free/reduced-price lunches.
  - *Minority Student Percentage*: The percentage of the district enrollment consisting of the total number of students in the following minority groups (minority percentage): African American, Hispanic, Asian, and American Indian.
- Teacher Assets
  - *High School Teacher Average Salary*: The average regular-term salary of teachers in the district. Fringe benefits were not included.
  - *Teacher with Master's Degree Percentage*: The percentage of teachers in a district with a master's degree or higher in any field.
  - *Teacher Asset Composite*: The combination of teacher average salary and master's degree percentage z-scores.
- District Financial Resources
  - *Cost per Student*: The district expenditures divided by average daily attendance.
  - *Local Revenue Percentage*: The percentage of district revenue from local sources. This is an indication of community financial resources and tax base.
  - *Financial Resource Composite*: The combination of cost per student and local revenue percentage z-scores.

The present study seeks to determine if district biology proficiency is a function of these student composition, teacher asset, and financial resource variables and whether the relationships vary depending on location within the state. Are districts with greater student poverty, higher minority enrollment, fewer teacher assets, and less district spending per student with reduced community financial support *consistently* associated with lower biology proficiency across the state or is there variation by region?

Methodology

Ordinary least squares regression (OLS) and geographically weighted regression (GWR) (Fotheringham 2009; Fotheringham et al. 2002) were used to examine the relationships between district-level biology proficiency and the student, teacher, and financial variables. GWR was used to determine whether variable relationships differed due to clustering of data by region and to account for spatial dependency when nearby districts were similar. The GWR procedure models geographically clustered data as an underlying continuous spatial process that can be portrayed on a map with geographic information system (GIS) software. A GIS produces maps by integrating spatial data (e.g., georeferenced coordinates such as latitude and longitude) and nonspatial data. Maps in the present study were generated with ArcMap10.1 (Environmental Systems Research Institute 2012) to show how the relationships varied across districts reflecting regional differences.

GWR was designed to incorporate the variation of local spatial relationships in the analysis approach (Fotheringham 2009; Fotheringham et al. 2002). An adaptive spatial kerning process was used to weigh data points as a function of their distance from a designated source, which in this case was a district centroid (see figure 6.1). Data points were assigned greater weights when they were closer to the designated source and smaller weights as the distance increased. GWR derived an optimum number of "nearest neighbors" by using

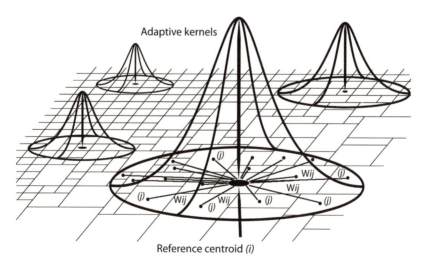

Figure 6.1. Adaptive spatial kerning process based on polygon centroids
Point (j) is polygon centroid. W_{ij} is weight for polygon centroid j in reference to centroid i. W_{ij} is a function of distance from j to i, with closer centroids having higher weights.

the spatial weights and calculating a local regression model for each geographic unit. Accordingly, based on each district's centroid in this study, GWR computed a local regression equation for every district from its data and surrounding nearest neighbors defined by spatial kerning (Fotheringham 2009; Fotheringham et al. 2002; Hogrebe and Tate 2012).

In GWR, the standard regression equation is revised to include geographic weighted reference points (u_i, v_i) (Fotheringham et al. 2002, 52):

$$y_i = \beta_0(u_i, v_i) + \beta_1(u_i, v_i)x_{i1} + \beta_k(u_i, v_i)x_{ik} + \varepsilon_i$$

The geographic weighted points (u_i, v_i) represent the coordinates of the ith point in space, which in this case is a reference district centroid. District centroids closer to the reference district centroid (i) have more weight in the parameter estimation. The adaptive spatial kerning process altered the kernel size depending on the number of districts in the area around the target district. For example, in order to identify the number of "nearest neighbors," a smaller kernel was generated for an area where a greater number of smaller districts surrounded the target district. The optimal number of nearest neighbor districts identified by the Akaike Information Criterion (AIC) was then used to generate a local regression equation for each district.

The first analysis examined the relationship of each variable with the Biology I score using both OLS and GWR in order to compare the overall R^2 values produced by each procedure. The local R^2 values generated with GWR for each variable combination were also mapped using ArcMap 10.1.

Next, a full model that included information from all variables was used to predict district Biology I scores. The full model district predictor variables were percentage of FRL students, percentage of minority students, teacher assets composite, and financial resources composite.

Because the teacher asset variables of salary and master's degree percentage had a moderately high correlation (r = .60) at the district level, they were combined into a single measure for teacher assets. The financial resource variables of cost per student and local revenue percentage had a similar correlation (r = .60) and were combined into a financial resources composite variable. The creation of the two composite variables consolidated the correlated variables and avoided the multicollinearity that would occur if these variables were entered separately into the same regression equation.

Using a full model that simultaneously includes all of the information allows for the determination of whether each predictor contributes unique information while controlling for the other variables in the equation. The full model is as follows:

Biology I scores = FRL % + minority % + teacher asset composite
+ financial resource composite

The local R^2 values from the full model were mapped with GWR to show how the relationship between the Biology I scores and variables representing poverty, teacher assets, and financial resources are a function of the underlying geographic spatial continuum.

Subsequently, an additional four maps were generated—one for each predictor variable in the full model. Each map shows the geographic regions where the local regression coefficients for that particular variable were statistically significant while controlling for the other three predictor variables. In these areas where coefficients were significant, the significance indicated that the variable contributed unique information to the prediction of Biology I scores when accounting for the other variables. The testing for significant regression coefficients was adjusted for multiple comparisons with the Benjamini-Hochberg procedure (Thissen, Steinberg, and Kuang 2002).

There are elementary and secondary schools in 445 unified districts in Missouri and elementary schools only in 73 districts. Although there are no secondary schools in the elementary-only districts, secondary students live in these elementary districts but attend high school in neighboring districts. The data for these high school students are not recorded in the elementary districts where they live but instead are reflected in the district data where they attend secondary school. For secondary students who lived in the elementary districts, areal interpolation (ArcMap 10.1) was used to estimate values for the elementary districts based on data in the surrounding unified districts. In order to maintain the underlying spatial continuum, this interpolation produced an average of nearby unified districts secondary school data values that were used as estimates for the elementary districts.

Results

The global (overall) R^2 values for the relationship between district Biology I scores and the student composition, teacher assets, and financial resources variables are shown in table 6.1. Results for both GWR and OLS models are reported as well as the adjusted R^2 values that show the expected R^2 shrinkage. For the GWR, the overall R^2 value for each model is conceptually the squared

Table 6.1   GWR and OLS results for variable relationships with district Biology I scores

Category	GWR results				OLS results		
	R^{2a}	Adjusted R^2	AIC[b]	Neighbors[c]	R^{2d}	Adjusted R^2	AIC
Full model[e]	.386	.321	3,311	153	.246	.241	3,345
Student composition							
Free/reduced-lunch percentage	.322	.286	3,321	125	.156	.154	3,402
Minority percentage	.358	.253	3,378	44	.054	.052	3,466
Teacher assets							
Teacher salary	.134	.095	3,451	143	.037	.035	3,476
Master's degree percentage	.321	.194	3,427	44	.067	.065	3,458
District financial resources							
Cost per student	.155	.099	3,455	107	.008	.006	3,493
Local revenue percentage	.296	.181	3,431	45	.025	.023	3,483

Note: AIC = Akaike Information Criterion; GWR = geographically weighted regressions; OLS = ordinary least squares regression.
[a] R^2 for all districts computed from observed and GWR predicted values at each location that gives a measure of model fit.
[b] Lower AIC values reflect better-fitting models.
[c] Optimum number of "nearest neighbors" that were used to derive the GWR local regression model for each district from a total of 518 districts.
[d] R^2 for ordinary least squares solution using all districts.
[e] Full model: Free/reduced-price lunch percentage, minority percentage, teacher assets composite, and district financial resources composite predicting biology end-of-course scores.

correlation between the observed district values and the predicted values based on the local models. This overall R^2 value provides an indication of model fit along with the AIC. Lower AIC values indicate better-fitting models and tend to reflect higher R^2 values. The R^2 values range from a high of 0.386 for the full model predicting Biology I scores to a low of 0.134 for teacher salary. Both student composition variables of FRL percentage and minority percentage had strong R^2 values (.322 and .358, respectively) in predicting Biology I scores, as did the teacher asset variable of master's degree percentage (.321) and the financial resource variable of local revenue percentage (.296). For every predictor variable, the GWR R^2 values were higher than the OLS R^2 values, and in most cases substantially higher, which indicates that variable relationships differ by location. Figure 6.2 transforms table 6.1 data into a bar chart comparing GWR and OLS R^2 results.

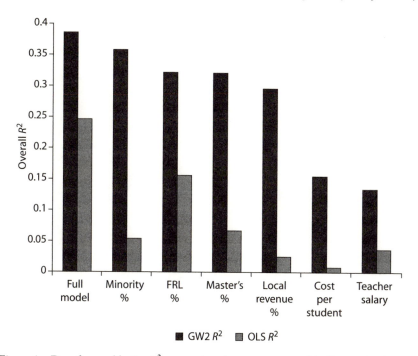

Figure 6.2. Data from table 6.1. R^2 comparison between geographically weighted regression and ordinary least squares for relationship between variables (left bar in pairs represents GWR)

The local R^2 values produced by the GWR analyses were mapped using GIS to demonstrate how the relationships between Biology I scores and student composition, teacher asset, and financial resource variables differed across districts throughout Missouri. Based on groups of "nearest neighbor" districts, GWR computes multiple local R^2 values (one for each district) that can be mapped in geographic space to represent variable relationships. Mapping the local R^2 values shows substantial heterogeneity in variable relationships across districts within the state that a global R^2 value fails to capture.

Mapping Local R^2 Values

Figure 6.3 maps the local R^2 values from the GWR for each variable to show the large variation across regions. In some areas, the relationship between the predictor variable and Biology I scores is very strong, for example, high local R^2 values (.40-.71) for minority percentage, while in many areas the relationships were much weaker (figure 6.3b). The strong relationship between minority per-

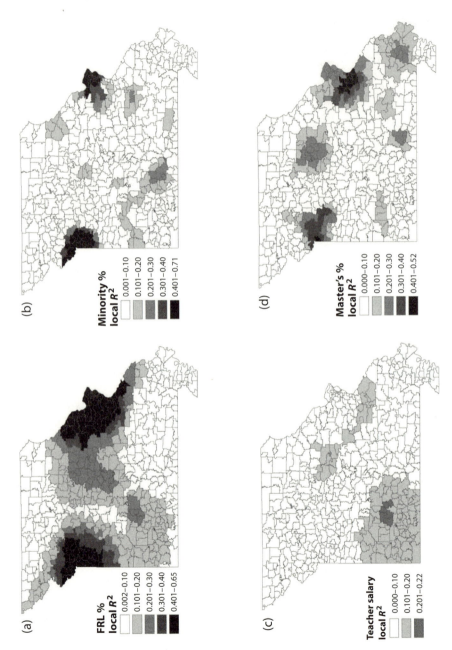

(b)

Minority %
local R^2

☐ 0.001–0.10
▨ 0.101–0.20
▨ 0.201–0.30
▨ 0.301–0.40
■ 0.401–0.71

(a)

FRL %
local R^2

☐ 0.002–0.10
▨ 0.101–0.20
▨ 0.201–0.30
▨ 0.301–0.40
■ 0.401–0.65

(d)

Master's %
local R^2

☐ 0.000–0.10
▨ 0.101–0.20
▨ 0.201–0.30
▨ 0.301–0.40
■ 0.401–0.52

(c)

Teacher salary
local R^2

☐ 0.000–0.10
▨ 0.101–0.20
▨ 0.201–0.22

Figure 6.3. Local R^2s for each variable predicting biology end-of-course scores

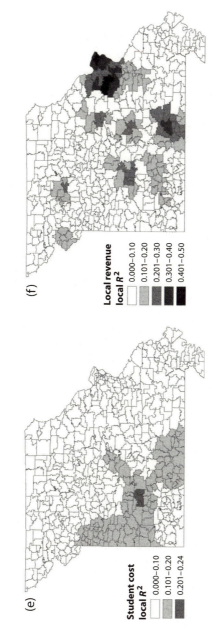

(e)

Student cost
local R^2

- 0.000–0.10
- 0.101–0.20
- 0.201–0.24

(f)

Local revenue
local R^2

- 0.000–0.10
- 0.101–0.20
- 0.201–0.30
- 0.301–0.40
- 0.401–0.50

Figure 6.3. (Continued)

centage and Biology I scores is concentrated in the St. Louis and Kansas City metro areas. This relationship is relatively weak across most other regions of the state. A similar regional pattern shows a strong relationship between Biology I scores and FRL percentage; however, the areas of higher R^2 values are much larger than for minority percentage (figure 6.3a). In these areas, districts that have greater percentages of FRL and minority students tend to have lower Biology I scores. For areas where the relationships are weak, one possible explanation is that Biology I scores are less related to FRL and minority percentages due to limited variability among districts that reflects similar local contexts. The other possibility is that even with adequate variability, relationships are weak.

The relationship between master's degree percentage and Biology I scores had a similar concentration of higher R^2 values around the larger urban areas along with some additional clustering in the central part of the state near Columbia (university town) and Jefferson City (capital) (figure 6.3d). Typically, more master's degree teachers are located in these larger urban areas. Interestingly, there is a cluster in the rural southeastern region of the state where R^2 values ranged from .10 to .30.

For teacher salary and cost per student predicting Biology I scores (figures 6.3c and 6.3e), the R^2 values for a small group of districts were lower (in the .10–.20 range). The majority of these districts tended to be located in the southwestern region of the state and not in the large urban areas of St. Louis and Kansas City. Finally, the relationship for local revenue percentage and Biology I scores had its largest R^2 values around the St. Louis region but failed to show high values in the Kansas City urban area (figure 6.3f). Evidently, there are differences between these two large urban areas as to the relationship of local revenue support on district Biology I scores.

The first map (a) in figure 6.4 shows the local R^2 values from the GWR full model that included FRL percentage, minority percentage, teacher asset composite, and financial resource composite predicting district Biology I scores. The results indicate substantial regional variation in the local R^2 values with the highest values concentrated in eastern and western regions radiating away from the large metro areas of St. Louis and Kansas City. The local R^2 values for the north-central and south-central regions were much lower and suggest a much weaker relationship between these predictor variables and Biology I scores in these areas.

Mapping Beta Coefficients for the Full Model

The next four maps in figure 6.4 show the geographic regions where the local regression coefficients in the full model were statistically significant for each predictor variable while controlling for the other variables. Each map displays the areas where one of the variables contributed unique information to the prediction of Biology I scores. The maps divide the t-test values for the beta coefficients into nonsignificant (white) and significant (shaded) areas at alpha .05 corrected by the Benjamini-Hochberg procedure discussed earlier.

The relationship between FRL percentage and Biology I scores while controlling for the other variables was statistically significant for 64% of the districts (figure 6.4b). For these districts, a higher percentage of FRL students was associated with lower Biology I scores. These districts formed a wide band across the central part of the state from east to west and extended downward through the southwest corner. The relationship was not significant across rural districts in the northern part of the state as well as a large rural section in the southeastern region.

For minority percentage, the relationship with Biology I scores was statistically significant for 31% of the districts while controlling for the other variables in the full model (figure 6.4c). A higher percentage of minority students was associated with lower Biology I scores across these districts. The first large region of significance begins on the eastern side of the state centered on the St. Louis region and expands mostly north and south but also to some districts to the west. The second region of significance starts with Kansas City–area districts and extends north to include the northwest corner of the state. Finally, a smaller area of significance is located along the southeastern border, a region with a larger minority population compared to other rural areas in the state.

The teacher asset composite variable had a significant relationship with Biology I scores across 73% of the districts. Apparently, for almost three-quarters of the districts a combination of higher teacher salaries and greater percentage of master's degrees was related to higher Biology I scores when controlling for the other variables. This relationship was not significant for a corridor of districts running approximately north-south in the central part of the state.

Finally, the relationship between the financial resource composite variable and Biology I scores was significant for 9.5% of the districts while controlling for the other variables. All but seven of these districts were clustered around the St. Louis metro region, where districts with a greater financial resource composite were associated with higher Biology I scores. Conversely, six of the remaining seven districts were clustered along the southern-central border in a rural area where higher financial resource composites were related to lower Biology I scores. So for this small group of districts, a combination of spending more per student and/or having more local revenue was associated with

(a)

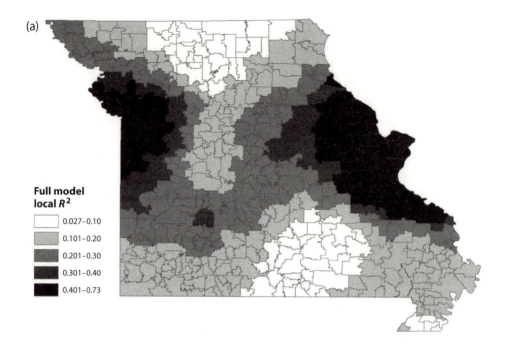

**Full model
local R^2**

☐ 0.027–0.10
▨ 0.101–0.20
▨ 0.201–0.30
■ 0.301–0.40
■ 0.401–0.73

(b)

(c)

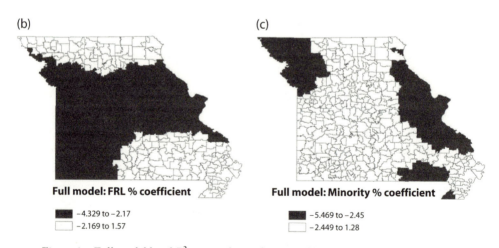

Full model: FRL % coefficient

■ −4.329 to −2.17
☐ −2.169 to 1.57

Full model: Minority % coefficient

■ −5.469 to −2.45
☐ −2.449 to 1.28

Figure 6.4. Full model local R^2 map and significant coefficients for each variable (corrected for multiple comparisons)

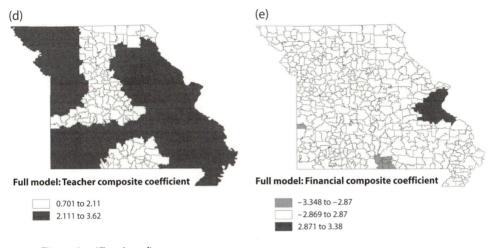

Figure 6.4. (Continued)

lower Biology I scores when considering other surrounding districts in the calculation of local R^2 values.

Discussion

The present study set out to determine whether student, teacher, and district measures associated with the poverty-financial affluence continuum were related to Biology I proficiency across Missouri school districts. The assumption was that the biology proficiency of students would be lower in districts that have greater student poverty, higher minority enrollment, fewer teacher assets, and less district spending per student with reduced community financial support. The results of the study supported this assumption for the most part, but they revealed that the relationships varied by regions across the state. The strength of the relationships depended on local contexts and geographic regions.

Policies and factors unique to local contexts in urban areas provide greater diversity and the opportunity for variable relationships to differ. In this study, a greater variety of local contexts in the larger urban regions tended to produce more statistically significant local R^2 values compared to fewer significant local R^2 values in the rural areas. In contrast, rural areas tend to be more homogeneous with fewer distinguishing local contexts and cover larger geographic areas.

More specifically, there were significant relationships between Biology I scores and district student composition, teacher asset, and financial resource variables, but the relationships varied by geographic region across the state.

Using GWR, which allows relationships to vary across the spatial continuum, substantially higher R^2 values were achieved than with the OLS models. An overall R^2 of .386 was produced with GWR when all four predictor variables were entered into the full model and each variable contributed unique information while controlling for the other variables *in specific geographic regions.*

FRL percentage accounted for unique information in 64% of the districts across the midsection and southwest part of the state in which higher FRL percentages were related to lower Biology I scores. However, FRL percentage was not related significantly to Biology I scores in 36% of the districts in the northern and southeastern portions of the state while controlling for the other variables. A higher minority percentage was associated with lower Biology I scores in 31% of the districts, again controlling for the other variables.

Higher levels of the teacher asset composite variable were related to higher Biology I scores across 73% of the districts. When taking FRL and minority percentages into account, higher average teacher salaries and/or a greater percentage of master's degrees was related to higher Biology I scores in almost three-quarters of the districts. This finding seems to suggest that the investment in teachers is producing better Biology I results for the majority of districts.

Interestingly, the combination of increased spending per student and/or higher local revenue percentage was only positively related to Biology I scores in fifty-three districts around the St. Louis metro area when controlling for the other variables. The positive relationship was not present in the other large urban metro region of Kansas City.

It is clear from this study that location and context affect how variables are related. The results emphasize the importance of allowing relationships to vary across geographic areas by accounting for spatial correlation and its underlying continuum. The finding that variable relationships are nonstationary across geographic regions is not unique to Biology I performance. An earlier study found that Algebra I performance in the state also varied by location in a similar urban-rural pattern (Hogrebe and Tate 2012). In addition, Thorne-Wallington (2014) reported similar patterns in the state of Missouri using reading outcome measures. Due to the diversity of local contexts in districts from urban areas and the relative homogeneity of many districts in rural settings, it is highly probable that other relationships will vary as a function of location. For example, variables may not be related in the same pattern for many high-poverty rural districts in a geographic region as they would be across a large urban area with clusters of both high- and low-poverty districts.

Our results are based on district-level variables and should not be viewed in the same fashion as individual models predicting biology performance outcomes. Instead, the results suggest that local and state policymakers need to carefully consider how to interpret state-level accountability measures as guides for biology-related interventions on learning. There is a definite need in the state of Missouri to tailor interventions based on regional models rather than uniform policy that assumes homogeneity of student groups across the state. This approach to intervention in science education is not new, yet it is rare today. For example, in the 1990s, the National Science Foundation funded urban and rural systemic initiatives across the country focused on improving science learning.[1] The program called for regional leadership to attend to the unique barriers to learning and opportunity in large urban school districts and rural school districts including collaborations of several smaller rural districts. The intent was to leverage resources in an aligned fashion within a region in pursuit of new learning pathways and supports. Our analyses and related research suggest that Missouri is in need of a similar plan for biology as well as for algebra and reading. Poverty is influencing learning in both urban and rural communities. Together, the current study and our past research point to the need for sustainable and adaptable improvements in science and mathematics education. Failure to act will jeopardize future cohorts of students living in urban and rural poverty and their access to emerging opportunities in the age of the New Biology and STEM disciplines.

NOTES

1. See http://www.nsf.gov/pubs/2000/nsf0034/nsf0034.htm and http://www.nsf.gov/funding/pgm_summ.jsp?pims_id=5463.

REFERENCES

Chaix, Basile, Juan Merlo, and Pierre Chauvin. 2005. "Comparison of a Spatial Approach with the Multilevel Approach for Investigating Place Effects on Health: The Example of Healthcare Utilisation in France." *Journal of Epidemiology Community Health* 59:517–26.
Environmental Systems Research Institute. 2012. *ArcMap10.1*. Redlands, CA: ESRI.
Fotheringham, A. Stewart. 2009. "Geographically Weighted Regression." In *The Sage Handbook of Spatial Analysis*, edited by A. Stewart Fotheringham and Peter A. Rogerson, 243–53. Los Angeles: Sage.
Fotheringham, A. Stewart, Chris Brunsdon, and Martin Charlton. 2002. *Geographically Weighted Regression: The Analysis of Spatially Varying Relationships*. West Sussex, England: John Wiley & Sons.

Gregory, Anne, Russell J. Skiba, and Pedro A. Noguera. 2010. "The Achievement Gap and the Discipline Gap: Two Sides of the Same Coin?" *Educational Researcher* 39 (1): 59–68.

Hogrebe, Mark C., and William F. Tate. 2010. "School Composition and Context Factors That Moderate and Predict Tenth-Grade Science Proficiency." *Teachers College Record* 112 (4): 1096–1136.

———. 2012. "Place, Poverty, and Algebra: A Statewide Comparative Spatial Analysis of Variable Relationships." *Journal of Mathematics Education at Teachers College* 3:12–24.

Hurd, Paul DeHart. 1997. "Scientific Literacy: New Minds for a Changing World." *Science Education* 82 (3): 407–16.

Kain, John F. 1968. "Housing Segregation, Negro Employment, and Metropolitan Decentralization." *Quarterly Journal of Economics* 82 (2): 175–97.

Missouri Department of Elementary and Secondary Education. 2013. *Missouri Comprehensive Data System, District and School Information*. Retrieved from http://mcds.dese .mo.gov/quickfacts/Pages/District-and-School-Information.aspx.

Naisbitt, John, and Patricia Adurdene. 1990. *Megatrends 2000*. New York: William Morrow & Company, Inc.

National Research Council. 2009. *A New Biology for the 21st Century*. Washington, DC: National Academies Press.

———. 2012. Education for Life and Work: Developing Transferable Knowledge and Skills in the 21st Century. Washington, DC: National Academies Press.

O'Connell, Ann, and D. Betsy McCoach. 2008. *Multilevel Modeling of Educational Data*. Charlotte, NC: Information Age Publishing.

Raudenbush, Stephen W., and Anthony S. Bryk. 2002. *Hierarchical Linear Models*. 2nd edition. Thousand Oaks, CA: Sage Publications.

Snijders, Tom A. B., and Roel J. Bosker. 2012. *Multilevel Analysis: An Introduction to Basic and Advanced Multilevel Modeling*. 2nd edition. London: Sage Publishers.

Tate, William F. 2008. "'Geography of Opportunity': Poverty, Place, and Educational Outcomes." *Educational Researcher* 37:397–411.

Tate, William F., Brittni Jones, Elizabeth Thorne-Wallington, and Mark C. Hogrebe. 2012. "Science and the City: Thinking Geospatially about Opportunity to Learn." *Urban Education* 47 (2): 399–433.

Thissen, David, Lynne Steinberg, and Daniel Kuang. 2002. "Quick and Easy Implementation of the Benjamini-Hochberg Procedure for Controlling the False Positive Rate in Multiple Comparisons." *Journal of Educational and Behavioral Statistics* 27 (1): 77–83.

Thorne-Wallington, Elizabeth. 2014. "Thinking Geospatially: How Variable Relationships with Reading Achievement Test Scores in the State of Missouri Vary by Geospatial Location." PhD diss., Washington University in St. Louis.

Tobler, Waldo R. 1970. "A Computer Movie Simulating Urban Growth in the Detroit Region." *Economic Geography* 46:234–40.

Wayne, Andrew J., and Peter Youngs. 2003. "Teacher Characteristics and Student Achievement Gains: A Review." *Review of Educational Research* 73 (1): 89–122.

Wilson, William J. 2012. *Truly Disadvantaged: The Inner City, the Underclass, and Public Policy*. 2nd edition. Chicago: University of Chicago Press.

Wiseman, Alexander W. 2012. "The Impact of Student Poverty on Science Teaching and Learning: A Cross-National Comparison of the South African Case." *American Behavioral Scientist* 56 (7): 941–60.

Wood, Nathan B., Frances Lawrenz, Douglas Huffman, and Matt Schulz. 2006. "Viewing the School Environment through Multiple Lenses: In Search of School-Level Variables Tied to Student Achievement." *Journal of Research in Science Teaching* 43:237–54.

7

Social Theory, Evidence, and Activism

Challenging Education Inequality in an Unequal Society

JEANNIE OAKES

I have spent more than three decades using research as a tool to understand educational inequality in the United States and to inform and guide the struggle for more equitable schooling. It has been an enterprise well worth engaging, and it has also been very sobering. Ours is a society intent on preserving inequality, and equity victories are typically partial and fragile. In this chapter, I lay out some of the most important lessons I have learned along the way, organized around six main ideas:

1. Educational inequality is not going away; even so, there are opportunities to make education more equitable.
2. Inequality is kept in place by structures, culture, and individual actions that "effectively maintain inequality," even in the face of workable technical solutions.
3. Inequality is a moving target. It manifests differently in response to efforts to make education more equitable and to changes in the larger ecology of inequality outside of schools.
4. Education reformers are most likely to lessen inequality, and actually make education better, if they approach their work with a mix of strong social theory, evidence, and activism. Absent this mix, their efforts will likely be ineffective, or, even worse, exacerbate inequality.
5. This equity reform mix requires that equity-minded scholars be public intellectuals and also passionate activists—taking on roles that go far beyond those of scholars working on more technical educational problems.
6. Equity-minded scholars must also persuade their universities, colleagues, and funders to recognize, reward, and nurture this work.

To elaborate and provide grounding for these ideas, I use examples from K–12 reform strategies over the past three decades. However, there are also equally potent examples that show these dynamics at work in efforts to make higher education and preschool more equitable.

Educational inequality is not going away; even so, there are opportunities to make education more equitable.

Like many other equity-minded researchers, I've focused my knowledge and skills on understanding educational inequality, investigating ways to end it, and communicating what I have learned to policymakers, educators, and activists who are committed to advancing policies and practices that will make schooling equitable. The most important thing I've learned, however, is that inequality in the United States is not going away, and education will remain inextricably entangled in it. Our nation's children of color enter a school system on unequal footing, they experience unequal schooling, and this inequality is manifest in their schooling outcomes and in their life chances that schooling helps to shape. Although the specifics may change over time, this fundamental cycle is repeated generation after generation.

This may seem like a defeatist conclusion to reach, but it is also very instructive. For many years, when confronted with the question of "What is your end game?" in regard to my commitment to education equity, I have said that I am helping to produce research that will specify elements of a fully equitable education system and will inform policymakers, educators, and communities as they develop strategies to adopt and implement more equitable policies and practices. Now, I have a more modest, better-informed goal. The "end game" now is to produce research that will inform and support collaborative efforts to mitigate the harmful effects of a fundamentally unequal system on those most negatively affected by inequality. I know now that "wins" result as much from political and cultural struggle as they do from rational decisions based on enlightening social science and are likely to be only partial and vulnerable. This process is what political scientist and economist Charles Lindblom (1990) has called "betterment."

Let me explain my seemingly defeatist conclusion about the durability of inequality. In March 2013 Nobel Prize–winning economist Joseph Stiglitz (2013b)—one of the most progressive, equity-minded economists in the nation—wrote in a *New York Times* opinion piece that stated that "a capitalist system will always yield some inequality" and "without it, there would be no

Figure 7.1. Democratic government requires equality

incentive for thrift, innovation, and industry." He's clearly right. Yet, at the same time, inequality is also deeply troubling to Americans, as we have seen quite dramatically over the past few years as the economic recession exposed the widening income and wealth gaps between the top 1% and the other 99% of Americans. Such inequality offends fundamentally our democratic rhetoric of "all men are created equal" and our cultural grounding in an "American Dream" wherein opportunities and hard work bring economic and social mobility and disrupt the intergenerational transmission of status.

The truth is, of course, that we live in a contradictory society. The functions of the democratic state, which requires political equality, are supported by a capitalist economy, which thrives on inequality (see figures 7.1 and 7.2). As a nation, we constantly juggle the often-contradictory requirements of a flat political system and a pyramid-shaped economy.

Most Americans believe that inequality is a normal part of economic, social, and political life. Even so, there is considerable disagreement in the United States about how much inequality is tolerable (or, even desirable) in a capitalist democracy, and this disagreement manifests every day in public policy debates. However, there is little disagreement about equal opportunity, a principle the public supports unequivocally as fundamental to American life. According to polls conducted by Pew Research Center (2011) over the past two decades, nearly nine in ten Americans agree that "our society should do what is necessary to make sure that everyone has an equal opportunity to succeed." Our national compromise is that all Americans deserve an equal opportunity to compete in a race for unequal economic and social life circumstances (see figure 7.3).

We see this dynamic in today's political discourse as Republicans have gained considerable traction with the argument that concerns about economic inequality are misplaced and that the "real" problem the country faces is an opportunity problem as evidenced by diminished social and economic mobility. And Democrats have learned through bitter experience that proposals to reduce inequality directly lead to charges of "class warfare" and worse; they,

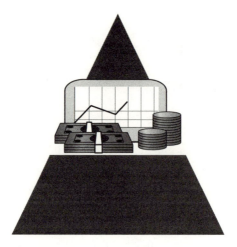

Figure 7.2. Capitalist economies require inequality

Figure 7.3. Equal opportunity to compete for unequal outcomes

too, find greater public resonance by calling for greater opportunities for those who work hard and play by the rules.

Even so, the nation seems to have fallen far short of achieving the degree of equity that most Americans think exists or find acceptable. When asked in 2007 to identify how wealth is distributed among quintiles of Americans, respondents to a survey dramatically underestimated the extent of wealth inequality that actually existed at the time. Even so, they reported that the extent of wealth inequality they thought existed was unacceptably skewed toward those at the top. At the time, the top quintile of Americans actually controlled more than 80% of the nation's wealth, and respondents estimated their share to be a considerably lower 60%. Most telling, respondents suggested that the appropriate share of wealth for the top 20% would be 30%—still unequally skewed to the top, but a dramatic 50% lower than was the actual case. Their erroneous estimates and more equitable preferences extended throughout the range of wealth distribution. It's worth noting that this survey was taken before the economic downturn, before the public discourse on the gap between the 1% and the 99%, and before the continued widening of these gaps in the years that followed (Norton and Ariely 2011).

The implications of these data for our cultural compromise—inequality under conditions of equal opportunity—are huge. They cast serious doubt on the view that the United States is a nation of equal opportunity and raise fundamental questions about the viability of the American Dream. Other analyses of social and economic mobility make clear that the United States has lower rates than almost any other developed nation (see Organisation for Economic Co-operation and Development 2010). To quote Stiglitz (2013a) again, "Today, the United States has less equality of opportunity than almost any other advanced industrial country. Study after study has exposed the myth that America is a land of opportunity."

Schools embody the contradictions between the requirements of capitalism and democracy and the cultural compromise of equal opportunity. This idea is not new, of course. It was the compelling social theory that economists Martin Carnoy and Henry Levin advanced in their 1985 book, *Schooling and Work in the Democratic State*. They argued that democratic societies must prepare each new generation with the knowledge and values needed to function effectively as democratic citizens, including the principles and practices of political and social equality. At the same time, capitalist societies must prepare young people to assume positions in the highly differentiated and unequal workforce that the economy requires. Schools are where this happens. Therein lies the root of the schooling contradictions we see all around us. In schools, as in the larger society, the cultural compromise is to provide a fair chance for all to compete for unequal outcomes (see figure 7.4).

Under the terms of this compromise, schools are expected to provide equal opportunities and meritocratic processes that allow young people to compete fairly for the unequal rewards of our economy. Thus, a fair competition makes unequal outcomes legitimate. This theory is not only conceptually elegant; it is extraordinarily useful for understanding the persistence of inequality in schools—and the potential for reducing it. It is even more useful now than in 1985, given the

Figure 7.4. Equal educational opportunity

increasing influence of the private sector in schooling. Carnoy and Levin (1985) help us understand why Americans both tolerate and are deeply troubled by educational equality, especially when it is connected to broader inequalities.

Carnoy and Levin's (1985) theory also helps us understand why our national concern about the "achievement gap" is far less about unequal outcomes per se than it is about the fact that the gaps are racial and socioeconomic. Our cultural expectation is that inequalities in outcomes are to be expected, even if all students have access to high-quality schooling and enrichment activities (although most would like to see all students do better). Gaps themselves can be fair if they are the result of a fair process. What's troubling to Americans is that the factors that create that inequality appear to be race and wealth based— factors that should not be skewing a fair competition.

Moreover, race and wealth combine in ways that, historically, have severely disadvantaged people of color and that, today, continue to make opportunities neither equal nor fair. Documented school-based sources of inequality (e.g., disparities in teacher preparation, experience, and attendance; class size; curricular rigor; school safety; and technology) exacerbate out-of-school-based sources of inequality (e.g., lower birth weight, hunger, mobility, lead exposure, parent availability, and education resources at home) (Barton 2003).

Of course, as uncomfortable as they are about racial and socioeconomic gaps, Americans have also found ways to rationalize such class- and race-based inequalities. Since Coleman (1966) found the achievement gap to be correlated more strongly with family background than with school conditions, the gap has been conventionally explained by a culture of poverty. Among the harms of poverty, the reasoning goes, are intergenerational, education-related dispositions and behaviors that limit students' ability to take advantage of educational opportunities and are mostly impervious to educators' interventions.

Carnoy and Levin's (1985) theoretical lens proves useful here, too. It helps us see that schooling actually contributes to the perpetuation of poverty as well as being a consequence of it. As such, it provides a strong counternarrative (and important complexity) to the commonly held and simplistic view that unequal schooling outcomes are caused by the conditions of poverty, as if these are somehow independent of schooling, and challenge our belief in the legitimacy of the educational inequality we see all around us. Their compelling theory, properly understood, together with the social science evidence that supports it, provides a platform on which to contest inequality and, more important, inform efforts to achieve more equitable policy and practice.

Yet it is sobering how foreign this idea is to most educators, reformers, and even researchers who care deeply about educational equity. Although it is increasingly popular among some education reformers to declare a "no excuses" stance that eschews poverty as a barrier to high achievement, this simplistic, even naïve, approach is unlikely to disrupt the vicious and reciprocal relationships among poverty, unequal schooling, and larger social and economic inequality. I return to this point later in this chapter.

Inequality is kept in place by structures, culture, and individual actions that "effectively maintain inequality," even in the face of workable technical solutions.

Inequality is not only an essential component of a capitalist economy; it is embedded in culture, policy, and social structures, as well as the product of individual actions. For example, consider how housing policies and school finance policies combine to perpetuate inequality over time. Researchers Becky Nicolaides and Andrew Wiese (2013) summed up this growing body of evidence succinctly in a commentary for the *New York Times* series on inequality:

> High property values support high-achieving schools, which in turn increase property values and personal wealth. Racial redlining holds property values down, limiting investment in schools and preventing families from building equity, disadvantages that pass to the next generation like a negative inheritance. The point is not simply that rich and poor people live in different places through a kind of class sorting in the marketplace. The places themselves help to create wealth and poverty. Because of this power of places to fix inequity over time, current patterns are likely to outlive their residents.

These relationships have been taken up by some education researchers. For example, Jean Anyon's (1997) and Pauline Lipman's (2002) insightful scholarship traces the long history of how schooling in Newark and Chicago has been nested in and profoundly shaped by the larger unequal political economy. Nevertheless, these relationships have not penetrated mainstream debates about education policy and school reform.

In education, the most painful evidence for the persistence of inequality comes from the nation's efforts to create diverse schools and classrooms. *Brown v. Board of Education* (1954) launched a decades-long effort to equalize education by dismantling the segregated structure of schooling. However, once integration was framed narrowly (and technically) as "busing," true equality became an impossible goal. Even the most elegant technical solutions—student assignment and "busing" plans—were not robust enough to change the cultural norms and individual actions that perpetuated segregation and inequality. In fact, by the early 1980s public opinion and court decisions had fundamentally undermined the nation's ability to achieve either integrated or equitable schools. This was a hearts, minds, and power problem that technical solutions could not overcome—a few effective examples notwithstanding.

Moreover, tracking and ability grouping—a longstanding feature of the comprehensive high school—became a structure for managing diversity within racially mixed schools. Research—mine and that of many others—made clear that tracking structures inequality, particularly in racially mixed schools, by allocating access to different content, pedagogy, and expectations. Tracking creates and reinforces unequal outcomes rather than ameliorating them (e.g., Lucas 1999; Oakes 2005). Still other research provided compelling evidence about the benefits of heterogeneous classrooms (e.g., Burris 2014; Burris and Garity 2008; Cohen and Lotan 1997; Mehan 2013; Oakes 2005; Watanabe 2012; Welner 2001). But, as was the case with desegregation, detracking reforms in racially mixed schools faced enormous resistance.

Amy Stuart Wells and I (with a team of incredible graduate students; Oakes et al. 1997), along with Kevin Welner (Oakes and Welner 1996), conducted several mixed-methods studies of detracking reforms. Looking at our data through the lens of social theory, we found that detracking was extraordinarily difficult because of the cultural and political challenges it made to the status quo of unequal schooling. Although not easy, the technical changes in structures and practices that the reform required were far less challenging, and many schools found effective ways to teach heterogeneous, detracked classes (Oakes 2005; see also Boaler 2002; Cohen and Lotan 1997). Yet powerful resistance was triggered consistently when:

- reformers rejected entrenched beliefs that students' academic needs and capacities differ enormously in ways that schools can't change;
- biases around race, language, and poverty cast doubt on the learning capacities of African Americans and Latinos; and
- classroom assignments threatened advantaged parents' efforts to ensure that their own children have a comparative advantage by getting the "best" the schools had to offer.

As was the case with desegregation, such resistance often stopped detracking reforms in their "tracks" (pun intended).

Early on, a colleague and gifted quantitative methodologist, Kenneth Sirotnik (1994), warned that rigorous evidence alone would not likely persuade policymakers or practitioners to abandon practices so rooted in cultural and political norms. And, in fact, social theorists have been deeply engaged in explaining this observation. For example, sociologist Samuel Lucas (2001) has demonstrated how advantaged members of society work actively to "effectively maintain inequality." Elites are more concerned, he explains, that their own children's opportunities are qualitatively *superior* to other children's than about the quality of the opportunities themselves. As a result, they actively work to keep *differentiation* in the system that effectively maintains their children's comparative advantage—even turning so-called equity reforms to their advantage—despite evidence of their widespread benefits (Lucas 2001).

Nevertheless, amazing educators have combined creativity, political savvy, and vigilance to detrack and create equitable schools in the face of this resistance. For example, Carol Burris (2014), principal of Southside High School on Long Island, New York, eliminated tracking at her school by offering more rigorous pathways for every student and increased both expectations and support. Using high-quality curriculum such as the International Baccalaureate, Southside saw 99% of all its students, including 95% of minority students, graduate with a Regents diploma in 2012. Similarly, racially diverse Evanston Township High School used detracking to enable a broad range of students to take challenging honors and advanced placement classes. Both schools regularly appear on the *Washington Post*'s list of the best high schools in America.

However, such schools are routinely dismissed as outliers that cannot be taken to scale. Ironically, unlike so-called "beat the odds" schools in racially segregated communities of concentrated poverty, these untracked, racially diverse high schools have not been held up as models to be replicated everywhere. Social theories such as those of Carnoy and Levin (1985), as well as Lucas (1999, 2001), help us understand why. Moreover, social theory and evidence help us understand why, in whack-a-mole fashion, "ability grouping" keeps popping up as a strategy, particularly in struggling urban schools, supported by strong advocacy but very weak studies, recent think tank reports (e.g., Loveless 2013b), and commentaries (e.g., Loveless, 2013a) picked up in newspapers and magazines (e.g., Elliott 2013; Garelick 2013).

It's clear. Educational inequality is not just an "engineering" problem that requires a technical fix—like a new structure or a teaching technique. Social theory, evidence, and activism are essential to understanding and confronting the cultural and political forces that keep inequality firmly in place. I return to this point in the following section.

Inequality is a moving target. It manifests differently in response to education equity efforts and changes in the larger ecology of inequality outside of schools.

Equity victories, even partial, cannot be assumed as permanent. They are often reshaped in ways that preserve inequality. For example, today's emphasis on having every high school graduate prepared for both college and career would appear to be a clear victory for detracking and equity. However, in many places it has become "better college prep for some" as differentiated course patterns or pathways create separate and unequal opportunities and outcomes. And, increasingly the goal itself has been challenged as "unrealistic" (e.g., Petrilli 2014), accompanied by a renewed emphasis on career and technical education for those unlikely to go to college.

Changes in the ecology of inequality outside of the education system, such as wealth, income, and race-based inequality, also trigger significant shifts in schooling inequality. Historically, there have been times when the nation has been better able than others to balance the imperatives of our unequal economic system with our democratic goals. One such time was in the 1970s when racial discrimination and poverty were called into question and resources and support were provided to change them.

The years after 1980 changed most of that. Policy and structural changes in the economy—deregulation, loosening protection for workers, "liberalizing" the finance industry—brought widening gaps in wealth and income, and contributed to the financial crisis we have experienced over the past five years. We have all seen charts depicting the widening economic gaps in the United States over the past four decades (Sherman and Stone 2010). We are now more out of balance than we have been in a century.

We have also seen the resulting impact of increasing economic inequality on children—by 2010 between thirteen million and sixteen million were living in poverty, and eight million of this number were living in extreme poverty (Aud et al. 2011). These increases are not race neutral, with the burden borne disproportionately by African American, Latino, and American Indian children who are six to nine times more likely to live in poverty than their White counterparts. Moreover, as Sean Reardon's (2011) recent analyses have shown, the widening gaps are also spatial—creating gaps that divide us physically and socially as well as economically. The percentages of families living in neighborhoods of concentrated wealth and in neighborhoods of concentrated poverty have doubled between 1970 and 2007, at the same time that the percentage of families living in middle income or mixed neighborhoods shrunk by a third. Neither of these growing spatial divisions is race neutral. By 2009, 37% of African American and Latino students attended high-poverty schools of concentrated poverty, in contrast to 6% of Whites and 12% of Asians. Patterns of attendance at schools with few poor students were almost exactly the reverse. As a consequence of this growing divide, schools have become increasingly segregated. They have also become increasingly unequal.

Robert Putnam's (2012) newest work reveals that the combination of economic and spatial inequality is shaping childhoods in ways that have devastating lifelong consequences, which puts the American Dream even further out of reach. Across racial lines, childhoods of those from the top third and the bottom third of the economic hierarchy have sharply diverged since the 1990s on out-of-school factors that support the development of cognitive and noncognitive skills and the cultural and social capital critical for life success. For example, increased spending by upper-income families on enrichment and learning opportunities in comparison to their less wealthy counterparts contributes to the growing achievement gap. Although lower-income families have increased spending on structured learning opportunities and enrichment for their children by an average of $480 per year, upper-income parents have increased their spending by nearly $5,300 (Reardon 2011).

In fact, the achievement gap between rich and poor kids born in 2001 was 30%–40% larger than it was for those born twenty-five years earlier (Reardon 2011). In the face of these changes—in combination with Draconian court decisions—more and more folks have come to believe that diversity reforms are futile and perhaps even wrongheaded. Increasingly, education reformers have focused their attention on making schools in high-poverty neighborhoods better. Starting with understandably angry activists of color who were convinced that their children could be educated well without the presence of white children, these efforts have been increasingly fueled by the activism of moneyed elites. For the most part, equity-minded theorists and researchers have been left on the sidelines.

Education reformers are mostly likely to reduce inequality if they approach their work with a mix of strong social theory, evidence, and activism.

Absent a mix of social theory, evidence, and activism working in concert, "equity" efforts fail or, even worse, exacerbate the problem. Theory gets dismissed as "just another opinion," and evidence gets "cherry picked" to the detriment of social justice. We have witnessed over the past several years a "reform" movement of neoliberals seeking to close the achievement gap by solving the "bad schools and bad teachers" problem—getting rid of those who let poverty and race be an excuse for not educating students. The reformers' primary tools are test-based accountability, school closures, teacher evaluation linked to test scores, and the expansion of choice and charters.

It is tempting to write this off as a nefarious privatization conspiracy by those who want to turn public education into a profit center. And certainly there is some of that. The education sector represents almost 9% of the country's gross domestic product (GDP). That is extraordinarily appealing in a capitalist society always seeking new markets. But my time at the Ford Foundation has shown me a more complicated side where well-meaning, very smart, privileged people from outside of education want desperately to use their power and privilege to make schools better for marginalized students because they believe the unequal status quo is horribly wrong. They bring to the problem their best analytic and strategic tools—borrowed mostly from corporate America—that, unfortunately, although well-intentioned, only make the fundamental problems worse.

This reform strategy is not a twenty-first century innovation. Since the early twentieth century, elites have sought to run schools like the private sector, and inequality persists. These reformers have a theory, but it is an eco-

Figure 7.5. Elite-driven educational reform (a reform process that mirrors the elite-driven strategies that improve the effectiveness and efficiencies of corporate America)

nomic theory that positions schools squarely on the capitalist side of the educational balance scale, as shown by the picture in figure 7.5. This economic, capitalist-driven theory is that education works best as a marketplace, where quality comes from high standards, well-managed human capital, "best practices" tied to the "bottom line" (measured by frequently tallied metrics), competition among providers, and savvy consumer choices informed by accountability data push failing enterprises out of business. With the right incentives and consequences in place, the theory goes: educators will work harder and stop making "excuses" (like poverty) for their failure. The theory also suggests that private providers, unshackled by needless regulation and the constraints of collective bargaining, are far more likely to succeed than are government agencies and unionized workforces.

And, in fact, this "reform" approach has created a few high-performing schools in high-poverty neighborhoods. Mostly charters, these schools are lifted up as proof that the "no excuses" reform can close achievement gaps.

Not surprisingly, this movement can be quite appealing to frustrated members of impoverished local communities who do not have other alternatives. But the success stories tend to be tops of a pyramid: inaccessible for most and the exception to the more common situation. They might be a life preserver for a handful of students, but as such they actually exacerbate, rather than reduce, inequality. A few lucky children from families who successfully negotiate a highly competitive system (picture the lottery in the 2010 feature film

Waiting for Superman) have high-quality learning opportunities and outcomes. The rest blame themselves for bad luck or lack of determination that locks them into so-called "failing" neighborhood schools, when in fact it is a broken system that perpetuates this type of inequality.

A closer and deeper look at these "no excuses" schools reveals that their higher quality and better outcomes often come from the extra learning time and resources bought with private money. And, of course, good outcomes are also made more likely when students who are not well matched to a "no excuses" approach are sent back to the regular public schools that fail to provide the same or similar type of educational opportunity.

Not only have these "reforms" failed to bring equity, but they have not led to better opportunities and outcomes improvements in the cities that serve as models for this approach. A new report from the Economic Policy Institute uses evidence from a range of studies of New York, Chicago, and Washington, DC, to demonstrate that, even on its own terms, market-based reform doesn't work (Weiss and Long 2013). Among their findings, Weiss and Long report that

- reform cities did worse than most others in closing achievement gaps;
- although the reformers claimed gains, those gains disappeared upon rigorous analysis;
- students who moved from "closed" failing schools did not move to better schools; and
- charters did not provide better options for most students, including the neediest.

This is not surprising. Absent strong social theory and evidence, the reformers have misunderstood the fundamental problems and misspecified the solutions. It is also not surprising that a reform theory and strategy borrowed from an economic system that depends on inequality fails to change deep structures, norms, and practices of unequal schooling.

So, what reforms could more effectively account for the complex relationship between educational inequality and the contradictions of capitalist democracies, confront the cultural and political resistance to equity-minded reform, and also develop effective technical solutions? With strong social theory and evidence as a guide, the substance of the needed reforms is quite obvious: policies that give the neediest students the learning opportunities, time, resources, and support they need to reach the increasingly high bar for school success and

Figure 7.6. Democratic educational reform (a reform process that prefigures equitable and democratic participation)

policies that give educators the learning opportunities, time, resources, and support they need to teach well in high-poverty communities. We actually find this agenda in several current projects, including the following:

- the Broader, Bolder Approach to Education Movement,
- the congressionally mandated Equity and Education Commission's report "For Each and Every Child,"
- the Schott Foundation's Opportunity to Learn Campaign, and
- Ford Foundation's More and Better Learning Time initiative.

Our Ford Foundation More and Better Learning Time (MBLT) initiative, for example, moves educational equity beyond the six-hour, 180-day year schooling that children receive in neighborhoods of concentrated poverty. The goal is to make more and better learning time a "normal" policy and practice in such communities and provide for children in the least advantaged neighborhoods and families the full range of learning resources, opportunities, and relationships that their more advantaged peers take for granted because their communities provide them and their families purchase them.

But it is not just the substance of what constitutes equitable schooling that must be different; the process must be as well. Equity is most likely when the reform process prefigures the full and inclusive participation that democracy requires—messy, open and participatory, very public and transparent, blending "expert" and local knowledge, and always accountable to the communities to whom the schools belong.

We actually have examples of this approach at work today, although they get far less attention or legitimacy than corporate-style reforms (see figure 7.6). In several cities, grassroots activists are using political power to stop top-down policies of school closings, teacher firings, and the proliferation of standardized testing. They are calling for local improvement strategies supported by resources and capacity-building that would allow schools to address the broad range of needs that affect educational success.

The efficacy of grassroots reform has been documented by numerous researchers (Mediratta, Shah, and McAlister 2009; Shirley 2010; Warren 2001; Warren and Mapp 2011) whose studies find that organizing builds social capital and changes the power dynamics in low-income communities in ways that support equitable schooling (see also Orr and Rogers 2010). The idea that such activism might be most powerful in combination with that social theory and evidence has been advanced compellingly by John Rogers, whose remarkable understanding of John Dewey's theorizing about participatory social inquiry and social change resonates so strongly with grassroots activism (Oakes and Rogers 2006). Paul Heckman's (1996) pioneering work in Arizona and our UCLA IDEA team's social design experiments have revealed more about the power of a reform strategy that combines evidence and activism. Michelle Renee has made clear the value and importance of scholarly knowledge and evidence to grassroots activists (Renee, Welner, and Oakes 2009).

Equity-minded scholars must also persuade their universities, colleagues, and funders to recognize, reward, and nurture this work.

Of course, grassroots activists cannot do this alone. They need allies who can support their use of social theory and evidence as a tool in their work to educate themselves and others and build public and political will. That is where education researchers are needed. First, we must go public. Equity-minded researchers must assume roles that go beyond those of researchers seeking to understand and solve more technical problems.

We must join with courageous colleagues who leave the safety of our privileged academic enclaves to become public intellectuals who advance ideas and evidence that change hearts and minds, as well as to serve as "experts" who inform policymakers and professionals. We must advance generative new concepts (social theories, even), make rigorous analysis accessible to public audiences, and tell compelling, evidence-based stories that mobilize policymakers, phi-lanthropists, and the public. We must also engage on equal status terms with those closest to and most negatively affected by inequality, providing relevant theory and evidence to inform equity struggles (Oakes and Rogers 2006). This is the only way to democratize expertise and help build knowledge tools that add power and efficacy to advocacy in policy debates.

As we play this role, however, our effectiveness and credibility demand that we remember who we are—researchers who balance our deep commitments to equity with our commitments to the highest standards of our profession. We also must remember and be humbled by the reality that activists are the ones who will take action on theory and research by making demands on policymakers, educational leaders, and the courts. They are also the ones whose work will sustain any reforms they achieve. In the end, this is not primarily about us.

Equity-minded scholars must also persuade our institutions, colleagues, and funders to recognize, reward, and nurture this work as legitimate forms of knowledge creation, dissemination, and use.

Finally, we must always keep in mind that the structures and cultures of universities (and philanthropies as well) operate in concert with other structures that serve to perpetuate current practices, norms, politics, and power dynamics. It is an existential dilemma for many equity-minded researchers who must derive at least some of their legitimacy from these traditional institutions while, at the same time, pursuing social justice agendas. That means, inevitably, that the creation and use of equity-focused research is constrained by currently narrow professional norms and standards governing what counts as scientific objectivity, respected methodology, worthy outlets for disseminating theory and evidence, and much more. This reality must not deter us from pressing our institutions to recognize and reward engaged scholarship seeking to advance equity. After all, just like schools, they must respond to the demands of democracy as well as capitalism.

ACKNOWLEDGMENTS

My thanks to Karen Hunter Quartz for introducing me to the relevance of Lindblom's work to education reform. Thanks to my Ford Foundation colleague Sanjiv Rao for this astute observation. Thanks to Annenberg Institute for School Reform at Brown University's Director, Warren Simmons, for this succinct framing, "bad schools and bad teachers."

REFERENCES

Anyon, Jean. 1997. *Ghetto Schooling: A Political Economy of Urban Educational Reform.* New York: Teachers College Press.

Aud, Susan, William Hussar, Grace Kena, Kevin Bianco, Lauren Frohlich, Jana Kemp, and Kim Tahan. 2011. *The Condition of Education 2011.* Washington, DC: U.S. Department of Education, Institute of Education Sciences, National Center for Education Statistics.

Barton, Paul E. 2003. *Parsing the Achievement Gap: Baselines for Tracking Progress. Policy Information Report.* http://www.ets.org/Media/EducationTopics/pdf/parsing.pdf.

Boaler, Jo. 2002. *Experiencing School Mathematics: Traditional and Reform Approaches to Teaching and Their Impact on Student Learning.* New York: Routledge.

Burris, Carol Corbett. 2014. *On the Same Track: How Schools Can Join the Twenty-First-Century Struggle against Resegregation.* Boston: Beacon Press.

Burris, Carol Corbett, and Delia T. Garrity. 2008. *Detracking for Excellence and Equity.* Alexandria, VA: Association for Supervision and Curriculum Development.

Carnoy, Martin, and Henry M. Levin. 1985. *Schooling and Work in the Democratic State.* Redwood City, CA: Stanford University Press.

Cohen, Elizabeth G., and Rachel A. Lotan. 1997. *Working for Equity in Heterogeneous Classrooms: Sociological Theory in Practice.* Sociology of Education Series. New York: Teachers College Press.

Coleman, James S. 1966. *Equality of Educational Opportunity Study.* Washington, DC: U.S. Department of Health, Education, and Welfare, Office of Education.

Elliott, Philip. 2013. "After Decade of Criticism, Student Grouping Rises." Associated Press. March 18. http://bigstory.ap.org/article/after-decade-criticism-student-grouping-rises.

Garelick, B. 2013. "Let's Go Back to Grouping Students by Ability." *The Atlantic.* March 26. http://www.theatlantic.com/national/archive/2013/03/lets-go-back-to-grouping-students-by-ability/274362/.

Heckman, Paul E. 1996. *The Courage to Change: Stories from Successful School Reform.* Thousand Oaks, CA: Corwin Press.

Lindblom, Charles E., ed. 1990. *Inquiry and Change: The Troubled Attempt to Change and Shape Society.* New Haven, CT: Yale University Press.

Lipman, Pauline. 2002. "Making the Global City, Making Inequality: The Political Economy and Cultural Politics of Chicago School Policy." *American Educational Research Journal* 39 (2): 379–419.

Loveless, Tom. 2013a. "Ability Grouping, Tracking and How Schools Work." *The Brown Center Chalkboard, Brookings Institute.* April 3. http://www.brookings.edu/blogs/brown-center-chalkboard/posts/2013/04/03-ability-grouping-tracking-loveless.

———. 2013b. *The Resurgence of Ability Grouping and Persistence of Tracking: Part II of the 2013 Brown Center Report on American Education.* Washington, DC: Brookings Institute. http://www.brookings.edu/research/reports/2013/03/18-tracking-ability-grouping-loveless.

Lucas, Samuel R. 1999. *Tracking Inequality: Stratification and Mobility in American High Schools.* Sociology of Education Series. New York: Teachers College Press.

———. 2001. "Effectively Maintained Inequality: Education Transitions, Track Mobility, and Social Background Effects." *American Journal of Sociology* 106 (6): 1642–90.

Mediratta, Kavitha, Seema Shah, and Sara McAlister. 2009. *Community Organizing for Stronger Schools: Strategies and Successes.* Cambridge, MA: Harvard Education Press.

Mehan, Hugh. 2013. *In the Front Door: Creating a College-Bound Culture of Learning.* Boulder, CO: Paradigm Publishers.

Nicolaides, M. Becky, and Andrew Wiese. 2013. "Suburban Disequilibrium." *New York Times.* April 6. http://opinionator.blogs.nytimes.com/2013/04/06/suburban-disequili brium/.

Norton, Michael I., and Dan Ariely. 2011. "Building a Better America—One Wealth Quintile at a Time." *Perspectives on Psychological Science* 6 (1): 9–12.

Oakes, Jeannie. 2005. *Keeping Track: How Schools Structure Inequality.* 2nd edition. New Haven, CT: Yale University Press.

Oakes, Jeannie, and John Rogers. 2006. *Learning Power: Organizing for Education and Justice.* New York: Teachers College Press.

Oakes, Jeannie, Amy Stuart Wells, Makeba Jones, and Amanda Datnow. 1997. "Detracking: The Social Construction of Ability, Cultural Politics, and Resistance to Reform." *Teachers College Record* 98 (3): 482–510.

Oakes, Jeannie, and Kevin G. Welner. 1996. "(Li)ability Grouping: The New Susceptibility of School Tracking Systems to Legal Challenges." *Harvard Educational Review* 66 (3): 451–70.

Organisation for Economic Co-operation and Development (OECD). 2010. *Education at a Glance 2010: OECD Indicators.* Paris: OECD Publishing.

Orr, Marion, and John Rogers. 2010. *Public Engagement for Public Education: Joining Forces to Revitalize Democracy and Equalize Schools.* Redwood City, CA: Stanford University Press.

Petrilli, Michael. 2014. "Kid, I'm Sorry, but You're Just Not College Material." *Slate.* March 18. http://www.slate.com/articles/life/education/2014/03/college_isn_t_for _everyone_let_s_stop_pretending_it_is.html.

Pew Research Center Publications. 2011. *The Elusive 90% Solution.* Washington, DC: Author. March 11. http://pewresearch.org/pubs/1925/elusive=90-percent-solution -gasprices.

Putnam, Robert. 2012. "Requiem for the American Dream? Unequal Opportunity in America." Presented at the ASPEN Ideas Festival, Aspen, CO, June 29.

Reardon, Sean F. 2011. "The Widening Academic Achievement Gap between the Rich and the Poor: New Evidence and Possible Explanations." In *Whither Opportunity: Rising Inequality, Schools, and Children's Life Chances,* edited by Greg J. Duncan and Richard J. Murnane, 91–116. New York: Russell Sage Foundation.

Renee, Michelle, Kevin Welner, and Jeannie Oakes. 2009. "Social Movement Organizing and Equity-Focused Educational Change: Shifting the Zone of Mediation." *Second International Handbook of Educational Change* 23:153–68.

Sherman, Arloc, and Chad Stone. 2010. *Income Gaps between Very Rich and Everyone Else More Than Tripled in Last Three Decades, New Data Show.* Washington, DC: Center on Budget and Policy Priorities.

Shirley, Dennis. 2010. *Community Organizing for Urban School Reform.* Austin: University of Texas Press.

Sirotnik, Kenneth A. 1994. "Equal Access to Quality in Public Schooling: Issues in the Assessment of Equity and Excellence." In *Access to Knowledge: The Continuing Agenda for Our Nation's Schools,* edited by John I. Goodland and Pamela Keating, 159–85. New York: College Board.

Stiglitz, Joseph. 2013a. "Equal Opportunity, Our National Myth." *New York Times.* February 16. http://opinionator.blogs.nytimes.com/2013/02/16/equal-opportunity -our-national-myth/.

———. 2013b. "Singapore's Lessons for an Unequal America." *The New York Times.* March 18. http://opinionator.blogs.nytimes.com/2013/03/18/singapores-lessons-for -an-unequal-america/?_php=true&_type=blogs&_r=0.

Waiting for Superman. 2010. Directed by Davis Guggenheim. Los Angeles: Paramount Vantage.

Warren, Mark R. 2001. *Dry Bones Rattling: Community Building to Revitalize American Democracy.* Princeton, NJ: Princeton University Press.

Warren, Mark R., and Karen L. Mapp. 2011. *A Match on Dry Grass: Community Organizing as a Catalyst for School Reform.* Oxford: Oxford University Press.

Watanabe, Maika. 2012. *"Heterogenius" Classrooms: Detracking Math and Science; A Look at Groupwork in Action.* New York: Teachers College Press.

Weiss, Elaine, and Don Long. 2013. *Market-Oriented Education Reforms' Rhetoric Trumps Reality: The Impacts of Test-Based Teacher Evaluations, School Closures, and Increased Charter-School Access on Student Outcomes in Chicago, New York City, and Washington, D.C.* Washington, DC: Broader, Bolder Approach to Education, Economic Policy Institute. http://boldapproach.org/rhetoric-trumpsreality.

Welner, Kevin G. 2001. *Legal Rights, Local Wrongs: When Community Control Collides with Educational Equity.* Albany: State University of New York Press.

8

The Challenge of College Readiness

WILLIAM G. TIERNEY

A great deal of discussion has occurred about the need for the United States to increase the number of students who enter a postsecondary institution and graduate with the requisite skills necessary to assume good-paying jobs. The logic of such an assertion is clear and sound. The United States once led the world in the percentage of students who went to and graduated from college and now lags behind other industrialized countries (Lewin 2010). The estimate of the number of jobs in a decade's time that will require skills learned in college far exceeds the estimates of graduates from America's postsecondary institutions. By current estimates, California, for example, in 2025 will have over one million jobs that cannot be filled—especially in the fields of science and technology—because the public postsecondary sector will be unable to meet demand due to capacity constraints and a mismatch between the skills students acquire in college and those skills needed for the workforce (Johnson and Sengupta 2009). To be sure, not everyone needs a four-year college degree, but the assumption has been that simply graduating from high school is no longer good enough (see figure 8.1). Such a point is particularly important for discussions pertaining to education's role in alleviating poverty. By 2020, 39% of workers are projected to need a bachelor's degree to meet economic demand. By 2025, that figure will increase to 41%.

A related problem is that too many students graduate from high school who are not college ready. Roughly 60% of students must take a remedial class in English or math when they enter college, and the percentage is even higher for community college entrants (Bailey, Jeong, and Cho 2009; National Center for Public Policy and Higher Education 2010). The related costs to postsecondary institutions of paying for non-credit-bearing courses and the time

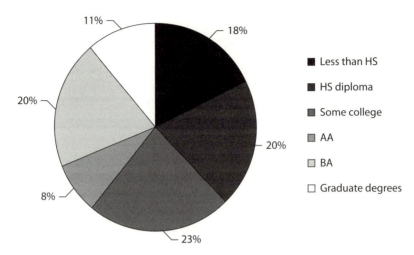

Figure 8.1. Educational attainment of California's workforce, 2010 (Johnson and Sengupta 2009)

involved for students in need of remedial education are considerable. And yet, we know that the lifetime earnings of someone who has a college degree is significantly higher than someone with a high school degree; we also know that during the last recession, unemployment for high school graduates was higher than those with college degrees (Carnevale, Rose, and Cheah 2013; Taylor et al. 2010).

The response to these issues has been twofold. On the one hand, President Obama, the Gates and Lumina Foundations, and numerous think tanks have issued calls for increasing college enrollment and decreasing the time it takes a student to graduate (Lumina Foundation 2013; White House n.d.). On the other hand, a great deal of discussion has been focused on creating a common core curriculum across the United States that will increase what students learn in high school so that they are better prepared for college. In this light, a common core curriculum might be considered a move toward "college for all," which is why some states have resisted the plans.

Nevertheless, the goals are straightforward and seemingly commonsensical: to increase the number of students attending college and to increase the number of students who graduate from high school college ready. The evidence demonstrates that college graduates earn more than high school graduates, which, in turn, increases tax revenues for states and the federal government (Tierney and Hentschke 2011). Presumably, if the country achieves its goal of

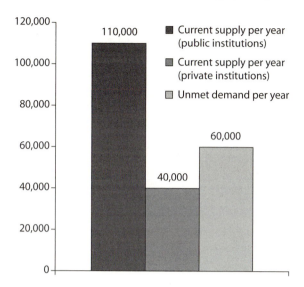

Figure 8.2. Baccalaureates issued per year by California institutions: Current supply vs. demand (Tierney and Hentschke 2011)

having more college graduates, it will be stronger economically, socially, and civically. It will also be better able to face the myriad issues of the twenty-first century.

Such a goal has met with two critiques. First, many have pointed out that such goals are unattainable. The state of American secondary schools will be unable to improve the college readiness of the least ready, argue some, and even if they did, argue others, postsecondary institutions have been unable to increase college capacity by traditional means—building more campuses— and are largely unwilling to consider alternative devices (e.g., online learning) to increase capacity (Tierney and Hentschke 2011; see figure 8.2).

Second, some, such as Richard Vedder (2012), have argued that there is no evidence that America needs more college graduates. Others have pointed to a credentialing phenomenon where people with advanced degrees are performing jobs that could be done by people with lesser credentials (Owen and Sawhill 2013). In effect, they are suggesting that rather than needing more college degrees, we need fewer. The assumption is that credentialing individuals drives up educational requirements that are entirely unnecessary to fill certain jobs.

As I elaborate in the following sections, both arguments have a degree of merit. The relationship between high schools and postsecondary institutions has been fraught with miscommunication for over a century. For example, only 10% of high school teachers believe that their students are not well prepared for college-level writing, as opposed to 44% of college faculty members (Sanoff 2006). High school teachers also believe that 63% of their graduating seniors are prepared for college-level coursework, while only 25% were shown to be college ready in ACT testing (Amelga 2012). Similarly, the capacity crisis in higher education has not occurred overnight; neither senior administrators nor faculty have offered long-term plans, however, that do not involve the state simply providing additional funds—something states will not do to a level necessary to meet demand.

The data that the credential proponents call upon are also true. A 2010 investigation of census data reveals that out of 41.7 million employed college graduates, 37% hold jobs that only require a high school degree (Vedder, Denhart, and Robe 2013). From this perspective, the country has workers who cannot find employment because better educated—not better qualified—workers have taken their positions. Moreover, new college-readiness requirements discourage students from taking career and technical education courses, and these requirements depress the ability of those who are trained for a particular job to find employment (Betts, Zau, and Bachofer 2013). From this perspective, it is less a need for more credentials and more a need to align skills with jobs.

Although these arguments are plausible, they also tend to miss the mark. Neither miscommunication nor an inability to increase capacity ought to suggest that the current situation is viable if it is not. If the country will be better off with more college graduates, ways need to be found that enable that to happen, either by policy directives at the state and federal level or through creative action on the part of P–12 schools and postsecondary institutions.

Data that show that some workers have assumed positions for which they are overqualified also does not take into account the fact that other positions are unfilled because of a lack of qualified workers. From this perspective, the problem is not that too many people have a college degree but that they have the wrong kind of degree. Whereas the United States has an urgent need for more individuals who hold degrees in science, technology, engineering, and math (STEM), it has an oversupply of individuals with other sorts of degrees. Those with other degrees may well have assumed positions for which they are overqualified, but they are unqualified for positions that require a bachelor's degree with a particular skill set. Thus, the country needs more college graduates with different degrees.

One question that has not been considered very much, which I turn to here, is a variation of the two critiques: how many high school students should not participate in the postsecondary sector? I wish to consider the consequences for those who do not go on to college. That is, although the data seem undeniable that more people need to participate in higher education, no one has suggested that everyone needs to attend college. The analysis of increasing access to higher education has been fine tuned to the degree that there is a good understanding of how many individuals will benefit from a four-year degree, how many need an associate of arts degree, and how many can get by simply with a postsecondary technical certificate. Such analyses not only help individuals consider what kind of skills they need for employment but also presumably can help the state develop an educational plan.

Such an understanding of the country's postsecondary needs is doubly useful. If one segment of the postsecondary sector only needs certificates, they should qualify for federal and state grants and loans, just like their advanced degree–seeking counterparts. However, such a projection also suggests that not everyone needs a four-year degree, or, for that matter, a two-year degree or postsecondary certificate. According to 2010 data, approximately 72% of the students who attend a postsecondary institution go to a public institution (U.S. Department of Education 2012). Virtually all students who demonstrate a financial need and who attend an accredited institution—public, private nonprofit, or for-profit—receive some form of financial aid (Tierney and Hentschke 2007). Coupled with state subsidies to public institutions, the public investment in higher education is considerable, although many suggest it is not enough.

But virtually no one suggests that public higher education should accommodate everyone who graduates from high school or has a GED. If the country was to support and fund postsecondary education in a manner akin to how public K–12 education is funded, the costs would be enormous. Recall my earlier comment in this chapter about California's situation. California needs to increase its college attainment rate from 31% to 41%, and an additional 20% need to have some form of postsecondary education (Johnson and Sengupta 2009). Such a goal accounts for 60% of high school graduates going on to college, and herein lies the problem I wish to consider in the remainder of this chapter.

A great deal of discussion has involved the need for increasing access to higher education, and it is fair to say that the policy-oriented dialogues have been largely supportive of such goals. The issues have revolved around what policies to take to enable the goals to be achieved. But what happens to those 40% of high school students in the United States who only need to graduate from high school? What becomes of them? Are we suggesting that a certain segment of society shall remain poor, even though additional educational avenues may lift them out of poverty? What are the consequences for them if the country enacts a "college for all" curriculum? And, perhaps most controversially, who decides which students need a college degree versus a high school degree?

Such questions are not only policy dilemmas but also go to the heart of how the country has defined education and democracy. The dilemma of individual achievement and communal responsibility has been an issue since the founding of the country. Accordingly, in what follows, I outline the educational issues surrounding a "college for all" curriculum for those who are least prepared. I consider the philosophical assumptions underpinning what should be learned in high school, even though those assumptions go unrealized. I then turn to a discussion of tracking to demonstrate historically who has gone to college and who has not, as well as who attends community colleges as opposed to four-year institutions. The data will be no surprise in the twenty-first century, but they stand in the way of an argument that says, all things being equal, anyone can go to college. I then contrast the data with how educational systems function in advanced, industrialized European countries to suggest an alternative model. I conclude not with a suggestion that one or another position is correct but that the current road we are on is untenable. As I elaborate later on, we must confront our philosophical inconsistencies before we are able to put forward strategic policies that help improve the country.

To advance this argument, I ground the discussion in delineating what happens to one hundred ninth grade students in California as a whole and in Los Angeles in particular.

The Philosophical Underpinnings of "College for All"

Assume one hundred students enter ninth grade. We know what happens to them now. An overrepresentation of students of color, first-generation, and low-income youth are less likely to graduate from high school and go on to college than Anglo and Asian, middle- and upper-class youth. Of those students who graduate from high school, an overrepresentation of middle- and upper-class, and Anglo and Asian students are more likely to go to a four-year institution than their low-income, first-generation Latino and African American counterparts.

Assume, however, that a degree of latitude exists, and the nefarious influence of tracking based on race and class is moot. What should be the assumption about the educational trajectory of those one hundred ninth grade students? Of related concern is who should determine that educational trajectory? Three primary philosophies undergird how one approaches these issues.

Individuals Have Equal Ability

One philosophic stance is that all children have equal ability if they are provided equal opportunity. From this perspective, if one hundred students enter ninth grade, and they are of unequal ability, it is because children have not been accorded equal opportunities. Those lacking quality educational experiences need to be provided with additional support to enable them to be on par with other children. If society provides adequate support, each child has the potential not only to graduate from high school but also to attend and graduate from a postsecondary institution.

The decision to go to college is made by the individual and his or her parents; that decision need not be made until the twelfth grade, although every opportunity should be afforded to children prior to their senior year so they are ready to apply. Society, as defined by the citizenry and taxpayers, should have a relatively insignificant role in sorting out who attends and who does not. Society has an obligation to pay for a student's education, but the assumption is that, as a public good, education should benefit all citizens equally. As opposed to other public goods, such as clean water or public safety, the assumption about education is that an individual's ability matters. There is no assumption that some people are better consumers of clean drinking water than others, or that how someone drinks water is variable. For other public goods, the quality of the consumer is irrelevant. The goal is to ensure that all individuals have access to the same quality drinking water.

Education, however, inevitably involves the user of the public good in a fundamentally different manner. The state not only needs to ensure that users have access to the public good, but, by ninth grade, if some students are lagging behind others, the state is obligated to provide the requisite resources to bring all students up to an acceptable level that enables them to graduate and, presumably, attend and graduate from a postsecondary institution. With other public goods, such as clean drinking water, the state does not need to train some users how to drink, or assume that some are better drinkers of water than others. Instead, the state simply needs to provide clean water to everyone.

Such an approach combines two public philosophies about the individual and the community. All individuals are alike, and the community's responsibility is to ensure not only equal opportunity but equal outcomes. The practical consequences of this approach are that a "college for all" curriculum should be implemented in all high schools. If all students can attend and succeed in college, the curriculum should be geared toward enabling every student to go to college.

Individuals Have Variable Ability (but Deserve Equal Opportunity)

A second philosophic stance is that those one hundred ninth graders are not all alike. Some are better qualified, as defined by standardized tests, grades, and teachers' judgments, than others. Consequently, some will graduate from high school and go to college, while others will not. However, all students should have the opportunity to attend college, and every effort should be made to enable participation in college. The result has been the creation of programs such as Upward Bound, Talent Search, and Math, Engineering, Science Achievement (MESA). Although many have questioned the effectiveness of such programs (e.g., Haskins and Rouse 2013), the assumption has been that all children need to be provided equal opportunity, which gets defined as the ability to go to college. Nevertheless, by the end of high school, if all students have been provided an equal opportunity, some will go to college and others will not. Moreover, some students will attend selective four-year institutions, whereas others will attend a two-year college; some will graduate with a bachelor's degree, whereas others will attain a postsecondary certificate. In some respects, the Master Plan in California (University of California 2007) was developed with this perspective in mind.

As with the previous stance, the individuals who determine whether a student goes to college are the student and his or her parents. However, where one goes is also shaped by tests that society has sanctioned by way of publicly supported institutions. How one performs on the tests is an indicator to the individual about what society is willing to pay. That is, one cannot simply decide to attend the postsecondary institution of his or her choice. Until twelfth grade, an individual has a great deal of leeway, but, ultimately, standardized tests will most likely be determinative.

Society's role is to enable equal opportunity via a tax structure that supports public education. Differentiation occurs, as judged by a student's ability, such that some will go to a community college and others to an elite four-year institution. The assumption has less to do with everyone having equal ability and more to do with the assurance that everyone has the opportunity to pursue whatever educational avenue they may desire, if they meet the requisite criteria.

This approach has two different stances about the individual and community. Individuals are different, but over time they will be able to sort out what they want to do. The community's responsibility is to ensure equal opportunities that will enable the individual to determine what to do. The result is that a "college for all" curriculum needs to be implemented in every school to ensure equal opportunity. When course offerings, such as Advanced Placement classes, the International Baccalaureate, and the like, are investigated, discrepancies will point out a lack of equal opportunity. What then needs to happen is to assure that students have the exact same educational opportunities. In Los Angeles, for example, what has come to be known as "A–G requirements" is a curricula aimed at students who desire to attend a postsecondary institution. Indeed, if a student successfully completes the A–G coursework, he or she must be admitted to a four-year institution. Until 2012, students had the option of not taking the A–G courses. With the vocal support of the school superintendent, the school board passed a motion in 2012 that stipulated, from 2014 onward, that all students will take the A–G curricula. Such a decision highlights the philosophy outlined here.

Individuals Have Variable Ability (and Should Be Tracked according to Their Ability)

A third philosophic stance is that the one hundred students have different abilities, and these abilities can be assessed by ninth grade. The standard way to determine intellectual difference is through standardized tests, grades, and teachers' evaluations. The result is ability grouping. Students are differentiated according to ability—some will take a college-focused curriculum, and others will take what used to be called vocational education, or a career-oriented curriculum. Thus, some students are expected to apply to four-year postsecondary institutions and receive a baccalaureate degree that prepares them for "white-collar" work, some will go to two-year community colleges for working-class jobs, and still others will only require a high school degree and find employment largely in the service sector.

Although hard work certainly plays a role in how this stance views ability, ultimately the assumption is that some are qualified and others are not. From this perspective, then, a desire to attend college should not play a role in the decision of who actually attends college. The arbiter is the school system, which interprets scores and tests for the state. The state's role is to ensure that the system is fair, equitable, efficient, and effective.

To be sure, the work of Howard Gardner (1993), following in the line of John Dewey (1916), offers a different interpretation. A case can be made that students do not have variable abilities but different abilities. Gardner and others reject standardized tests because they examine one form of intelligence rather than multiple forms. While there is much to be said for this line of work, the ideas have not been implemented. Indeed, high-stakes testing has taken on only increased importance over the last several years, which sorts students into those who are college bound and those who are not.

A long history exists about the misguided attempts to track students according to race, class, gender, and religion rather than ability. A considerable literature also exists about the limited successes of ability grouping (Ansalone 2001; Archbald and Farley-Ripple 2012). A fair amount of research, for example, suggests that high-ability students do just as well in mixed groups, and low-ability students do better in mixed groups rather than in a group of their peers. Others have pointed out the state's long history of privileging the children of the wealthy rather than the poor.

At the same time, the data presented earlier highlight the fact that although we need more people participating in higher education, we surely do not need everyone attending college. Literature also points out that a "college for all" curriculum is more likely to push students who are the least ready out of high school; courses that are oriented for students likely to attend college are also likely to bore students who have no desire to keep studying academic subjects (Rosenbaum, Stephan, and Rosenbaum 2010; Samuelson 2012).

The Consequences of Tracking and Detracking
Tracking

I have described philosophical positions that are absent, if possible, of ideology. That is, I have assumed that we live in a perfect world and put forward positions as if underlying issues such as racism, sexism, and classism do not exist. Absent the history of such issues, a policy analyst may suggest one of these philosophical stances and proceed to implement it. However, one need merely look at college admissions to discover the pernicious outcomes of ability grouping, or what has come to be known as tracking (Ansalone 2001; Oakes 1985, 1987).

The Master Plan for Higher Education in California is a useful case in point (Douglass 2011; Geiser and Atkinson 2013; University of California 2007). Enacted in 1960, the plan has been viewed as a prototype for other states and even foreign countries. Although many suggest that the plan is in need of an overhaul a half a century after its creation, the basic tenet has been widely lauded as a democratic ideal: if an individual wanted to attend a postsecondary institution, then the state would find a place for him or her in the public system. Such an idea is laudable, and moved the ideal of equity forward when the Plan was initiated, yet the implementation of the plan has not been free of the often-implicit, and occasionally explicit, consequences of discrimination.

Even today, for example, African Americans and Latinos are overrepresented in community colleges and underrepresented on the ten campuses of the University of California (UC). Similarly, the poor are overrepresented in two-year institutions and underrepresented at the UC. Within an institution, we also know that poor people of color and women tend to be underrepresented in high-status STEM fields and overrepresented in lower-status fields, such as education and nursing.

To be sure, one possible interpretation of such data is that the postsecondary sector sorts people out in a meritocratic manner. Indeed, a meritocracy is ostensibly what has driven American education for a century. The idea of a meritocracy is, in part, laudable. At the turn of the century, some postsecondary institutions implemented quotas so that they did not have an overrepresentation of Jews in their institutions. Hence, the assumption of a standardized test was that anonymity would sort people according to their ability, rather than by their religious affiliation. Over time, of course, the citizenry came to realize that if attending college was based solely on a standardized test, then some would be privileged and others harmed. As a corrective, programs such as Head Start and public policies such as affirmative action were created. Public policies that tend to help underperforming students have nevertheless come under attack and have largely been curtailed, underfunded, or eliminated.

Those who call for a return to a meritocracy never really face the probable outcome, however. Assumptions that individuals have variable ability and should be tracked accordingly will likely vary by race, income, and gender. That is, the trends that have occurred in a society that has given lip service to the idea that everyone should have equal opportunity are likely to be exacerbated. No one seriously would believe, for example, that equal percentages of poor and upper-class students will be taking Advanced Placement classes, even if they should in theory. Insofar as schools are embedded in a society that provides inherent advantages to some and disadvantages to others, the likely result is that the poor and students of color will be even more overrepresented among non-college-goers, as well as at less elite institutions in the postsecondary sector.

Indeed, even though the most pernicious effects of tracking have ended, many will argue that structural tracking remains (Lucas 1999). From this perspective, the overt placement policies of the 1960s and 1970s that cordoned off educational opportunity for the poor and students of color have largely ended. As Lucas (1999) points out, "Chicago schools used a four-track system composed of honors, regular, essential, and basic programs. All students were assigned to one of the four tracks, and that track assignment determined students' courses" (6). Investigations of this sort of assignment underscored how students in largely middle- and upper-class neighborhoods received one kind of curricula, while students in poorer neighborhoods received another. Although formal segmentation has ended, careful analyses have pointed out how structural inequality enables it to continue; in effect, a hidden curriculum has replaced what was once demonstrably clear. Advanced Placement classes in low-income neighborhoods, for example, may now exist. However, the number of students in those neighborhoods who actually take Advanced Placement tests, much less receive scores high enough to get college credit, is less than half of the number in upper-class neighborhoods.

Others have argued that those who are tracked fall within an "oppositional culture" (Ogbu 2008). According to this position, minority students assume that succeeding in high school conforms to the majority culture and that academic advancement requires Black and Latino students to "act white." Even though this thesis is provocative (and some students may adhere to such an idea), the careful work of Angel Harris (2011) and others has largely debunked the notion of an "oppositional culture." The Black-White achievement gap, he argues, can be more likely attributed to opportunity rather than to any internalized oppression on the part of students of color. In effect, tracking by way of a hidden curriculum in low-achieving schools is what stymies educational opportunity.

Detracking

An alternative view has to do with the consequences of assuming that everyone should take a "college for all" curriculum. Students currently enter ninth grade with varying abilities. In the past, students had varying opportunities to choose college-preparation curricula, but the assumption of "college for all" is that every student—all one hundred students in my hypothetical model—will take such a curriculum. In effect, success in high school gets defined as being prepared for college. Research has shown, however, that a "college for all" curriculum actually may increase the dropout rate in schools (Berliner 2006; Rosenbaum et al. 2010; Rumberger 2011). It is also true, as noted earlier, that all jobs will not require a college certificate or degree (Carnevale, Smith, and Strohl 2010). The result is that an increasing number of scholars have questioned a one-size-fits-all curricular model that expects all students to be prepared to go to college (Symonds, Schwartz, and Ferguson 2011).

Conversely, a fair amount of research questions the utility of a "college for all" curriculum (Roderick, Nagaoka, and Coca 2009). Underperforming students are also at risk of being pushed out of the traditional school system if they do not do well on high-stakes tests (Lin 2006). The San Jose Unified School District, for example, mandated a college preparatory curriculum; the result was that Black and Latino students were disproportionately moved to alternative high schools (Lin 2006). Others point out that at a time when technology and social media have vastly broadened options—consider how citizens receive news and information—that to offer fewer options in education seems wrongheaded.

Many argue that career and technical education increases attendance rates, decreases dropout rates, and improves high school completion rates (Balfanz and Byrnes 2012; Bishop and Mane 2004). As I elaborate in the following paragraphs, international comparisons demonstrate that countries with variable curricular options, including vocational education, have higher completion rates than the United States (Cardoza 2012). From this perspective, then, the curricula of other industrialized countries should be adopted in our schools.

If a potpourri of options exists, the likelihood that students will graduate from high school and assume a variety of careers may increase. One example that Russell Rumberger (2011) has pointed out is Big Picture Learning High Schools. In these schools, Rumberger notes that "learning is tailored to the interests and goals of each student and pursued through a combination of individualized school-based and work-based learning experiences" (272). The point is not merely that students have multiple curricular options but that their graduation is dependent upon what they need to know in their areas of interest. A student who wants to study physics, for example, will not only have a very different curriculum from a student who wishes to be a chef, but what the future physicist needs to master to graduate from college will differ from what someone who wishes to be a chef will need to master. This approach assumes that noncognitive skills (e.g., motivation, grit, time management) are as important as cognitive skills for some students (Heckman, Stixrud, and Urzua 2006). Thus, rather than assume that ability grouping tracks students into a dichotomy of "haves" and "have-nots," this approach argues that, in the twenty-first century, multiple career paths need to be open to students. A one-size-fits-all curriculum is not only wrong for the job market of the twenty-first century but also may increase the dropout rate and drive students away from successful educational opportunities and job employability.

At the same time, "multiple paths" also need to mean the same thing in different locales. Children of the middle and upper classes are not often introduced to career paths in the vocational and service sectors, for example, or encouraged to attend a community college. If by "multiple paths" all that occurs is that children in low-income neighborhoods have a few additional opportunities that are regularly afforded to all children in upper-income families, then very little will change. One of the challenges for the poor is that they frequently are not able to see the sorts of career opportunities that exist. The potential exists that greater curricular offerings can broaden horizons and, in doing so, educational and economic opportunity.

A European Alternative to "College for All"

The United States has had a long history of the twin ideas of American exceptionalism and individual ability. Indeed, since the founding of the country, a discourse has developed around the idea that America is unique and that an individual can do whatever he or she desires if the government does not intrude. Such an assumption, in part, has led to the idea that everyone should have the same opportunity for college. Furthermore, if individuals have the same opportunity, they "will be all they can be," to paraphrase a popular jingle. One alternative, however, is how education and opportunity have been conceived in Germany and other European countries.

Comparative data with OECD countries highlight how America's current educational structure is neither exceptional nor geared for individual opportunity. Youth unemployment is higher, and the number of youth in stable employment five years after leaving education is lower than in other advanced industrialized economies (Hoffman 2011, 3). One assumption that European countries and the United States share is that youth with low skills and low educational levels are at risk. As outlined earlier, the countries diverge with regard to America's position vis-à-vis educational opportunity and Europe's specific policies aimed at vocational training for youth. Such training links education to labor market needs and includes workplace learning. Students in high schools in Germany go outside the school to be trained for specific skills in the workplace that will enable them to assume a career.

The integration of work and learning is something that has been critiqued quite severely in the United States, in large part because of a history of discrimination against particular groups of individuals—racial and ethnic minorities, in particular. A great deal of research has pointed out how individuals in the early twentieth century were trained for the workforce in a manner that suggested the purpose of education was to make individuals submissive workers (Bowles and Gintis 1976). Such a critique suggested that the schooling that America provided ran counter to the ethos of individualism. The same line of research continued through the 1980s, where the important work by Jeannie Oakes (1987) on tracking highlighted how ability grouping largely failed, and those who were tracked were the same sort of individuals who were tracked at the start of the century—students of color.

European countries also have been concerned with tracking. It is worth quoting Nancy Hoffman (2011) at length here:

> Concern about the potentially pernicious effects of early tracking continues to preoccupy the OECD countries. They keep data and are sensitive to the relationship between parental education and income and schools results. . . . Tracking takes two forms in the OECD countries: in Austria, Germany, Switzerland, and the Netherlands students choose or are placed into a vocational or academic pathway between the ages of 10 and 12. The Nordic countries and Australia have comprehensive schools through the end of lower secondary school, with everyone following the same curriculum. Then at age 15 students and their families have a choice of a university or vocational pathway. (18)

Although European countries attempt to avoid the sorts of tracking that concern those in the United States, the outcomes remain relatively the same. Three differences, however, exist between the United States and a country such as Switzerland or Germany. First, those who are tracked find jobs and careers, rather than dropping out or being unemployed, as is frequently the case in the United States in the twenty-first century. Second, wages for the working class tend to be higher in European countries than in the United States; one of America's problems is the huge discrepancy in wages and income. Third, the apprenticeships and traineeships offered in Europe are more advanced than what was once defined as vocational education. In Europe, high-tech, cutting-edge training tends to be part of the vocational framework rather than part of tertiary education.

Here's how the German apprenticeship model works. Students are apprentices at an employer four days a week; they are in school only one day a week. As in the United States, this form of training is free, and the training lasts about three years. The employer pays minimum wage for the students, and they provide on-the-job training. But they also have a say in what the curricula and training should be. When the training is over, the student and the employer can continue the job, but neither the student nor employer is stuck with the other. The engagement between school and businesses is quite firm and set in a way that is rare in the United States. As one observer of the training that Germany provides has commented, "On-the-job training is likely the biggest lever America can pull to close the skills gap. Sadly, only a handful of American companies operate anything resembling an apprenticeship program" (University Ventures 2013, 2).

In a school-to-work system, employers play a significant role in what students learn and how they are trained. They also may pay for part of the training or apprenticeship. Such a relationship has frequently been resisted in the United States, in part because of a fear that a corporate agenda would train "workers" in a manner that would make them compliant. Although one may agree with such sentiments, a sustained and systemic relationship with school systems and employers is largely absent in the United States. The result is that America's college graduates leave school without being prepared for a particular career. Two-thirds of all Germans, however, have an occupational qualification by the time they are twenty (Hoffman 2011, 100).

My purpose here is neither to give an extended exegesis on German education nor to suggest that such a model is perfect. In Europe, for example, there tends to be an overreliance on a single indicator, such as performance on a standardized test. However, as Norton Grubb (2008) and others have noted (Grubb and Lazerson 2012), viable alternatives exist to the increasingly common assumption that all one hundred ninth graders should be prepared and go to college, and if they do not, either something is wrong with the system or something is wrong with them. As Ben Levin and Lauren Segedin (2011) have noted, "Studying what other systems do is a worthwhile activity not because it gives us answers, but because it gives us questions and ideas. . . . It tells us that there are other ways to get to a goal and broadens our thinking about what these might be" (7). Hence, a variety of possibilities might exist that actually better serve the populace and the individual than the assumption that everyone should go to college.

The reasons for dropping out of high school tend to be similar across countries and schools—academic ability, boredom, a lack of relevant curricula, and personal problems, to name a few—but the solutions to resolving these problems differ. Countries other than the United States have a viable alternative to mainstream education geared toward college preparation. Linkages to the labor market and a career get set early in a child's schooling in Europe, whereas career-based discussions, in the United States, largely take place in postsecondary education.

Conclusion

This is a text without a conclusion, or, at least, I am unconvinced of the appropriate solution, much less what the appropriate policies might be to advance a solution that pertains centrally to our theme of rethinking education and poverty. The United States is on the horns of a dilemma. Unquestionably, the country needs to make dramatic strides in improving access to higher education. More students need to be college ready, and more students need to graduate from two- and four-year institutions. But roughly 40% of the population does not need to attend higher education. This population's attendance will neither raise overall wages nor employment, and the citizenry cannot afford the revenue necessary for everyone to participate in higher education. Additionally, a college preparation curriculum is likely to increase dropout rates in high school.

However, the history of inequality that has existed in the United States is likely to ensure certain outcomes. The poor, students of color, and other historically marginalized populations would likely be overrepresented in the non-college-going populations. The pervasive strength of those among the entitled classes will surely strengthen social capital for their children (Bourdieu 1986), whereas college-going networks will not be so strong in low-income neighborhoods.

A country that prides itself on the idea of educational opportunity needs to come to grips not simply with schooling, but with wealth inequality. In a fair society where people are paid similar wages, attending college would not be nearly as critical as it is today. College-educated workers earn almost twice as much an hour as their high school–educated counterparts (Tierney and Hentschke 2011). Education has long been seen as a route out of poverty and into the middle class. But it seems clear that education also should prepare people for a wide array of careers and citizenship. There has recently been a great deal of discussion about measuring academic readiness for college (Maruyama 2012; Porter and Polikoff 2012). To be sure, what one needs to succeed in college must be investigated and refined. But perhaps an additional priority ought to be a fulsome discussion about what the opportunities should be when students graduate from high school and how these opportunities might be more closely targeted to particular careers and employment. Such a discussion also needs to be linked to a larger conversation in the country about wealth disparities and how to reduce income inequality.

ACKNOWLEDGMENTS

The author wishes to thank Shaun Harper, Adrianna Kezar, James Minor, and Laura Perna for helpful comments on an earlier draft of this chapter.

REFERENCES

Amelga, Makeda. 2012. *College and Career Readiness: A Quick Stats Fact Sheet*. Washington, DC: National High School Center at the American Institutes for Research. http://www.businessweek.com/articles/2012-04-09/why-college-isnt-for-everyone.
Ansalone, George. 2001. "Schooling, Tracking, and Inequality." *Journal of Children and Poverty* 7 (1): 33–49.
Archbald, Doug, and Elizabeth Farley-Ripple. 2012. "Predictors of Placement in Lower Level versus Higher Level High School Mathematics." *High School Journal* 96 (1): 33–51.
Bailey, Thomas, Dong Wook Jeong, and Sung-Woo Cho. 2009. *Referral, Enrollment, and Completion in Developmental Education Sequences in Community Colleges* (CCRC Working Paper No. 15). New York: Teachers College, Columbia University.
Balfanz, Robert, and Vaughan Byrnes. 2012. *The Importance of Being in School: A Report on Absenteeism in the Nation's Public Schools*. Baltimore: Johns Hopkins University Center for Social Organization of Schools.
Berliner, David C. 2006. "Our Impoverished View of Educational Reform." *Teachers College Record* 108 (6): 949–95.

Betts, Julian R., Andrew C. Zau, and Karen Volz Bachofer. 2013. *College Readiness as a Graduation Requirement: An Assessment of San Diego's Challenges*. San Francisco: Public Policy Institute of California. http://www.ppic.org/main/publication.asp?i=1049.

Bishop, John H., and Ferran Mane. 2004. *Raising Academic Standards and Vocational Concentrators: Are they Better Off or Worse Off?* (CAHRS Working Paper No. 04-12). Ithaca, NY: Cornell University, School of Industrial and Labor Relations, Center for Advanced Human Resource Studies. http://digitalcommons.ilr.cornell.edu/cahrswp/16/.

Bourdieu, Pierre. 1986. "The Forms of Capital." In *Handbook of Theory and Research for the Sociology of Education*, edited by J. G. Richardson. 241–58. New York: Greenwood Press.

Bowles, Samuel, and Herbert Gintis. 1976. *Schooling in Capitalist America: Educational Reform and the Contradictions of Economic Life*. New York: Basic Books.

Cardoza, Kavitha. 2012. "Graduation Rates Increase around the Globe as U.S. Plateaus." *American University Radio*. February 21. http://wamu.org/news/morning_edition/12/02/21/graduation_rates_increase_around_the_globe_as_us_plateaus.

Carnevale, Anthony P., Stephen J. Rose, and Ban Cheah. 2013. *The College Payoff: Education, Occupations, Lifetime Earnings*. Washington, DC: Georgetown University Center on Education and the Workforce.

Carnevale, Anthony P., Nicole Smith, and Jeff Strohl. 2010. *Help Wanted: Projections of Jobs and Education Requirements through 2018*. Washington, DC: Center for Education and the Workforce, Georgetown University. http://cew.georgetown.edu/jobs2018/.

Dewey, John. 1916. *Democracy and Education: An Introduction to the Philosophy of Education*. New York: Macmillan.

Douglass, John Aubrey. 2011. "Revisionist Reflections on California's Master Plan at 50." *California Journal of Politics and Policy* 3 (1): 1–36.

Gardner, Howard. 1993. *Multiple Intelligences: New Horizons in Theory and Practice*. New York: Basic Books.

Geiser, Saul, and Richard C. Atkinson. 2013. "Beyond the Master Plan: The Case for Restructuring Baccalaureate Education in California." *California Journal of Politics and Policy* 4 (1): 67–123.

Grubb, W. Norton. 2008. "Challenging the Deep Structure of High School: Weak and Strong Versions of Multiple Pathways." In *Beyond Tracking: Multiple Pathways to College, Career, and Civic Participation*, edited by Jeannie Oakes and Marisa Saunders, 197–212. Cambridge, MA: Harvard Education Press.

Grubb, W. Norton, and Marvin Lazerson. 2012. "The Education Gospel and Vocationalism in U.S. Higher Education: Triumphs, Tribulations, and Cautions for Other Countries." In *Work and Education in America*, edited by Antje Barabasch and Felix Rauner, 101–21. New York: Springer.

Harris, Angel L. 2011. *Kids Don't Want to Fail: Oppositional Culture and the Black-White Achievement Gap*. Cambridge, MA: Harvard University Press.

Haskins, Ron, and Cecilia Elena Rouse. 2013. *Time for Change: A New Federal Strategy to Prepare Disadvantaged Students for College*. Princeton, NJ: Princeton University-Brookings Institute. http://www.brookings.edu/research/papers/2013/05/07-disadvantaged-students-college-readiness-haskins.

Heckman, James J., Jora Stixrud, and Sergio Urzua. 2006. "The Effects of Cognitive and Noncognitive Abilities on Labor Market Outcomes and Social Behavior." *Journal of Labor Economics* 24 (3): 411–82.

Hoffman, Nancy. 2011. *Schooling in the Workplace*. Cambridge, MA: Harvard Education Press.

Johnson, Hans, and Ria Sengupta. 2009. *Closing the Gap: Meeting California's Need for College Graduates*. San Francisco: Public Policy Institute of California. http://www.ppic.org/main/publication.asp?i=835.

Levin, Ben, and Lauren Segedin. 2011. *International Approaches to Secondary Education*. Toronto, Canada: Higher Education Quality Council of Ontario.

Lewin, Tamar. 2010. "Once a Leader, U.S. Lags in College Degrees." *New York Times*. July 23. http://www.nytimes.com/2010/07/23/education/23college.html.

Lin, Barbara. 2006. *Access to A–G Curriculum at San Jose Unified School District*. Center for Latino Policy Research Brief 2 (1): 1–2. http://escholarship.org/uc/item/92k987pp.

Lucas, Samuel R. 1999. *Tracking Inequality: Stratification and Mobility in American High Schools*. New York: Teachers College Press.

Lumina Foundation. 2013. *A Stronger Nation through Higher Education*. http://www.luminafoundation.org/stronger_nation/.

Maruyama, Geoffrey. 2012. "Assessing College Readiness: Should we be Satisfied with ACT or other Threshold Scores?" *Educational Researcher* 41 (7): 252–61.

National Center for Public Policy and Higher Education. 2010. *Beyond the Rhetoric: Improving College Readiness through Coherent State Policy*. http://www.highereducation.org/reports/college_readiness/CollegeReadiness.pdf.

Oakes, Jeannie. 1985. *Keeping Track: How Schools Structure Inequality*. New Haven, CT: Yale University Press.

———. 1987. "Tracking in Secondary Schools: A Contextual Perspective." *Educational Psychologist* 22 (2): 129–53.

Ogbu, John U., ed. 2008. *Minority Status, Oppositional Culture, and Schooling*. New York: Routledge.

Owen, Stephanie, and Isabel V. Sawhill. 2013. *Should Everyone Go to College?* Washington, DC: Brookings Institute.

Porter, Andrew C., and Morgan S. Polikoff. 2012. "Measuring Academic Readiness for College." *Educational Policy* 26 (3): 394–417.

Roderick, Melissa, Jenny Nagaoka, and Vanessa Coca. 2009. "College Readiness for All: The Challenge for Urban High Schools." *Future of Children* 19 (1): 185–210.

Rosenbaum, James E., Jennifer L. Stephan, and Janet E. Rosenbaum. 2010. "Beyond One-Size-Fits-All College Dreams: Alternative Pathways to Desirable Careers." *American Educator* 34 (3): 2–13.

Rumberger, Russell W. 2011. *Dropping Out: Why Students Drop Out of High School and What Can Be Done about It*. Cambridge, MA: Harvard University Press.

Samuelson, Robert J. 2012. "It's Time to Drop the College-for-All Crusade." *Washington Post*. May 27. http://articles.washingtonpost.com/2012-05-27/opinions/35456501_1_college-students-josipa-roksa-private-colleges-and-universities.

Sanoff, Alvin P. 2006. "A Perception Gap Over Students' Preparation." *Chronicle of Higher Education*. March 10. http://chronicle.com/article/A-Perception-Gap-Over/31426.

Symonds, William C., Robert B. Schwartz, and Ronald Ferguson. 2011. *Pathways to Prosperity: Meeting the Challenge of Preparing Young Americans for the 21st Century*. Cambridge, MA: Harvard University Graduate School of Education. http://dash.harvard.edu/bitstream/handle/1/4740480/Pathways_to_Prosperity_Feb2011-1.pdf?sequence=1.

Taylor, Paul, Rich Morin, Rakesh Kochlar, Kim Parker, D'Vera Cohn, Mark Lopez, Richard Fry, Wendy Wang, Gabriel Velasco, Daniel Dockterman, Rebecca Hinze-Pifer, and Soledad Espinosa. 2010. *How the Great Recession Has Changed Life in America*. Washington, DC: Pew Research Center.

Tierney, William G., and Guilbert C. Hentschke. 2007. *New Players, Different Game: Understanding the Rise of For-Profit Colleges and Universities*. Baltimore: Johns Hopkins University Press.

———. 2011. *Making It Happen: Increasing College Access and Attainment in California Higher Education*. La Jolla, CA: National University System Institute for Policy Research.

University of California. 2007. *Major Features of the California Master Plan for Higher Education*. Oakland, CA: Author. http://www.ucop.edu/acadinit/mastplan /mpsummary.htm.

University Ventures. 2013. "The Skills Gap and the Spit-Take." *UV Letters* 3 (21). http://universityventuresfund.com/publications.php?title=the-skills-gap-and-the -spit-take.

U.S. Department of Education. 2012. *Fall Enrollment Survey*. Washington, DC: National Center for Education Statistics, Integrated Postsecondary Education Data System. http://nces.ed.gov/programs/projections/projections2021/tables/table_20.asp.

Vedder, Richard. 2012. "Why College Isn't for Everyone." *Bloomberg Businessweek*. April 9. http://www.businessweek.com/articles/2012-04-09/why-college-isnt-for-everyone.

Vedder, Richard, Christopher Denhart, and Jonathan Robe. 2013. *Why Are Recent College Graduates Underemployed? University Enrollments and Labor-Market Realities*. Washington, DC: Center for College Affordability and Productivity. http:// centerforcollegeaffordability.org/uploads/Underemployed%20Report%202.pdf.

White House. (n.d.). "Higher Education." http://www.whitehouse.gov/issues/education /higher-education.

9

Poverty, Privilege, and the Intensification of Inequalities in the Postsecondary Admissions Process

LOIS WEIS, KRISTIN CIPOLLONE, AND AMY E. STICH

Since the middle of the twentieth century, the United States has witnessed an unprecedented expansion of educational opportunities, allowing more people than ever before—particularly disadvantaged groups—access to postsecondary options. Yet, while opportunities for postsecondary education have increased dramatically, these opportunities have not been equally or democratically distributed (Mullen 2010; Reay 2011; Stich 2012). In fact, deep differentiation and stratification have accompanied the widespread expansion, predominantly serving to reproduce/reify existing social and economic inequalities (Shavit, Arum, and Gamoran 2007).

Given recent research in K–16+ education, this finding is not surprising. For example, Reardon (2011) argued that the achievement gap between low-income and high-income children has grown by 30%–40% between children born in 2001 and those born in 1976. Significantly, Bailey and Dynarski (2011) concluded that gaps in college entry, persistence, and completion have also grown. Drawing on data from the National Longitudinal Surveys of Youth (U.S. Bureau of Labor Statistics 1979, 1997), they note that "rates of college completion increased by only four percentage points for low-income cohorts born around 1980 relative to cohorts born in the early 1960s, but by 18 points for corresponding cohorts who grew up in high-income families" (117). Moreover, the majority of low-income students enrolled in higher education attend two-year and less selective four-year institutions, wherein rates of retention and completion are the lowest (Bastedo and Jaquette 2011; Long and Kurlaender 2009; Melguizo 2008; Niu and Tienda 2013).

Clearly, where one goes to college is linked to differential ability to pay for higher education, as well as varied opportunities for academic preparation in elementary and high school. However, the intensified production of inequalities in postsecondary access and outcomes must also be understood as increasingly tied to the ways in which differently situated students, parents, and schools are able and willing to harness/actualize all available capitals to *position* for postsecondary entrance at a time of deepened internal stratification in higher education (e.g., Bowen, Chingos, and McPherson 2009; Leslie et al. 2012; Thomas and Bell 2008). In this way, the opportunities and experiences of low-income students are inescapably tethered to what is happening among those with privilege. As relatively privileged families intentionally move to consolidate future class position via access to particularly located postsecondary destinations (Weis, Cipollone, and Jenkins 2014), poor, working-class, and even lower-middle-class students are increasingly left behind.[1] This is linked to the structural abandonment of the U.S. poor and working class (Lipman 2011), as well as the everyday actions and activities of the relatively privileged as they drive toward "distinction" in economic and social circumstances that produce intensified anxiety throughout the class structure (Bourdieu 1984; Weis et al. 2014).

In this chapter, we turn our attention to the "college-linking" process (Hill 2008; McDonough 1997; Weis et al. 2014), as this constitutes a critical, determining moment relative to one's educational, occupational, and life chances. This process, not unlike the system of education itself, is highly differentiated by type and amount of capital available for exchange, resulting in deeply divided perceptions, experiences, opportunities, and outcomes. More specifically, we explore key school, family, and student-level mechanisms through which inequalities in relevant outcomes are produced on the ground of actual practice. We focus our discussion on: (1) opportunity structures within two differentially positioned secondary schools, (2) student identities and their formation in relation to available school-based opportunity structures and the types and amounts of capital possessed by their families, and (3) the role of parent involvement with respect to the transmission of advantage or disadvantage at the point of college admissions. Our basic premise is that the marked intensification of inequalities in access to postsecondary education must be understood as linked both to the relative abandonment of children of poverty and the commensurate escalation of particular kinds of "class-positioning work" among relatively privileged populations, both within schools and by families.

Data affirm what Lucas (2001) and others (e.g., Shavit, Arum, and Gamoran 2007) call "effectively maintained inequality" (EMI). In the case at hand, this means that the massification of postsecondary education leads to an intensification of inequalities rather than a narrowing of such inequalities. EMI is a framework that recognizes that educational expansion at any given level is often accompanied by increasing institutional differentiation and/or heightened internal systemic stratification, thereby rendering the *status* of any given institution within a range of hierarchically possible options increasingly important. Put another way, the battle over *qualitative* distinction in educational opportunities can be expected to intensify, as more generalized access to any given level of education is achieved.

Data are drawn from two large-scale, ethnographic investigations, as follows: (1) a study of the opportunity structure and linked college applications and admissions process in two privileged secondary schools (one private/one public) that serve largely but not entirely White students (Weis et al. 2014)[2] and (2) a comparably conceived study of the opportunity structure and linked college applications and admissions process in eight urban, nonselective secondary schools, four of which are located in a similar geographic region. All four have free/reduced-lunch rates of 70%–80% and serve a high proportion of racial minorities, particularly African American and multigenerational Latino/a.[3] Given space limitations, we draw on data from one privileged school (Cannondale) and one nonselective urban school (STEM Academy). Both schools exhibit a targeted focus on the college admissions process.[4] Focal students are drawn from the top of their respective classes, as measured by grade point average (GPA) and/or test score data.[5]

Two Schools, Two Opportunity Structures

For many, the American dream, and the ideology of meritocracy on which it is based, is a powerful explanatory framework for justifying the social hierarchy (Hochschild and Scovronick 2003). The idea that working hard and playing by the rules will lead to success is one subscribed to by people across the social spectrum (Johnson 2012). Under the assumption that schools "level the unequal playing field," schooling is seen to play a central role in making the American dream a reality, ensuring that students' family backgrounds do not unduly advantage or disadvantage individuals in terms of opportunities.

In the face of this powerful ideology, an extensive body of research suggests that schools play a pivotal role in reproducing the very inequality they are tasked to eliminate (e.g., Anyon 1980; Oakes 1985). Not only do students within the same school receive different academic opportunities by virtue of placement in the track structure (Kelly 2008; Oakes 1985), thereby contributing to the long-noted "within school variance" with respect to achievement outcomes (Coleman et al. 1966; Jencks 1972), but students in different schools/districts receive dissimilar educations as well (Lee and Weis 2012). Given that K–12 education sets one up for postsecondary opportunities and future life outcomes, understanding the ways in which schools and families work to position students for college is essential.

Despite being located in comparable geographic regions, the two schools we focus on have notably different academic and sociocultural environments. Cannondale High School (CHS) is an affluent, suburban, public, comprehensive high school located in the northeastern United States. The student population is overwhelmingly White, and while not all students in attendance are affluent, the town in which the school is located is. CHS has a reputation as a "good school," a key factor in drawing families to settle in the area. The school has a 99% graduation rate and over 90% of the graduating class matriculates into college immediately upon high school completion. The curriculum offered is rich and varied. The school boasts more than fifteen Advanced Placement (AP) classes, an array of International Baccalaureate (IB) courses,[6] college credit–bearing courses (set up through an articulation agreement with a local four-year, highly reputable college), honors, and electives in addition to the state-required curriculum. The extracurricular opportunities are equally as varied, with close to one hundred clubs, sports teams, and organizations from which students can choose.

College is an integral part of CHS's organizational habitus. Embedded into the very fabric of the school, the importance of college physically manifests itself everywhere. As lead counselor Tom Cherub explains, college "hits you over the head." Teachers and counselors proudly display pennants and degrees from their alma maters; academic departments devote entire bulletin boards to where faculty went to college; and the school counseling department arranges numerous displays detailing college information, visits from college representatives, test prep information, interactive maps highlighting where students in the previous class matriculated, and daily announcements share college-related information. College is ever present, and the expectation is that students will not only attend college but will attend four-year schools.

While Cannondale serves a relatively privileged and highly capitalized student body, STEM Academy serves an entirely different clientele and offers vastly different opportunities. As an urban "College Board School," STEM

Academy aims to prepare its students (largely African American and low income) for college admission through a pervasive college-going discourse, early exposure to postsecondary institutions (e.g., field trips to local colleges), targeted extracurricular activities, and Advanced Placement courses; however, despite being college preparatory in name, opportunities for college preparation are, in fact, quite limited. Relative to course offerings, a very small number of AP options actually exist (two, in fact), and extracurricular opportunities are hard to come by. While STEM Academy was conceived with an eye toward increasing college and high-level STEM opportunities for low-income students, the school struggles to maintain its intended vision and offerings, which, at the time of the study, did not differ at all from the city's non-STEM-focused, comprehensive urban secondary schools. Despite this, STEM Academy takes the college admissions process very seriously, and two school counselors (also responsible for grades 5–8 in addition to 9–12) work through a litany of general counselor duties (scheduling, counseling, paperwork) (McDonough 1997; Perna 2008) while also working with seniors to fill out financial aid forms correctly, complete college applications, write essays, and meet deadlines. As a result of such efforts, the majority of graduating seniors attend local nonselective four-year and two-year schools.

Dominant themes around the college applications and admissions process are noticeably different between the two sites. While some elements of the process work across schools (e.g., students have to fill out application forms; financial aid forms, as relevant; sit for college entrance tests, as relevant; and the like), focusing on major narratives within each institution with respect to what we have come to call the "co-production of the college admissions process" reveals sharp differences. Although parents, students, and school personnel, particularly guidance counselors, are involved in such "co-production" in each institution, they are involved in different ways and to notably different extents, ultimately producing vastly different postsecondary matriculation outcomes.

In the next section, we examine student identities vis-à-vis the college admissions process. We argue that the working apparatus of the school, as coupled with parental and community expectations for college, serves to shape students' understandings of the kinds of colleges that are "right" for them. Such identities are instrumental to how one approaches the college admissions process and highlight the mechanisms through which inequalities between advantaged and disadvantaged groups are produced on the ground.

College-Going Identities and College Admissions

As Ball (2003) so eloquently articulates:

> Parents' commitment to providing for their children what Allatt (1993, 153) calls a "landscape of possibilities" has to be set against the deeply inscribed grammars of aspirations which circumscribe choice. For some families certain possibilities are unthinkable. The "transgenerational family scripts" (Cohen and Hey 2000, 5) of some middle-class families "exert prospective and regulative influence on actual life chances and choices" (Cohen and Hey 2000, 5). They are pursuing what Du Bois-Reymond (1998) calls a "normal biography"; although on occasion these can be resisted. Normal biographies are linear, anticipated and predictable, unreflexive transitions, often gender- and class-specific, rooted in well-established life-worlds. They are often driven by an absence of decisions. (65)

While all focal students across the two sites envisioned a future that included college attendance, what "college" meant and how students incorporated post-secondary education into their identities varied markedly.

The "decision" to attend college for participants from Cannondale can be characterized in very much the same way as Ball previously describes—as more of a nondecision, a predictable and nonreflexive transition (Mullen 2010). From the time students can remember, they always envisioned themselves as college bound. Illustrative of this point is the fact that Cannondale students needed clarification when asked the question: "When did you first start thinking about college?" (Ball 2003; Riegle-Crumb and Grodsky 2010). STEM Academy students, in contrast, could immediately provide concrete time frames, as college attendance does not comprise the next step in a well-codified "transgenerational script." Cannondale students Chloe and Michael, who have grown up in environments where aspiring to/attending college is just the norm, state that this is "just what my family does."

Nicholas, also from Cannondale, talks about how going to college is the "natural tendency" for students "like him." Parents and the larger school community scaffold the transfer of this "normal biography," affirming and facilitating adoption by students while marking four-year college attendance as "simply normal." Within this college-going habitus—assuming they will go to college, attend specific types of institutions (four-year, selective), and that college is what *naturally* follows high school—students develop a particular identity. Given this identity, focal students' academic and extracurricular lives become purposively organized and, in more cases than not, *explicitly organized for* postsecondary entrance (Stevens 2007). Students interpret college as the mechanism for success and social status, modeling the trajectories they have witnessed among parents, siblings, and other relatives. While the option not to attend college is certainly present (as is the option to pursue employment that does not require a college education), it has never been presented as a "real" option for these students, who altogether reject this as a viable alternative (Kaufman 2005). Not going to college is subsequently marked as the reality of "other" students, students who they perceive to be less motivated, hardworking, deserving, and academically able.

Building upon entrenched family expectations, student identities are further shaped in relation to their own position within the high school opportunity structure. Focal students at CHS are used to being in the most advanced classes with the same group of students, which acts to additionally shape both how they conceive of themselves and how they construct others. As Brantlinger (2003) reminds us, "Those who excel have a sense of superiority and entitlement," sentiments that are clearly exhibited in the lengthy focus group exchange that follows:

> *Kristin:* What about the courses you select? Does that have anything to do with—
> [preparing for college]? Like the courses that you took and why you took them?
> *Brad:* Yeah, oh yeah!
> *Kristin:* Oh yeah? Say more . . .
> *Nicholas:* Well, I took IB, and part of IB was the college stuff. It has good
> recognition—growing recognition at colleges, and I think that is a way to
> differentiate myself from students that may have similar academic qualities,
> let's say [. . .]
> *Brad:* Yeah . . . I am trying to think; you know, I do all the honors and AP stuff,
> and that might just be for college, but it is also for me to know that I can do it
> and feel good about myself, too (*snickers*).
> *Karina:* And I don't feel good in, like, state[7] classes because I feel like a lot of time
> the stuff is commonsense.
> *Brad:* And also, some of those kids . . . I am taking health, which is, like, my first,
> like, state-level class in a long time, and I am like, "Where did all these douche
> bags come from?"
> [. . .]
> *Karina:* But it has that reputation, like state English. Like, I haven't been in state
> English in, like, a long time, but the essays, like, I will see my friends' essays and

they will get a 100 on them, but I'll look at it and be like, "Seriously?" *I feel like I was writing like that in eighth grade* (emphasis added). And then we are graded so much harder in AP and then it's just, well, this is completely different, but our school [grades] is unweighted (difficulty of courses is not taken into account when calculating GPA's), which kind of sucks for our average but [. . .]

Nicholas: But, I would have to say, I mean a lot of them, like, if you are taking [grade] 7 honors, [grade] 8 honors, you are just expected to take [grade] 9 honors, and then [grade] 10 honors, and 11 AP, and then 12 AP.

All: Yeah, yeah.

Nicholas: I mean, this is just the next path; like, if they don't offer honors, you move up to AP; it's just sort of the steady progression upward.

Karina: And it would be like you failed if you went from AP last year into a state level this year, you know, you are just like, "Oh, did you do really bad last year?"

Brad: It's like a drop down. It's like all your peeps (people who surround you; friend group and family), all your parents went to college and whatnot and you didn't, it's like, "What's wrong? You were in honors and now you are not." [. . .]

Nicholas: . . . but most of the electives I have taken when I have been in with all the, I have been intermingled with all the rest of the—

Karina: Normal people.

This exchange between Brad, Nicholas, and Karina is particularly revealing. To begin, we see the conscious moves made by students as they strive to create "distinction" in order to position themselves for potential acceptance at particularly located colleges. As Nicholas states, "(Taking) IB . . . was the college stuff. It has good recognition—growing recognition at colleges, and I think that is *a way to differentiate myself* from students that may have similar academic qualities." Second, we see the ways in which the available opportunity structure of the school, and particularly one's own located position in the opportunity structure, works over time to encourage students to draw further distinctions between themselves and others in this already-privileged community.

Brad and Karina are perhaps most direct when talking about state-level courses, classes they perceive to consist of mostly "commonsense" and where the standards are framed as considerably lower than what they experience in their AP and IB classes ("I feel like I was writing like that in eighth grade"). Taking state-level classes, particularly after one has been on an accelerated track, is perceived as a step down and therefore an embarrassment, a common sentiment among focal students.[8] When asked to compare how state-level courses compare to AP courses, AP students expressed the notion that students in state-level courses are "lazy" and less willing to work hard. By positioning students in state courses in this way, focal students simultaneously affirm their *own* identities as hard workers who go the extra mile to achieve. Explicitly positioning themselves as students who take the AP and IB courses because they want to challenge themselves and "feel good about themselves," they simultaneously mark others as "going through the day just to get out of school." Top students come to see their own position within the academic hierarchy (as well as the lesser status of their peers) solely in terms of their *own* efforts, contributing to a strong sense of superiority and entitlement (Yonezawa and Wells 2005).

Importantly, these students are not solely a product of their background with respect to their academic identities and college desires. Rather than *simply* following a "transgenerational script" with respect to college attendance, they rework that script, ultimately *coming to script themselves* and adopting identities that mark them as "highly selective college goers" by virtue of being in the top track. In so doing, they actively position themselves psychologically and practically for entrance into America's most highly valued postsecondary institutions. Importantly, such identity can only be understood as constructed at the nexus of family privilege, available opportunity structure, and their own located position within the opportunity structure in a given classed location.

In stark contrast, STEM Academy focal students, who were, by methodological design, similarly drawn from the top of the class, were often first-generation college students, and in some cases they were the first in their extended families to graduate high school. While they expressed a desire to attend college because they, like focal students at Cannondale, saw it as necessary to obtain a "good job" or "be successful," their lives were not encased by the college admissions process as were those of Cannondale students. Without comparable "transgenerational scripts" to follow, the college process took shape and form largely as a *reactionary set of practices* rather than a dominant, longitudinally driven process. For example, when asked when they first started thinking about college, the majority of STEM Academy students replied that they started thinking about it when they first arrived at the school—a school that evidences deep discursive and behavioral commitment to college-going activities (e.g., taking students to visit colleges). Aubrey, in his sophomore year at STEM Academy, recalls the first time he considered going to college, linking this consideration to an internal dialogue about his own college-going identity:

Amy: Did you always see yourself as someone who'd go to college?

Aubrey: At one point I wasn't because I was, like, I don't think I'm gonna be able to do this "cause of the way I was slackin'." An' I was, like, my grades, I don't think I'll be able to make it because, uh, how terrible my grades was.

Amy: Mm-hm.

Aubrey: So, I'm, like, I'm prob——probably not gonna get into a good college, so, if any at all. So, I was always worried about that.

Amy: Okay, at what age? Or what grade level?

Aubrey: Last year.

Amy: Last year, you started to worry about it?

Aubrey: Yeah, last year.

Amy: Okay, okay.

Aubrey: An' once I got to high school, I just—I dunno, it was, like, boom!

As was the case with many of his STEM Academy peers, Aubrey's moment of realization/worry was followed by a reactive set of practices characterized by fits, starts, and unpredictability, often accompanied by a false sense of simplicity and ease (though not without its own stress). Unlike the co-production of college admissions that characterizes more privileged environments, wherein parents, students, and school personnel collectively work to co-produce an "admissions subject" and accompanying dossier/portfolio to present to college admissions staff, the college admissions process at STEM Academy devolves into a largely one-sided endeavor driven by the guidance counselor. Given the one-sided nature of this process, counselors express frustration and concern for student futures:

Amy: What are the biggest challenges that you face, and that the school faces, in helping them actually go on to college? Or are there any? I mean, it seems fairly smooth.

Michelle (Lead Counselor at STEM): I think it is. I mean, here being a small school and having only whatever I have, thirty, say, thirty-five seniors to work with. I mean, you could hold thirty-five hands, *and you do. You just hold their hand every step of the way.* I think the hardest part, to be honest, and I think this is horrible and I think it is a system-like failure—failing systems to these kids. . . . (So), for now, we have to hold their hand. Otherwise, it is not going to get done, and it is all great and your numbers look great (number of students who go on to college), you know, you feel really accomplished. . . . We know our percentages that went to college and didn't. So for instance, these [are] all just line graphs (*shows Amy*). So, for instance, 73% of our kids that graduated in the class of 2012 went to college, which is really high; 73% for a low-income school. Fifty percent went in 2010, which was our first graduating class. And I'm really proud of that. Now the problem—the problem, I think, is [that] they walked into the [college] door, [and] no one held their hand for one single thing. So I sat here and I had to hold their hand this year in order to get it done [get them in the door], except for Robert. [Only one student in the class did any of the work on his own.]

Michelle homes in on a very important point. As noted previously, the college process is co-produced in privileged environments.[9] In Cannondale, for example, a trifecta of parents, counselors, and students are fully engaged, focused on the common goal of college admissions. While Cannondale students are expected to "own the process" (as counselors like to stress), they do so surrounded by an arsenal of parents, teachers, and counselors who stand ready and willing to assist with any and all aspects of the co-production. At STEM Academy, only a very small number of students "own" any part of the process at all, meaning that they enter college without having had an important experience that arguably helps to prepare them for independent college work, no matter which college they attend. As Michelle states, we can get them in, but when they enter college, *no one stands ready to "hold their hand"*—a situation about which she is justifiably concerned, given low rates of persistence and graduation among low-income students.

Parental Involvement and the College Process

The extent to which parents use their class-based resources to intervene in the college applications process (if they intervene at all) comprises our third lens for understanding how inequalities are (re)produced vis-à-vis the college applications process. Parents at Cannondale are extremely knowledgeable about the process and consciously utilize their college-related capital to advance their children's admission to highly selective colleges. Parents at STEM Academy also do what they can on behalf of their children's college opportunities, though the form this "classwork" takes differs significantly from that of their privileged counterparts. Hoping that their children will go to college, just as much as privileged parents do, STEM Academy parents are, in contrast to those parents with a range of relevant capitals, structurally positioned to stand entirely on the sidelines. A further examination of parental actions is illustrative.

Although parental micromanagement of the college admissions process has been shown to characterize some privileged secondary schools (Weis et al.

2014), Cannondale parents evidence a somewhat "hands-off policy" with regard to the admissions process itself. Parents of CHS focal students tend to engage a very distinct form of "upfront classwork," as they take great care to purchase homes in particular catchment areas and subsequently work to position their children for accelerated/gifted and talented programs at the elementary and middle school levels (Lareau 2000, 2003). This is not to suggest that parents abdicate all intervention at the high school level; on the contrary, parents are still heavily involved, but their involvement takes on a decidedly "behind the scenes" nature.[10] Parents spend a great deal of effort laying a foundation for their children that emphasizes academic achievement, high expectations, and college admissions. Additionally, they put a tremendous amount of effort into cultivating particular identities and skill sets early on, which results in the normalization of these values and identities and, ultimately, as we suggest earlier, the adoption of highly selective college oriented identities that students embrace *as their own*. Once students are on the "right" academic trajectory, parents take a step back, confident that students and the school (which has been structured to benefit the top students) will continue to position them favorably. This is clear in the comments of Frank Penn, who shared that if Michael had not been "on the right path or wasn't applying to the schools of his caliber, then we might have intervened."

Cannondale parents engage in intense and sustained "classwork" that begins at a very young age and continues throughout high school, albeit in markedly altered form. By the time their children reach the college admissions process, these same parents who engaged in highly intensive "upfront classwork" willingly take a step back and allow their children to "drive the process." In the midst of a well-articulated stance that can be characterized as "watching and waiting to intervene," Cannondale parents proof their children's college admissions essays, arrange for college visits and tours, hand over their credit cards for application fees and plane tickets, and freely express their opinions with respect to where they think their children will best thrive. In the final analysis, they willingly activate any and all class capitals whenever necessary.

The situation at STEM Academy is strikingly different. For this former "College Board" school, the "college for all" mantra penetrates all facets of student life but does so without critical depth and is not buttressed by the types of parental capital that scaffold access to college. Although some programs and preparatory structures are apparent within the school, students learn mostly surface knowledge relative to the college process such as filling out applications, financial aid forms, and learning definitions of college-related terms. Even among parents who had some higher education, there is heavy reliance upon the school to drive the process and ensure that their children go on to college.

Though data indicate that both parents and students are woefully underinformed about pathways to college, parents continue to believe in the power of higher education to mobilize their children beyond their familial class position, and they consistently offer heavy doses of emotional support and encouragement. Dion, a student at STEM Academy, talks to his mother about his college aspirations. In contrast to Cannondale parents, Kim Bailey, Dion's mother, just wants him to go to college, regardless of where:

> *Amy:* Do you talk to anyone else about college? Family, school counselor?
> *Dion:* Like me and my mom, like she'll ask me questions about college once in a while.
> *Amy:* Okay.
> *Dion:* She'll ask me how I feel about going to college and things like that.
> *Amy:* Right, right. Does she want you to go anywhere in particular?
> *Dion:* She said that she just don't, she don't, like, I don't think she cares, she just want me to go.

As the vast majority of STEM Academy students do not have parents who possess knowledge of the college process, student and parent narratives surrounding college admissions stand in sharp contrast to the extensively orchestrated co-productions evidenced at Cannondale. Rather than letting students "go at it alone," however, guidance counselors step knowingly into the void and do it for them—filling out applications, continually reminding students of financial aid forms, and the like. As noted earlier, the long-term consequences of this intervention remain unknown.

Conclusion

The overall landscape of higher education in the United States has changed dramatically since the 1980s. Epenshade and Radford (2009) stated that "college admissions angst has probably never been greater, mainly because more students are now competing for relatively few spots at the nation's most prestigious colleges and universities" (15). While colleges and universities are now more open in their admissions than they were in the past, and while more students than ever before are applying to college (Epenshade and Radford 2009), the system itself is increasingly marked by noticeable stratification, particularly in terms of family income (Bowen et al. 2009). Karen (2002) argued that due to this increase in college applicants and attendees, one must attend more prestigious schools in order to reap the advantage that a college education presumably provides, a position that affirms notions of "effectively maintained inequality."

In response to broadened access and the established "value added" of particularly located institutions (Bowen and Bok 1998; Bowen et al. 2009; Rumberger and Thomas 1993; Stephan, Rosenbaum, and Person 2009; Thomas 2000; Thomas and Zhang 2005), privileged schools and families increasingly activate any and all available capital as they position their children for postsecondary entrance. Admittance to particularly located postsecondary institutions is now conceptualized as *the lynchpin* for future class status, and those with privilege engage in well-orchestrated "class warfare" designed to capture and/or retain privilege for the next generation (Weis et al. 2014).

Data presented in this chapter must be understood in this context. Although we worked with the very top students in each school, STEM Academy and its students cannot compete with Cannondale with respect to the college admissions process. Although this is obviously connected to how much money any given family can devote to a college education, it is far more complicated than that. As we see in this chapter, available school-based opportunity structures, academic identities, and the ability of parents to mobilize and actualize varying forms of capital work collectively to produce an architecture of capital accumulation that *inevitably* privileges those with existing privilege. In light of new global economic circumstances (Brown, Lauder, and Ashton 2011) and intensified stratification within the postsecondary sector itself (Leslie et al. 2012), anxiety among those with privilege encourages a highly ramped-up drive for "distinction" as students approach the college admissions process. This begins earlier, of course, but takes on heightened shape and form as students, parents, and schools drive toward the postsecondary sector. Ironically, in times of broadened access to higher education, it becomes increasingly difficult for poor, working-class, and even lower-middle- and middle-class students to find ground to compete.

Importantly, it is our comparative ethnographic lens that puts this in sharp relief, as everyone associated with these schools is doing all they can to position the next generation for college. Given that selectivity of institution *in and of itself* matters with regard to postsecondary outcomes (above and beyond the characteristics of entering students),[11] the extent to which and the ways in which poverty and privilege are jointly implicated in the current production of inequalities are causes for deep concern. For the groups under consideration here—all of who have "done it right" and taken the college process seriously— the college admissions "game" is markedly different. While both STEM Academy and Cannondale are ramping up the process, evidenced "class warfare" is clearly skewed in favor of the privileged. While all Cannondale focal students may not "win" the competition for most and highly selective college admissions, their chances are much better than those of comparably situated students at STEM Academy. While we may only conjecture at the consequences that result from differential patterns of college access, what is evident is that the intensified and sustained "classwork" on the part of the privileged, in combination with the vast differences in opportunity structures in affluent and low-income schools, renders those without privilege on substantially shakier ground when competing for college admissions.

NOTES

1. In discussing privileged families in this chapter, we are not referring to the top 1%, whose extensive wealth enables them to preserve class position through transference of massive capital. Rather, we are referring to the professional and managerial class (what is generally referred to as the upper-middle class), who fall within the top 80% of the wage structure (Piketty and Saez 2003) and increasingly invest their existing economic capital in carving out what we refer to as a "new upper-middle class" by heavily investing in particular kinds of experiences and education for their children (Kaushal, Magnuson, and Waldfogel 2011; Weis, Cipollone, and Jenkins 2014).

2. Although these schools serve a relatively privileged population, in the sense that students are largely upper-middle class, the two privileged schools under consideration here do not have the status or prestige of schools that serve highly capitalized populations that reside in cities of far more extensive capital and wealth. More specifically, these two schools are not comparable to private day and/or boarding schools, such as Trinity, Horace Mann, Choate, Andover, St Paul's, and the like, or public schools located in parts of Westchester. For an extensive discussion of this point and its meaning with respect to privileged populations in the United States, see Weis, Cipollone, and Jenkins (2014).

3. Access to STEM is often expected to offer "real" opportunities for low-income minorities (Ferrini-Mundy 2013; Means et al. 2008; National Research Council 2011) and was therefore crucial to our understanding of opportunity/opportunity structures in a low-income school district. We also note here that one of our nonselective urban schools serves a high proportion of recent immigrants and refugees. The other schools are heavily, if not entirely, intergenerational African American and Latino/a. All names of schools, personnel, parents, and students are de-identified and pseudonyms are employed.

4. Research in the nonselective urban schools was supported by a grant to Margaret Eisenhart and Lois Weis. Portions of the research in the privileged institutions were supported by a grant from the Spencer Foundation to Lois Weis. All errors

of interpretation rest with the authors. Data from the other three non-selective schools that serve comparable low-income underrepresented minorities will be reported elsewhere. Data from the second privileged institution are reported in Weis, Cipollone, and Jenkins (2014).

5. At Cannondale, the affluent public school in our sample, students were drawn from the top 10% due to the large class size (over six hundred students). STEM Academy has significantly smaller class sizes (closer to one hundred); therefore, we drew our sample from students who fell into the top 20%. In-depth details with regard to research design, data collection, and analysis for both large-scale ethnographic investigations are reported at length elsewhere (Cipollone 2012; Weis, Cipollone, and Jenkins 2014).

6. The IB program is a rigorous course of study focused on the development of critical thinking and analytical and research skills, and was brought to the district for a number of reasons, one being to raise the academic profile of the school and make students more competitive in the college process (conversation with IB Director, July 2009). For a complete overview of the program, see http://www.ibo.org/.

7. State classes are classes that require a state exam at their conclusion and are considered quite basic at a school such as Cannondale. Students need to pass a certain number of state-level classes in order to graduate. Many students, such as those in this study, begin taking state-level tests in eighth grade and by tenth grade have more than exceeded the required amount. Additionally, many of the honors-level classes will conclude with the state test.

8. It should be noted that health is a required course for graduation, and no honors or AP version of the course exists.

9. The extent to which parents, and particularly mothers, are involved in the co-production of the college admissions subject is particularly evident at the second of our two privileged institutions. For in-depth discussion of the co-production of the college admissions subject at Matthews Academy (a private co-educational day school), see Weis, Cipollone, and Jenkins (2014).

10. This narrative about parents differs somewhat from what we see at Matthews Academy, where anxiety around college positioning is higher than at Cannondale and parental micromanagement of the college admissions process is far more evident (see Weis, Cipollone, and Jenkins 2014).

11. An important caveat here is that contrary information exists with regard to STEM (Science, Technology, Engineering, Mathematics) majors, where, as Arcidiacono (2004) suggests, majoring in STEM fields of study predicts short- and long-term outcomes of interest to a greater extent than does institutional selectivity. Economists report that differences in returns to majors are much larger than differences in returns to college quality, suggesting that, as James et al. (1989) noted, "while sending your child to Harvard appears to be a good investment, sending him to your local state university to major in engineering, to take lots of math, and preferably to attain a high GPA is an even better private investment" (251–52).

REFERENCES

Allatt, Pat. 1993. "Becoming Privileged: The Role of Family Processes." In *Youth and Inequality*, edited by Inge Bates and George Riseborough, 139–59. Buckingham, UK: Open University Press.

Anyon, Jean. 1980. "Social Class and the Hidden Curriculum of Work." *Journal of Education* 162 (1): 67–92.

Arcidiacono, Peter. 2004. "Ability Sorting and the Returns to College Major." *Journal of Econometrics* 121 (1): 343–75.

Bailey, Martha, and Susan Dynarski. 2011. "Inequality in Postsecondary Education." In *Whither Opportunity? Rising Inequality, Schools, and Children's Life Chances*, edited by Greg J. Duncan and Richard J. Murnane, 117–32. New York: Russell Foundation.

Ball, Stephen J. 2003. *Class Strategies and Education Markets: The Middle Classes and Social Advantage*. London: RoutledgeFalmer.

Bastedo, Michael N., and Ozan Jaquette. 2011. "Running in Place: Low-income Students and the Dynamics of Higher Education Stratification." *Educational Evaluation and Policy Analysis* 33 (3): 318–39.

Bourdieu, Pierre. 1984. *Distinction: A Social Critique of the Judgment of Taste*. Cambridge, MA: Harvard University Press.

Bowen, William G., and Derek Bok. 1998. *The Shape of the River: Long-Term Consequences of Considering Race in College and University Admissions*. Princeton, NJ: Princeton University Press.

Bowen, William G., Matthew M. Chingos, and Michael S. McPherson. 2009. *Crossing the Finish Line: Completing College at America's Public Universities*. Princeton, NJ: Princeton University Press.

Brantlinger, Ellen. 2003. *Dividing Classes: How the Middle Class Negotiates and Rationalizes School Advantage*. New York: RoutledgeFalmer.

Brown, Phillip, Hugh Lauder, and David Ashton. 2011. *The Global Auction: The Promise of Education, Jobs, and Income*. New York: Oxford University Press.

Cipollone, Kristin. 2012. "Leveraging Privilege: The College Process and the Mobilization of Social Advantage in an Affluent Public High School." PhD diss., University at Buffalo, State University of New York.

Cohen, Phil, and Valerie Hey. 2000. *Studies in Learning Regeneration: Consultation Document*. London: University of East London and Brunel University.

Coleman, James S., Ernest Q. Campbell, Carol J. Hobson, James McPartland, Alexander M. Mood, Frederic Weinfeld, and Robert York. 1966. *Equality of Educational Opportunity*. Washington, DC: U.S. Government Printing Office.

Du Bois-Reymond, Manuela. 1998. "'I Don't Want to Commit Myself Yet': Young People's Life Concept." *Journal of Youth Studies* 1 (1): 63–79.

Epenshade, Thomas J., and Alexandria Walton Radford. 2009. *No Longer Separate, Not Yet Equal: Race and Class in Elite College Admission and Campus Life*. Princeton, NJ: Princeton University Press.

Ferrini-Mundy, Joan. 2013. "Driven by Diversity." *Science* 340 (6130): 278.

Hill, Lori Diane. 2008. "School Strategies and the College-Linking Process: Reconsidering the Effects of High Schools on College Enrollment." *Sociology of Education* 81 (1): 53–76.

Hochschild, Jennifer L., and Nathan B. Scovronick. 2003. *The American Dream and Public Schools*. Oxford: Oxford University Press.

James, Estelle, Nabeel Alsalam, Joseph C. Conaty, and Duc-Le To. 1989. "College Quality and Future Earnings: Where Should You Send Your Child to College?" *American Economic Review* 79 (2): 247–52.

Jencks, Christopher. 1972. *Inequality: A Reassessment of the Effect of Family and Schooling in America*. New York: Basic Books.

Johnson, Heather Beth. 2012. "Schools: The Great Equalizer and the Key to the American Dream." In *Schools and Society: A Sociological Approach to Education*.

3rd edition, edited by Jeanne H. Ballantine and Joan Z. Spade, 271–85. Thousand Oaks, CA: Pine Forge Press.

Karen, David. 2002. "Changes in Access to Higher Education in the United States: 1980–1992." *Sociology of Education* 75 (3): 191–210.

Kaufman, Peter. 2005. "Middle-Class Social Reproduction: The Activation and Negotiation of Structured Advantages." *Sociological Forum* 20 (2): 245–70.

Kaushal, Neeraj, Katherine Magnuson, and J. Waldfogel. 2011. "The Nature and Impact of Early Achievement Skills, Attention and Behavior Problems." In *Social Inequality and Educational Disadvantage*, edited by Greg J. Duncan and Richard Murnane, 187–205. New York: Russell Sage Foundation.

Kelly, Sean Patrick. 2008. "Social Class and Tracking within Schools." In *The Way Class Works: Readings on School, Family, and the Economy*, edited by Lois Weis, 210–24. New York: Routledge.

Lareau, Annette. 2000. *Home Advantage: Social Class and Parental Intervention in Elementary Education*. Lanham, MD: Rowman & Littlefield.

———. 2003. *Unequal Childhoods: Class, Race and Family Life*. Berkeley: University of California Press.

Lee, J., and Lois Weis. 2012. *High School Pathways to Postsecondary Education Destinations: Integrated Multilevel Analyses of NELS, ELS and NCES-Barron's Datasets*. Final Report to the Association of Institutional Research.

Leslie, Larry L., Sheila Slaughter, Barrett J. Taylor, and Liang Zhang. 2012. "How Do Revenue Variations Affect Expenditures within U.S. Research Universities?" *Research in Higher Education* 53 (6): 614–49.

Lipman, Pauline. 2011. *The New Political Economy of Urban Education: Neoliberalism, Race, and the Right to the City*. Routledge: New York.

Long, Bridget Terry, and Michal Kurlaender. 2009. "Do Community Colleges Provide a Viable Pathway to a Baccalaureate Degree?" *Educational Evaluation and Policy Analysis* 31 (1): 30–53.

Lucas, Samuel R. 2001. "Effectively Maintained Inequality: Education Transitions, Track Mobility, and Social Background Effects." *American Journal of Sociology* 106 (6): 1642–90.

McDonough, Patricia M. 1997. *Choosing Colleges: How Social Class and Schools Structure Opportunity*. Albany: State University of New York Press.

Means, Barbara, Jere Confrey, Ann House, and Ruchi Bhanot. 2008. *STEM High Schools: Specialized Science Technology Engineering and Mathematics Secondary Schools in the U.S.* A Report to the Bill and Melinda Gates Foundation. Menlo Park, CA: SRI International. http://www.sri.com/sites/default/files/publications/means_et_al_istem _narst_2013_4_1_13.pdf.

Melguizo, Tatiana. 2008. "Quality Matters: Assessing the Impact of Attending More Selective Institutions on College Completion Rates of Minorities." *Research in Higher Education* 49:214–36.

Mullen, Ann. 2010. *Degrees of Inequality: Culture, Class, and Gender in American Higher Education*. Baltimore: Johns Hopkins University Press.

National Research Council. 2011. *Successful K–12 STEM Education: Identifying Effective Approaches in Science, Technology, Engineering, and Mathematics*. Washington, DC: National Academies Press.

Niu, Sunny X., and Marta Tienda. 2013. "High School Economic Composition and College Persistence." *Research in Higher Education* 54:30–62.

Oakes, Jeannie. 1985. *Keeping Track: How Schools Structure Inequality*. New Haven, CT: Yale University Press.

Perna, Laura. 2008. "Understanding High School Students' Willingness to Borrow to Pay College Prices." *Research in Higher Education* 49:589–606.

Piketty, Thomas, and Emmanuel Saez. 2003. "Income Inequality in the United States, 1913–1998." *Quarterly Journal of Economics* 118 (1): 1–39.

Reardon, Sean. 2011. "The Widening Academic Achievement Gap between the Rich and the Poor: New Evidence and Possible Explanations." In *Whither Opportunity? Rising Inequality, Schools, and Children's Life Chances*, edited by Greg J. Duncan and Richard J. Murnane, 91–116. New York: Russell Sage Foundation.

Reay, Diane. 2011. "Schooling for Democracy: A Common School and a Common University? A Response to 'Schooling for Democracy.'" *Democracy and Education* 19 (1): article 6.

Riegle-Crumb, Catherine, and Eric Grodsky. 2010. "Racial-Ethnic Differences at the Intersection of Math Course-Taking and Achievement." *Sociology of Education* 83 (3): 248–70.

Rumberger, Russell W., and Scott L. Thomas. 1993. "The Economic Returns to College Major, Quality and Performance: A Multilevel Analysis of Recent Graduates." *Economics of Education Review* 12:1–19.

Shavit, Yoshi, Richard Arum, and Adam Gamoran. 2007. *Stratification in Higher Education: A Comparative Study*. Redwood City, CA: Stanford University Press.

Stephan, Jennifer L., James E. Rosenbaum, and Ann E. Person. 2009. "Stratification in College Entry and Completion." *Social Science Research* 38 (3): 572–93.

Stevens, Mitchell L. 2007. *Creating a Class: College Admissions and the Education of Elites*. Cambridge, MA: Harvard University Press.

Stich, Amy. 2012. *Access to Inequality: Reconsidering Class, Knowledge and Capital in Higher Education*. Lanham, MA: Lexington Books.

Thomas, Scott L. 2000. "Deferred Costs and Economic Returns to College Quality, Major and Academic Performance: An Analysis of Recent Graduates in Baccalaureate and Beyond." *Research in Higher Education* 44 (3): 263–99.

Thomas, Scott L., and Angela Bell. 2008. "Education and Class: Uneven Patterns of Opportunity and Access." In *The Way Class Works: Readings on School, Family and the Economy*, edited by Lois Weis, 273–87. New York: Routledge.

Thomas, Scott L., and Liang Zhang. 2005. "Changing Rates of Return to College Quality and Academic Major in the United States: Who Gets Good Jobs in America?" *Research in Higher Education* 46 (4): 437–59.

U.S. Bureau of Labor Statistics. 1979. *National Longitudinal Survey of Youth 1979 (NLS79)*. Washington, DC: U.S. Department of Labor.

———. 1997. *National Longitudinal Survey of Youth 1997 (NLS97)*. Washington, DC: U.S. Department of Labor.

Weis, Lois, Kristin Cipollone, and Heather Jenkins. 2014. *Class Warfare: Class, Race and College Admissions in Top-Tier Secondary Schools*. Chicago: University of Chicago Press.

Yonezawa, Susan, and Amy Stuart Wells. 2005. "Reform as Redefining the Spaces of Schools: An Examination of Detracking by Choice." In *Beyond Silenced Voices: Class, Race, and Gender in United States Schools*. Revised edition, edited by Lois Wise and Michelle Fine, 47–61. Albany: State University of New York Press.

10

Museums, Theaters, and Youth Orchestras Advancing Creative Arts and Sciences within Underresourced Communities

SHIRLEY BRICE HEATH

Public intellectuals, as well as academic scholars, generally address topics related to those living in poverty through data and analyses related to instrumental outcomes. Research as well as opinion features related to the poor invariably take note of the absence or lack of economic opportunities, which in turn implies poor healthcare, underfunded schools, inadequate transport, and insufficient access to jobs that pay a living wage and make possible health-enriching leisure-time choices. Indeed, the chapters in this text accurately reflect many of the challenges the poor face and how education might aid them in overcoming these obstacles. I wish to add to our discussion about poverty by way of how the arts might also play a role not simply in improving one or another outcome but also increasing civic engagement.

In the United States, in an era when education policymakers stress improving standardized test scores for children living in underresourced neighborhoods, proposing alternative approaches provided in the arts and sciences by cultural organizations such as museums and regional theaters seems an impossible dream. However, other nations, such as England, Scotland, Ireland, Finland, and Denmark, have found ways to expand learning environments for those living in underresourced areas. In addition, these nations have opened the doors of their museums, theaters, and music centers to recent immigrants, asylum-seeking child soldiers, and residents of communities that have lost mines, mills, and local merchants and now face high unemployment. The United States began to take some steps in this same direction in the second decade of the twenty-first century.

This chapter explores some of those steps in a comparative analysis over the following three sections. The first argues the human development benefits of learning through arts and science for all children, but most especially for those who grow up in underresourced environments. This section lays the groundwork for the mid-portion of the chapter, which provides examples from several modern economies, including the United States, of cultural centers that have taken themselves seriously as learning environments for those living in underresourced communities. In doing so, these cultural venues have partnered with individuals and families from these communities to create performances of play and work based in both the arts and sciences. The final section addresses the essential role of research, as distinct from evaluation, in the sustainability of these learning environments. My intent is neither to dismiss the critical issues raised in the previous chapters nor to suggest that what follows is a different part, or even orthogonal to what has been discussed. Instead, as Bill Tierney has noted in the introduction, a concerted effort needs to incorporate multiple approaches, and the arts is one central avenue.

Why Are Play and Exploration through the Arts and Sciences So Important to Human Development?

A growing body of evidence tells us that the very steps that modern education systems (led in many cases by the United States) have taken to boost academic test scores have eliminated fundamental activities that keep children's emotional and cognitive health in balance. Near the end of the twentieth century, policymakers in the United States put in place school reforms that forced children, especially those from impoverished families, to focus on "basic" or instrumental sequential skills. Support for this idea came from claims that future employment opportunities would follow when such children could "catch up" with their middle- and upper-class counterparts in skills fundamental to academic success. These educational policies (primarily No Child Left Behind and Race to the Top) in all their iterations led to the systematic removal of classes and after-school participation in the arts as well as hands-on science explorations within schools serving underresourced communities. In short, the "basics" in skills and information accumulation crowded out activities vital to sensory-emotive learning.

Just how is such learning vital in early human development? From infancy through the life span, learning that engages visuospatial, emotive, haptic, and linguistic neurostructural resources of the brain are proving to be vital to balanced physical and mental health. Young children's socialization must therefore include habituating practices essential to the evolution of the brain's neurostructuring; otherwise, normal brain development cannot occur. Exploratory and creative play and work make possible the brain's early pruning and dedicating of neuronal pathway creation for visuospatial, cognitive, and linguistic development. For example, infants need to be able to use their hands and forearms to engage with malleable objects so they can develop the haptic or touching resources through which they internalize signals that come from form and texture. Visual exploration reinforces these haptic cues, making possible an envisioned and remembered image of what the infant has explored and perceived. From infancy, humans can learn through their "thinking hands" (Pallasmaa 2009, 2012).

As children mature and have opportunities to turn their envisioned images into sketches, drawings, and three-dimensional models or objects (again using their hands), they create representations of what they have known through eye and hand, enhancing the ability to move from the particular to the general in long-term memory. Later linguistic development allows children to label or name forms and objects they know to be "real." This knowledge provides a base from which children tie reality to the abstractions of concepts and categories of objects, conditions, and phenomena. Sorting out the world through the direct sensory input afforded in play and exploratory pursuits leads children to guess, imagine possibilities, and make hypotheses about what and how things work and people think and feel. Thereby, the neurologically normal human brain takes up its potential for lifelong learning.

As humans interact, they benefit from "like-me equivalence" made possible through mirror neurons (Meltzoff 2013). Infants and young children acquire information and habituate skills through imitating and adapting what they see others around them do. Infants are born with the need to reach out (quite literally) and to see and imitate what is being done by others in their environment. This deeply embedded need to experience both emotively and by sociomotor means what the environment holds is fundamental to human development. Regular supportive interactions with others who model and tutor various ways to explore this environment continue throughout the life span.

In the rush of many modern economies to school the young in academic "achievement," parents and teachers have little time to emphasize in early child socialization modeling and encouraging social play in which children build, design, destroy, and redo projects, and explore substances, textures, and environments rich in sensual stimulation. Deprivation of such interactions intensified after the turn of the twenty-first century in modern economies inclined to align their education policies with school reform in the United States. As the portion of young mothers with graduate degrees increased in these nations, and daycare and early childcare program used by these parents grew, families had less and less time to play with their children or plan outings that included explorations on playgrounds and nature walks or the achievement of joint home projects. Thus, across socioeconomic classes, children entered their primary years of school with relatively little art and science preparation through using their eyes and hands to explore and create in environments around them (Heath 2013). Teachers could not fill the void left from the early years of deprivation because school reform measures pushed them insistently toward academic test preparation of children at an earlier and earlier age.

This well-documented turn away from play affected children from all social classes, so why single out the special situational needs of children who grow up in underresourced communities? The answer lies in the fact that these families must persistently struggle to meet basic needs such as food and shelter. Family members often work several jobs, lack reliable means of transport, and have little discretionary time or money. Worries often push out the joy in play, laughter, and long walks or castle construction in sandboxes. Their children generally experience few opportunities to travel beyond their immediate neighborhoods to places of playful exploration. Children are also likely to have relatively little leisure-time reading of a wide range of written sources with highly literate adult readers. Caregiving adults living in underresourced circumstances must go to extraordinary lengths to find the time to model and tutor drawing and sketching, molding and sculpting, talking and writing, and creating garden or building projects at home. Thus, their children may not hear on a regular basis the expanded language of guidance, critique, planful behavior, and hypothetical thinking. Without extensive practice in hearing and producing such language, children tend to fall behind in competency with several structured symbol systems, including those of language and enumeration.

Young children growing up in families and communities that have neither time nor financial resources to access or create playful, imaginative, language-rich exploration opportunities often enter school without feeling they "own" fundamental ways of learning. It is this sensation that feeds children's curiosity, eagerness to explore, and willingness to imagine beyond what is given. These children feel uncertain about undertaking agentive roles related to learning and acquiring expertise, particularly when tasks and situations call for experience with structured symbol systems such as written language or numerals.

Curiosity, as well as the desire to know more and to become more skilled, develops in most instances as an individual gains the sense that he or she needs information and skill improvement in order to play a current or desired role (Donald 2001). Behaviors within such roles become envisioned, and individuals imagine (and experience deep within the brain related locomotor impulses) they are actually carrying out movements essential to these roles. Consider the long hours young boys and girls spend on sports fields, basketball courts, or ice rinks in order to gain the skills they need to take on specific roles. Similar impulses are needed for all types of learning. Individuals need to see and think consciously about themselves taking on roles and using knowledge and skills to earn authentic critique and praise.

Neuroscientists can now show us what happens in the human brain as individuals perceive themselves playing a role or undertaking a specific set of skills. The emotive, linguistic, and cognitive resources brought to bear under these circumstances enhance memory, intensify depth of comparative analysis, and even help advance complex learning during very short periods of participation (Supekar et al. 2013). As many in both poetry and neurology have said in one way or another, "the mind is embodied" (Gibbs 2006). We must use our bodies (and emotions) to engage our minds. One of the most mysterious gifts human beings have is the ability to play multiple roles and hold several identities or states of feelings simultaneously. In other words, as we mature, we gain competence in *playing* and *working* the mind and body in layered richness. Children living under the restricted conditions that poverty imposes in terms of parenting time for play, role-building, and co-construction talk and action miss out on opportunities vital to developing a sense of competence. Parents with financial and transport resources, but little time to play with their children, often ensure that they have sustained opportunities on sports teams as well as the programs of children's theaters, museums, musical ensembles, libraries, parks, and botanical gardens. Children of the poor miss out on these compensating but vitally reinforcing learning environments.

Thinking in Place and the Role of Learning Environments

The mid-portion of this chapter offers some examples of cultural centers that have taken seriously their responsibility as complementary learning environments for those living in underresourced circumstances in modern economies. These programs illustrate the practice-rich and mastery-driven nature of such learning opportunities. Most of these, such as ensemble music and dramatic programs, as well as science and art museums, are available at no charge to participants. All reflect decidedly strong policy decisions by their institutions to undertake an identity as "learning environment" for *all*.

For example, many museums, such as the Tate Museums in England, have eliminated their traditional walk-through visits for schoolchildren and replaced these with ongoing learning studios in which children and other interested learners gain expertise on subjects related to coming or current exhibitions. Museums of art, history, and science have thus begun eliminating one-time visit opportunities that have traditionally been bound to the bureaucracies of formal schooling. Prior departments of education and outreach in museums have shifted to become "programs of learning and participation" that provide open studio access. Topics of these open studios change in relation to activities within the museums, engaging scientists, artists, curators, and local innovators, and business concerns. Identifying and solving problems in relation to particular aspects of coming exhibitions focus on studio learning. Sought out to take part are storytellers, young performance artists, and tinkerers of all ages. In those nations, such as England and Denmark, who helped reduce the number of children seeking asylum from civil-war-torn African nations in the 1990s and first decades of the twenty-first century, museums have developed special programs of inclusion.

Theaters have also emerged as major learning environments for cross-age groups with special interests in topics such as climate change, domestic abuse, racial conflicts, and xenophobia. These theaters have done so in order to bring thinking and consciousness to the forefront in disenfranchised communities. In 2013 the Public Theater in New York City brought five community centers into partnership to produce a free performance of William Shakespeare's *The Tempest* as a musical at the Delacorte in Central Park—the city's largest theater venue. Themes within the play (e.g., the isolation that comes from displacement to an unknown island, the poisonous effects of revenge, and the power of faith in the next generation) brought a metacognitive awareness of the timeless themes of dramatic literature to community participants and audience alike.

The Public Theater initiated the community participatory program of Public Works, which renewed founder Joseph Papp's vision of a theater "of, by, and for the public." This vision called for a public theater that would be open and accessible to everyone. Directed by Lear deBessonet, Public Works provides classes throughout the preceding year in acting, dance, choral music, and musical theater in preparation for six to eight weeks of intensive rehearsal before a performance such as *The Tempest*. Community partners, consisting of locally based organizations committed to hosting classes, rehearsals, and theater promotions in a three-year arrangement with the Public Theater, included five community organizations located in the five boroughs. The first was the Fortune Society, a community organization of formerly incarcerated individuals working and learning to find their way back into employment and civil life after years of imprisonment. These individuals often compared themselves to Prospero, the duke of Milan, who was wrongfully cast out of his place and onto a remote island by his power-seeking brother. He had once sought revenge but transformed as he learned how to live both forgiven and forgiving. From Staten Island came members of the Domestic Workers Union (many of whom were immigrants), who were employed throughout the city of New York as both nannies and domestic workers. From the Bronx came young people living in communities with few public schools that offer rich in-school or after-school opportunities in arts studios or science laboratories. These young people find their way to the Dream Yard, a community organization dedicated to immersion in the arts for all young people and their parents. Other young people, many of whom had been foster children, came from the Children's Aid Society, where they had taken part in choral music ensemble work throughout the year. Elders came from the Brownsville Recreation Center, where they had been taking part in dance and exercise classes throughout the year prior to the Delacorte performance. Two hundred of these community members joined with five Equity actors in the production of *The Tempest*. In addition to work in singing and dancing groups, some community members played leading roles in the play.

Research with the community members throughout the rehearsal process indicated changes in several hard-to-alter behavioral and attitudinal areas of learning. Participants of varying ages indicated an increase in reading participation both in direct relation to the play and beyond. Additionally, individuals without prior experience with the public transport systems on other islands of New York City learned to navigate new and additional portions of the subway system, predict transport times to different rehearsal venues, and study ahead to learn which stations provided accessible entry and exit from the underground.

Additionally, individuals across different age groups showed a strong shift in attitude regarding their own capabilities. Initially, during joint rehearsals that brought community members from all five boroughs together, participants shared their stories with one another during the long wait times of rehearsals with litanies of "I never thought I could . . . [do any of this, get up and perform before a crowd, be willing to speak in public, have this kind of hope, meet a real expert]." As rehearsals continued over several weeks, participants ceased talking about their past fears and feelings of inadequacy. Instead, in their conversations with others, they began to share and celebrate stories of their past individual achievements.

> "I was featured in a documentary about immigrants."
> "I do films in Latin America that have won prizes there."
> "I used to work at The Public. When Joe Papp was here, I was a docent, and then I became a carpenter working on sets right here at the Delacorte."
> "I'm a singer who's never done acting before."
> "I've got the lead in the play at my high school this next term."
> "I used to teach dance to kids."

The sense of respect that came from Equity actors as well as the directing staff of The Public also emerged as a frequent topic of conversation among community members. They also noted new understanding of metaphors, analogies, and the poetry of Shakespeare's language. These realizations seemed to inspire highly generalized statements about their amazement at seeing and thinking about the world in such different ways: "Being here opened me up to being alive." "I cannot believe this is happening to me—the respect, expectation of excellence, and assurance that I am needed to make this play happen."

Participation in Public Works affirmed for community members not only personal growth but also solidarity in being somehow "different" from individuals they knew who could not imagine taking part in such a public and high-risk event as the performance of *The Tempest* before an audience of two thousand on three consecutive evenings in Manhattan. Participants expressed in their comments the view that different life experiences and income levels in New York City meant that people across the city tended to live segregated lives. Yet this production brought communities together in a vision of what the city *could* be—united as either participant or audience members for this public performance. One participant remarked about the "bringing together" achieved through the diversity of the different community partners, none of which knew anything about any of the others before they all united in Manhattan in mid-July to start rehearsals for the early September performances. She wondered aloud: "Where else are you going to have an older gentleman who has been to prison working together with a prep school ballerina and some kids from the Bronx and feeling like family?" Indeed, the language of "family" and "love" became pervasive and was used by ensemble members to affirm their unity with other cast and staff members.

Coexisting with this enthusiasm for unity across diversity was the realization that in this production they found other individuals who, like them, had always felt a sense of difference. For some participants, the very act of reading and performing Shakespeare was itself radical. Many had never heard of or read Shakespeare and were daunted by the language of the play. Yet when asked whether they might have preferred to do something more contemporary or "urban," most responded that they preferred the challenge that Shakespeare gave them. One community member who had a speaking role in *The Tempest* explained: "For me, it's like I'm translating all of this from Shakespeare's language into something that people will understand. First, I have to figure out what he's trying to say, and then I have to figure out how to say it with those words but in a way that people who don't get that at all will understand. So it's like I'm a translator."

Others noted that they had never imagined that they would either read *or* perform Shakespeare. Now, however, they felt as though they had come to understand something they never suspected before they began to work with the production: "It's the kind of story everyone can understand, you know?"

"Thinking in place" metaphorically captures much contained within the Public Works production and similar experiences designed with community partners, young and old. One's "place" within not only certain given "high education" pursuits such as performing Shakespeare but also within a high-risk, highly visible performance for an entire city translates into philosophical reflections. From the primary school participants to the elders, their conversations portrayed a meta-awareness of the importance of their learning and of taking on new roles, literally and figuratively. They gained a new and different sense of responsibility for what they could and should do in the future. Teenagers in particular seemed struck by the need for them to reconsider their prior views of groups such as the formerly incarcerated, gays, "old people," and their own parents. In several instances, parents and children took part in *The Tempest* together. In the majority of these cases, either the child or the parent initially agreed to audition and was chosen. Thereafter, the other decided to try out in later auditions. The shared experience of rehearsals, unique to both parent and child, led to sustained conversations between older and younger, opening, in the eyes of parents, "a way for [them] to talk with [their child] about something neither [had] ever imagined [they] would or could be doing."

Moving about the city via an unfamiliar transport system also gave participants a new sense of the geography of New York City. Many expressed that they learned that their persistent sense of "feeling poor" lifted when they saw what the rest of city dwellers and subway riders were like. "Getting to know this place [primarily Manhattan] tells me all the poor people like me don't live where I live. There are folks like me all over this city."

The specifics of a sense of space and place apply in similar ways to other programs and learning environments designed for inclusive and full participation by individuals living in underresourced communities. In ensemble music learning, this issue has received considerable attention from both social historians and neuroscientists. For more than two centuries after the Enlightenment, the view prevailed that creating and appreciating ensemble music (particularly instrumental music) mark individuals as financially secure and "well rounded." However, since the last decades of the twentieth century, this attitude has shifted to favor the democratic view that opportunities to learn ensemble music can and should be available to *all* children, including those living in impoverished communities around the globe.

During the Enlightenment, the view that auditory and visual experience contributed to knowledge formation accompanied the swell of emphasis on pedagogy for children and the public alike (Stafford 1999). A leisure industry burst onto the scene in the late seventeenth century, only to become widely accepted as normative by the mid-eighteenth century. What came to be known as a "middle class" developed rapidly as people traveled and sought out theaters, lectures, museums, and sites of musical performance. Literacy spread through these forms of public pedagogy, as well as the broadening introduction of children's literature and music books for children. Members of the merchant class as well as the intelligentsia and those of landed wealth ventured out to learn what travelers to faraway places had collected and learned.

Parents and the public prized works created with the fingers and hands that resulted in products and performances that left no doubt of long hours of practice toward perfection. Proper posture disciplined the body during these pursuits so that public performances or presentations would be offered with a modest, albeit "proper," bearing. Tools of arts production, ranging from easels and paint boxes to musical instruments, became normative household display items, along with artifacts attesting to literacy, such as book stands, book cases, and ceramic figures and paintings that portrayed individuals reading, painting, and playing music. Recognition of the legitimacy of individual interpretational powers in music paralleled the eighteenth century Protestant culture of reading and writing on "one's own."

Beliefs surrounding the artful science of creating music that became normative during the Enlightenment firmly held into subsequent centuries and also among many upper- and middle-class families in modern economies today. This collective ideology embraces musical learning for its powers to further children's learning of specific qualities of mind: individual interpretive creativity, development of mental and physical discipline, competence in reading into and beyond literate sources, acquisition and care of material objects, and practice and instruction leading to mastery. Those of the upper and middle classes holding these beliefs then and now look ahead to individual success for their children. They know that learning to play an instrument or sing well enough to be included in a group requires many hours of practice as well as years of lessons. Much valued is the belief that such learning within groups instills the value of working together to produce something beautiful and creative that audiences will appreciate.

Yet since the final decades of the twentieth century, these opportunities, long cherished by those of substantial financial means, have become available for children living in some underresourced communities in nations around the world. Democracy as an international ideal for all people and all nations led many to embrace goals of social justice and equity for children living in poverty around the world. As a consequence, the idea spread that music, and indeed all arts, should be available to all children, regardless of class background. This view accelerated along with the conviction that the arts, especially music, can change lives for the better (Tunstall 2012).

The United States is a modern economy that has no exemplary history of equitable distribution of nonschool enrichment learning opportunities in music except to those involved in religious institutions. Moreover, the costs in time and financial outlay for underresourced families as well as schools and communities have long seemed prohibitive. Music lessons, along with the purchase or rental of instruments (and their storage and use in at-home practice sessions), have generally exceeded the discretionary incomes and spatial resources of working-class or working-poor families in the United States. Furthermore, as migratory labor patterns for immigrant families accelerated with agribusiness development, transport of large and fragile musical instruments for these families was entirely unrealistic.

As budgets for public education faced increasing cuts with the turn of the new century, access to music teachers or ensemble groups remained available primarily to students enrolled in private or independent schools. The only public schools able to retain the arts were those located in upper-income residential areas where parents formed foundations to support art in their schools. Moreover, in these communities, parents carpooled to ensure additional practice and rehearsal time for their children's participation in arts programs.

Families living in communities of more limited means had no such opportunities. Moreover, even when public transport was available, working-poor parents were often reluctant to send their children across town to unfamiliar sites for long hours of practice and rehearsal. These parents often worked two jobs and only rarely in positions offering flexible hours for transporting children to lessons or rehearsals or for attending afternoon or weekend concerts.

In short, especially since the turn of the twenty-first century, youngsters living in locations that could not offer music education either during or beyond school hours had little hope of growing up with sustained participatory experience in music ensembles. When news of Venezuela's phenomenal success with its El Sistema programs reached the United States about this time, musicians and educators who had previously served primarily upper- and middle-class families wondered, "Why can't the Venezuelan phenomenon happen here in this country?" Debates and deliberations followed, with ample recognition of the many differences between the culture, geography, and economic patterning of leisure time in the United States and Venezuela. Yet as individual programs of what was initially termed "El Sistema USA" emerged in different parts of the United States, means of resourcing and promoting these opportunities came through the time and resources of individuals from middle- and upper-income families, many of whom held the democratic and social justice views noted previously. Moreover, as the declining effectiveness of U.S. public education for children living in poverty became more widely recognized, enthusiasts for arts and science programs, including ensemble instrumental music programs, found motivation in the long-standing view that such learning positively affects all learning. Moreover, many individuals felt that ensemble music could uniquely promote high learning demands for children and adolescents living in underresourced communities unlikely to provide such learning for local children during after-school hours.

With the spread of El Sistema–inspired programs, both during and after school in the United States, neuroscientists increased their attention to how ensemble music participation advances learning. At the same time, social scientists intensified their focus on nonclassroom learning contexts—studios, rehearsal zones, and laboratories, for example. Some learning scientists addressed the issue of voluntary expertise development (sometimes termed "informal learning") by young and old. In these instances, individuals or small groups determined the need or desire to learn something and set about finding combinations of ways to learn and work together. The field of "citizen science," for example, became as active as community music, theater, and arts festivals had become in communities around the United States and Europe. Some of these researchers wanted to know, in particular, the effects of voluntary expertise development opportunities for children living in communities with few resources of time, space, material goods, or local experts in highly specialized art forms.

Five primary features of the learning environment of ensemble music increasingly drew the attention of researchers in the learning sciences. These factors account for the depth and retention of learning that lie at the center of creating music for mastery. These affordances are generally invisible and out of awareness for accomplished musicians. Working within an ensemble environment forces individuals to hone their memory for details. The context demands as a matter of course visual attentiveness, mental quickness, and collaborative skills. Such skills are also those required in an information-based and technology-driven world where academic advancement, employment, medical care, and other critical aspects of daily life rely on quick and ready use of these same skills.

Within ensemble music learning, whether choral or instrumental, the following key features of learning indicate the relevance of "thinking in place."

1. Rehearsal zones support kinesthetic and haptic exploration as well as an accumulation of information and skills that encourage self-monitoring.
2. These places of learning demand visual attentiveness to multiple cues and sources of cues within the immediate environment plus development of the ability to tune out visual distractions.
3. Ensemble music requires participants to tolerate and understand the need for repetition and redundancy both in the music itself and in routines of practice.

4. Rehearsal zones demand simultaneous attention to several structured symbol systems.

5. These places foster acceleration of empathy and a sense of caring—for others within the ensemble as well as for instruments and relations between the music and the audience.

Practice Spaces

One of the first vehicles for learning to create music is space—rehearsal zones and studios in particular (Heath, Paul-Boehncke, and Wolf 2007; Hetland et al. 2007). Close examination of these spaces brings to our attention not only the visual and auditory nature of practice spaces but also kinesthetic and haptic learning.

In *kinesthetic learning*, individuals observe the body in motion—their own and others'. Alignment of the individual body as well as positioning in relation to others in the group conveys critical information in ensemble music. This information indicates whether individuals are mutually attending to the same stimulus, working in rhythm and with synchrony when called for, and anticipating future moves of either specific members or sections of the full group.

Haptic learning is generally thought of as learning that derives from touching or gaining information through the "eyes of the skin," particularly with the hands and forearms as well as the fingers. In some art forms, such as dance, haptic learning involves several portions of the body at once. Architects consider in their designs the haptic learning that derives from the "feel" of the entire body within particular spaces where walls or divisions differ in their exterior surfaces (Pallasmaa 2009, 2012). Musicians echo this sentiment when they speak of the "feel" of certain concert spaces as well as the acoustics of these venues.

But beyond this general sense of "feel" in a space are the minute aspects of haptic understanding (Wilson 1998). Advances in fMRI (functional magnetic resonance imaging) technologies now permit neuroscientists to see what happens to internal visual images in the brain when individuals grip, hold, or touch what they see. The haptic, or hand-guided, feedback that young musicians gain when they grip a bow, drum stick, or the neck of a violin, viola, or cello enhances the act of mentally visualizing, of envisioning what lies beyond the current moment. Gripping with the hand sends what neurologists call "force patterns" to those portions of the brain that enable individuals to envision what lies ahead (Reiner 2000, 2008). Children learn to verbalize this sense of "nextness" when they grip objects in their hand. They learn to think before and as they carry out actions.

Guided Practice

Guided practice is essential, however, for individuals to continue to improve visual (as well as auditory) perception of multilayered details in the midst of seeming chaos, messages, and signals to different sections of the ensemble, as well as demonstration by the conductor that may seemingly be directed toward only one section of the ensemble. Visual discernment reduces the number of struggles the cognitive system faces in attempting to sort out irrelevant cues from those pertaining directly to one section or another, one portion of a page of music, or one part of an instrument. Being attentive and alert comes through not only practice but also maturation.

Researchers who examine rehearsal zones give particular attention to how spaces become "instrumental" to the creative work of musicians as well as dancers and actors. The acoustics of spaces enhance the listening possibilities for members seated in various parts of the ensemble (as well as audience members). Musicians also need to have within their rehearsal spaces a sense of the mutual tuning in by others to the sounds in the immediate space. Joint attention of the group has to grow for individuals to achieve mastery. No individual player or singer can "zone out" or lose focus, for if they do so, the sense of togetherness is lost for others.

The importance of space to learning goes largely unnoted for many sites other than those in which the practice of the arts or sciences take place. Similarly, when assessing resources for young children's growth, developmentalists rarely note the importance of spaces—both indoor and outdoor. Young learners living in crowded housing conditions and neighborhoods without either open spaces or buildings suitable for music rehearsals have few opportunities to learn how to "listen to space." Families without discretionary income or time to learn within dedicated spaces (in either their homes or local neighborhoods) can rarely attend to their children's interpretive skills for either spatial knowledge or awareness of tactile, haptic, or kinesthetic cues.

Visual Attentiveness

Perhaps most obvious about ensemble music is the fact that learners who want to become members must develop habits of sustained attentiveness and observational awareness to what seems to be *everything*. Much of the work of learning in music comes through imitation. Novices want to do what others do, and they need to do as others do in many ways. Critical, however, is learning which players to imitate.

To the experienced musician, it is obvious, for example, that reading a sheet of music differs for those who play different instruments. This distinction is learned as novice musicians sense their own belonging within a section or as an alto or tenor within a choral group. Timing, interpretation, and much else about performance relies then on imitation as a starting principle. Yet mastery relies on depth of understanding of distinctive roles, parts, and styles. As individuals gain mastery, they also grow more sensitive to nuances of coordination of these differentiated contributions from various parts of the ensemble (Levitin 2006; Zbikowski 1997). For example, individuals within the string section must attend to what others in this section do with specific parts of the body, but they must also pay attention to notes, rhythm, pace, and the conductor's movements, and detect these as cues that must be met with action in order to bring about desired outcomes for their section. Both direct and peripheral vision matters for beginners as well as for the most accomplished musician. Cues to be followed seem to be everywhere all at once.

With maturity and experience, young musicians gain in their ability to "think" with and through the complementarity of being visually attentive to what goes on around them and also in controlling their own hands and body for purposeful actions. Cognition becomes grounded as children gain practice in motor-dependent production from what it is that they see, anticipate, or envision. They also learn to assess their own actions as they do so. Cognitive neuroscientists use the term "grounded cognition" to refer to the extent to which the brain's modal systems ground internal representations of what others refer to as "concepts" (Barsalou 2010). In ensemble music, this grounding or conceptual understanding comes about through simultaneous input from the environment, body, and situational emotive stimuli grounded through the brain's modal systems.

Habituated Tolerance of Redundancy

Within instrumental and choral ensembles, learners experience constant repetitiveness. They see within their music an order that is created by repeated patterns within particular segments of a set of lyrics or stretch of notes or portions of a fugue or sonata. With practice comes repetition of these patterns in multiple attempts to improve and to "get it right." Individuals become accustomed to hours and hours during which they must tolerate repetition. They thereby become habituated, albeit subconsciously, to the fact that the practice it takes to improve and move toward mastery is vital.

As young learners gain familiarity with hearing and foreshadowing in their heads repetition of notes as well as bars and stretches of musical scores, they internalize stretches of this patterning. Only through hearing and taking part in stretches of music again and again will this habituation enable learners to move to a level of automaticity in recall, as well as recognition of how one repetition differs from another. Such is the case in many fields of intellectual mastery. Learners move into an unfamiliar space with dissimilar language uses, material items, and individuals playing roles that seem highly disparate. With practice, the environment becomes familiar and routines develop. Such habituation is critical to master the skills needed to compare these dissimilar items and roles, identify patterns, grasp the meaning of metaphors, understand particulars in relation to a whole, and figure out order and system (Rothstein 2006).

As noted previously, this kind of mastery applies in any type of engagement with information or technology worlds. For example, scientists in all fields rely, just as musicians do, on sorting out patterns and order as they carry out their work. Repetitive movements of any phenomena that scientists study (whether celestial beings or geophysical structures) carry meaning. But to know these phenomena, scientists, as well as musicians, repeatedly look again, try to work out patterns, and determine how trying again may bring new results. They know the value of looking and listening closely to detect segments of phenomena that differ from time to time or under varying circumstances in only one element or detail (e.g., the vitality of one note or the shaping of a single molecule).

The Layering of Structured Symbol Systems

Learning the vital role of repetition enables musicians to identify, even at a young age, parts and grasp the ways in which parts contribute to the whole. The arrangement of the many parts or elements involved in the production of music, whether choral or instrumental, amounts to layers of structured symbol systems, with notes, sounds, and numerals being only the most obvious of these. What is on a page of music presents several systems (arrangement of lines and spaces along with musical notes, indications of time through both words and numbers, and, for choral groups, the words to be sung).

It is only the structuring of symbol systems that allows humans to detect meaning. As infants and toddlers learn to recognize and produce language(s), they can do so only because the symbols (sounds) of every language make meaning through their structuring. Later, children learn to read and count because they come to understand the structuring within their particular script system, whether alphabetic or otherwise. It is therefore no surprise that research in music learning continues to emphasize the extent to which the "language" areas of the brain work during the creation of music (Levitin and Menon 2003).

Youngsters in ensemble music must learn to read the several-layered structured symbol systems simultaneously—a stronger cognitive demand than is the case when reading the written script system of any language. Beyond the page of music before them, children must also interpret movements of the conductor's baton. They must read, encode, and translate all of these symbol systems to produce sounds that reflect timing, pace, emotional interpretation, and physical and musical coordination with the conductor's wishes, as well as with the actions of others in one's section and the ensemble group as a whole.

A further point is often overlooked when researchers talk about the layering of different symbol systems in music. Young musicians must learn to grasp the meaning of highly abstract terms that conductors use to refer to aspects of interpretation that cannot be rendered directly in symbol systems or literal language. This demand has been termed "cross-domain" learning (Zbikowski 1997). For example, characterizations of musical pitch as "falling" or "rising" have no necessary relation to the actual vertical placement of notes on the printed page or the vertical orientation of the page. Essentially, much that happens in music relies on metaphorical interpretation and the suspension of belief in the literal. Other domains must then be called up to interpret music. Musicians have to "map" what they know about the real world onto specific usages of words and phrases in music and learn to act accordingly. "Text painting," or mapping the semantic meaning of lyrics onto notes, is familiar to those in choral groups as well as to instrumentalists who play such music. In such "painting," melodies often "ascend" and "descend" in relation to semantic meanings of accompanying lyrics. In particular, musicians have to translate into specific actions metaphors reflecting concepts used in music, such as "beauty," "mystery," and other "emblems" of what some consider the "inner life" of music.

This "inner life" of music is often expressed by conductors and aficionados alike in terms of emotion or aesthetic quality with verbs such as *ascend*, *descend*, and *lift* as well as nouns such as *texture*, *integrity*, *truth*, and so forth. Moreover, conductors sometimes urge young musicians to an aesthetic effect by providing analogies or metaphors, asking them to "play that feeling you get when you run in the wind" or "show here the release you get when you achieve something you struggle hard to do." Again, just as scientists sometimes use words or phrases that rely on metaphorical interpretation, so must musicians.

Empathy and Caring Work

This environmental feature often seems too obvious to merit mention in treatises on the life and meaning of learning music. Yet being within a space that becomes familiar over time and involves the same group of people in the act of creating music brings a sensual reality to the meaning of words such as *collaboration* or *cooperation*. Staying attuned to others through having to be mindful of their movements at all times brings about a sense of empathy over time (Singer 2006). Being in a group where one person's error, absence, or lapse of attention has consequences for specific others as well as for the group as a whole builds empathetic responsiveness.

Children who participate within ensemble groups must learn to care not only for their instruments but also for others within the group. This type of caring refers to attention giving, as with coordinating movements of bows in the string section. *Caring* in this sense refers to "being alert." This meaning is the same as that which we convey in the caution to "take care." The further sense of "care about" also applies in ensemble music. The need for continuous care that comes with playing musical instruments is unique. Picking up cues, interpreting emotion through sounds and action, and responding appropriately constitute core aspects of singing a part as well as playing an instrument. These skills cannot come through solitary practice. They can evolve only through observing and being with other singers or players whose expertise grows through years of practice in "taking care" and "caring about." Both uses of *care* point to the potential to make a difference in the state or condition of something or someone else.

Moreover, the need to care for an instrument conveys special meaning for children of families living in small spaces, communities with high crime rates, or in neighborhoods without reliable public transport. Each time a youngster picks up his or her musical instrument, that instrument requires attentive care—whether tuning and adjusting or checking on the alignment of components. The interdependence between the player and instrument is established at the moment a child is given responsibility for an instrument. Learning to care about it comes along with learning to play. Without this care, the instrument will fail them, and they, in turn, will fail both *to take care* and *to care about* the instrument as well as the ensemble.

Reflections on Research and Evaluation

Education reforms after the start of the twenty-first century in the United States and other modern economies intensified the need for schools to take responsibility for student and teacher performance as measured through standardized tests of academic achievement. Justification for expenditure in support of supplementary learning opportunities for children living in underresourced communities needed to include evidence of gains on standardized test scores, particularly in reading and mathematics.

In several nations, federal and state or regional bureaucracies, as well as private funding sources, increasingly called for "evaluation" of any learning opportunity offered to children both within and after school. Consulting firms and evaluation teams collected school scores and attendance records, surveyed parents and educators, and often asked children for self-reports of satisfaction with their learning experiences. Everyone seemed eager to use these evaluations to "prove" that certain programs or approaches "improved" academic achievement by children living in poverty conditions. Priorities in funding centered on programs of tutoring to eliminate deficiencies and raise standardized test performance.

Thus, any practice-based arts or science program faced increasing pressure to provide evidence of "boosts" to academic test scores and grades. As has been noted elsewhere in the text, the generally shallow work of evaluation overshadowed the specific knowledge and skills gained by young and old taking part in sustained participatory learning in museums, theaters, or ensemble music. Features of learning environments went unnoted by evaluators, for they generally thought little about child development and the role of the professional guidance and extensive practice in the "head, hand, and heart" work of learning in the arts and sciences. The behavioral, visual, auditory, haptic, and interpretive practice that such learning demands gives much more than an ability to create and make art or develop curiosity in science.

Research carried out by scholars in several disciplines of the learning sciences, such as cognitive psychology, anthropology, and the neurosciences, continues in a steady stream to identify the complex ways in which practice-based arts and sciences make core differences in learning processes. The general goal of learning scientists is to understand what happens in different types of learning environments that reinforce behaviors possible at certain maturational levels. At what age, for example, can young children translate into action highly abstract metaphors or read the intention of a conductor? This area of research by learning scientists tends to center on contexts of voluntary expertise development in which participants must meet high demand, take risks in performance, and undergo regimens of practice in order to acquire even mid-level mastery.

Researchers in cognitive neuroscience or the learning sciences do not offer judgments on conditions or claim causal influence on behaviors unrelated to the learning context studied. To be sure, they do compare learning environments, but they do so primarily to identify specifics of certain environments that co-occur with patterns of observed behaviors. They also compare the extent and nature of learning by individuals as behavioral changes take place over time. These changes are, in many instances, compared with data on maturational changes. In other words, learning science researchers can indicate the extent to which patterns of behavior *differ* in pace for children working in arts and sciences learning situations from the developmental trajectory human developmentalists regard as "normal" for children who have no such opportunities.

Moreover, the interdisciplinary research of learning scientists leaves no doubt that claims of specific functional outcomes, such as performance on standardized academic tests, tell us very little about what actually happens in the brains, bodies, and emotions of learners involved in practice-based arts and sciences learning environments.

Evaluations that primarily rely on standardized test scores cannot capture what learning sciences researchers are rapidly documenting and analyzing about the differential effects on learning in various types of environments. When evaluators and educators go after only functional, surface-level, and often-temporary and contingent kinds of learning gains, they shortchange what happens in any deep learning, such as that in ensemble music. Changes in levels of mastery can be observed, noted, and analyzed in co-occurrence with shifting development of musical knowledge and skill. These research findings are supported through annual administration of specific tests that measure growth in visual perception, detection and memory of patterns, categorization and language processing skills, and interpretation of metaphors and abstractions related to emotional responses.

For those who grow up and live in underresourced communities, families can rarely provide the intensity and professional guidance of practice toward performance and exhibition that the arts and sciences demand. When cultural centers and other support sources step in to make such learning possible across communities and age groupings, the learning that results brings lifelong and life-wide consequences. Moreover, skills acquired in these sites increasingly appear at the top of lists of characteristics predicted to be essential to successful participation in the twenty-first-century economy. Such skills have been identified by employers and researchers working in the worlds of wellness and health, as well as industries linked with information technologies. In list form, the skills sound so simple as to be unworthy of notice in the everyday world. Yet the cumulative effects are what matters: seeing and hearing patterning of parts in relation to the whole, reliable interpreting of multiple symbol systems as well as metaphors and abstract references, maintaining interpersonal and intrapersonal behavior in accordance with situational circumstances, and developing and sustaining mentally challenging activities that call for visual and auditory perception as well as long-term memory for details and patterning.

In short, the very skills and concepts that become manifest with extended participation in the learning ecology of practice-based arts and sciences are central to effective learning, now and into the future, not only for children living in underresourced communities but for *all* young learners. Just as Abedi highlights in his chapter the pernicious effects of poverty on academic achievement and Snipp homes in on the challenges that indigenous populations face with regard to achieving traditional educational outcomes, I have raised a concern about how underresourced communities also need opportunities such as access to museums, theaters, and musical orchestras. Those from poorly endowed communities are less likely than their wealthier counterparts to live in symbol-rich environments with regular intense cognitive and linguistic demands that call for highly specific listening, interpretive, and motor skills. Moreover, impoverished families can rarely provide their children close, supportive, sustained association with experts and other learners working toward the same goal of mastery in performance.

REFERENCES

Barsalou, Lawrence W. 2010. "Grounded Cognition." *Annual Review of Psychology* 59:617–45.
Donald, Merlin. 2001. *A Mind So Rare: The Evolution of Human Consciousness.* New York: W. W. Norton.
Gibbs, Raymond. 2006. *Embodiment and Cognitive Science.* Cambridge: Cambridge University Press.
Heath, Shirley Brice. 2013. *Words at Work and Play: Three Decades in Family and Community Life.* Cambridge: Cambridge University Press.
Heath, Shirley Brice, Elke Paul-Boehncke, and Shelby Wolf. 2007. *Made for Each Other: Creative Sciences and Arts in the Secondary School.* London: Creative Partnerships.
Hetland, Lois, Ellen Winner, Shirley Veenema, and Kimberly M. Sheridan. 2007. *Studio Thinking: The Real Benefits of Visual Arts Education.* New York: Teachers College Press.
Levitin, Daniel J. 2006. *This Is Your Brain on Music: The Science of a Human Obsession.* New York: Penguin.
Levitin, Daniel, and Vinod Menon. 2003. "Musical Structure Is Processed in 'Language' Areas of the Brain: A Possible Role for Brodmann Area 47 in Temporal Coherence." *Neuroimage* 20:2142–52.
Meltzoff, Andrew N. 2013. "Origins of Social Cognition: Bidirectional Self-Other Mapping and the 'Like-Me' Hypothesis." In *Navigating the Social World: What Infants, Children, and Other Species Can Teach Us,* edited by Mahzarin R. Banaji and Susan Gelman, 139–44. New York: Oxford University Press.
Pallasmaa, Juhani. 2009. *The Thinking Hand.* New York: Wiley.
———. 2012. *The Eyes of the Skin: Architecture and the Senses.* New York: Wiley.
Reiner, Miriam. 2000. "The Nature and Development of Visualization: A Review of What Is Known." In *Visualization: Theory and Practice in Science Education,* edited by John K. Gilbert, Miriam Reiner, and Mary Nakhleh, 25–29. Surrey, UK: Springer.
———. 2008. "The Validity and Consistency of Force Feedback Interfaces in Telesurgery." *Journal of Computer-Aided Surgery* 9:69–74.
Rothstein, Edward. 2006. *Emblems of Mind: The Inner Life of Music and Mathematics.* Chicago: University of Chicago Press.
Singer, Tania. 2006. "The Neuronal Basis and Ontogeny of Empathy and Mid Reading: Review of Literature and Implications for Future Research." *Neuroscience and Biobehavioral Reviews* 30:855–63.
Supekar, Kaustubh, Anna G. Swigarta, Caitlin Tenisona, Dietsje D. Jollesa, Miriam Rosenberg-Leea, Lynn Fuchsb, and Vinod Menon. 2013. "Neural Predictors of Individual Differences in Response to Math Tutoring in Primary-Grade School Children." *Proceedings of the National Academy of Sciences* 110 (20): 8230–35.
Stafford, Barbara Maria. 1999. *Artful Science: Enlightenment Entertainment and the Eclipse of Visual Education.* Cambridge, MA: MIT Press.
Tunstall, Tricia. 2012. *Changing Lives: Gustavo Dudamel, El Sistema, and the Transformative Power of Music.* New York: W. W. Norton.
Wilson, Frank. 1998. *The Hand: How Its Use Shapes the Brain, Language, and Human Culture.* New York: Random House.
Zbikowski, Lawrence. 1997. "Conceptual Models and Cross-Domain Mapping: New Perspectives on Theories of Music and Hierarchy." *Journal of Music Theory* 41 (2): 11–43.

11

Education, Poverty, and East Asian Development Miracles

SIMON MARGINSON

This chapter discusses higher education and science systems in a specific group of nations that have evolved out of macro poverty since World War II. It explores the miracle of accelerated educational and socioeconomic development in the post-Confucian societies of East Asia, societies that all share a common Sinic state tradition and common Confucian educational legacy: Japan, South Korea, Singapore, Taiwan, and China. It also reflects on Vietnam, which shares some of the Sinic underpinnings but has yet to share the educational fluorescence of its neighbors. Is education key to the East Asian postpoverty miracle? Is education and science the cause, condition, associate, or product of accelerated social and economic development? The chapter explores factors shaping the dynamism of education in the region and considers the question of whether there are lessons for other nations.

Megatrends: Growth of Tertiary Participation and Spread of Science

The last two decades have seen major expansion in the role of higher education[1] in human society, encompassing both the emergence of mass participation in higher education as a national norm, with age participation rates trending to 50% and beyond, and the spread of scientific and technological capacity through the emergence of research universities in an increasing number of countries. While only a minority of students participates in science-intensive (Science, Technology, Engineering, and Mathematics—STEM) tertiary programs, the spread of the research university to middle-income countries is a significant democratization of access to science on a world scale. The two megatrends, the growth of participation and spread of science, are uneven by region and country and within countries, but the overall patterns of growth in participation and the distribution of capacity in science are clear. These megatrends are associated with the three other megatrends in modernization: the relative growth of knowledge-intensive work, urbanization, and the burgeoning of the middle class.

The capitalist economy continues to absorb precapitalist rural sectors in Asia, Africa, and Latin America. The proportion of the world population in cities has exceeded 50% for the first time. The European Union Institute for Strategic Economic Studies estimates the size of the global middle class (persons with $10–$100 per day) will increase from 1.8 billion in 2009 to 4.9 billion in 2030, when it will be more than half the world's population (Vasconcelos 2012). The majority of this growth in the middle class will be in Asia, mainly China and India. The combined size of the Asian middle classes will grow from 0.6 billion people in 2009 to more than 3 billion people in 2030. The members of the middle class will want higher education for their children. As seen in the past, a small proportion of middle-class families will seek education abroad, partly because of the positional advantages international education can bring. The overwhelming majority will participate at home.

Tertiary Participation

Between 1995 and 2011, the world gross tertiary enrollment ratio (GTER) rose from 15% to 30% (see figure 11.1). The GTER increased substantially in every world region. While the quality of tertiary educational participation varies significantly between and within countries, it is apparent that the world is moving inexorably everywhere toward high tertiary education participation societies, even though in Sub-Saharan Africa and South Asia there is still far to go before majority participation is achieved. This is a major change in human affairs.

Participation is approaching universal levels only in Europe—it more than doubled in Eastern Europe during the sixteen-year period—but is moving toward 50% in Latin America and the Caribbean, and in East Asia it exceeds the 50% mark except in China. In East Asia and the Pacific, the GTER rose by a factor of three, from 10% to 30% in sixteen years, with the vast demography of China driving the regional numbers (United Nations Educational, Scientific and Cultural Organization [UNESCO] 2014).

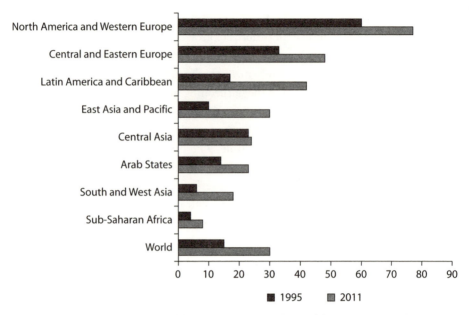

Figure 11.1. Gross tertiary enrollment ratio (GTER) by world region, 1995 and 2011 (Source: UNESCO 2014)

The Spread of Science

The growth in science research has been almost as spectacular as the growth in tertiary education, though national science systems are yet to become as universal as mass tertiary education systems. Again, the worldwide secular trend is from low participation/distribution toward high participation/distribution, with no end in sight to the process of growth. Strategically, science has been moved from the margins of state-building—something that only highly developed countries in North America, Europe/United Kingdom, and Japan could afford as an expression of their leading global role to part of the normal business of established and emerging states. This is a striking change. It seems that all nations now need a developed capability in science and technology, even though not all can yet afford to pay for it.

Because of the spread of technology in industry, including agriculture, and the importance of innovation in production, nations now need an indigenous science infrastructure and trained personnel just as they need clean water, stable governance, and a globally viable financial system. As a part of this growth, they need universities that can "participate effectively in the global knowledge network on an equal basis with the top academic institutions in the world" (Altbach 2011). Nations and cities that lack the capacity to interpret and understand research, a capacity that rests on trained personnel themselves being capable of creating research, find themselves in a position of continuing dependence.

The common growth of research systems is sustained by the globalization of knowledge within one-world English language science. It takes the competitive form of an "arms race in innovation" as nations seek advantages through research and development (R&D) investments. Global research rankings continually compare nations' performances and signify their competitive position. In 1997 there were thirty-nine nations whose citizens published over one thousand research papers in globally recognized science journals, which is a proxy indicator for the presence of an indigenous capacity in research science. As table 11.1 shows, by 2011, fourteen years later, there were fifty-one such nations. The new science nations include Croatia, Serbia, Slovenia, Chile, Malaysia, Thailand, Tunisia, and Iran. The output of published science grew faster in Iran than in any other country, increasing at a remarkable 23.0 per annum between 1997 and 2011.

In sum, both high-participation tertiary education and research science have spread from high-income countries to middle-income countries. Some poorer countries are expanding tertiary participation, though they have yet to begin building science systems. Education and science are among the factors associated with the evolution of nations out of economies characterized by rural labor and a low-skill, high-underemployment urban economy. Nations that are moving out of poverty develop their tertiary education systems and, later, their science systems. The spread of aspirations for secondary and tertiary education is part of the process of lifting all economic and social aspirations. As states become more competent and affluent, governments advance the supply of higher education.

Note that the two sets of changes—the growth in participation in tertiary education and the spread of science—are interdependent. As educational participation expands, it is associated with the differentiation of programs into more disciplines and the growth of capital-intensive professional training, including engineering and information technology. Governments subsidize the STEM disciplines more readily than most other fields because of the perceived association between STEM capacity, industrial innovation, and economic growth (Freeman, Marginson, and Tytler 2014). Further, in fostering science-based education at the tertiary level via "world-class" science universities,

Table 11.1 Nations publishing more than one thousand science papers in 2011

Anglosphere	European Union	Non-EU Europe	Asia	Latin America	Middle East	Africa
USA 212,394	Germany 46,259	Russia 14,151	China 89,894	Brazil 13,148	Iran 8,176*	South Africa 3,125
UK 45,884	France 31,686	Switzerland 10,019	Japan 47,106	Mexico 4,173	Israel 6,096	Egypt 2,515
Canada 29,114	Italy 26,503	Turkey 8,328	South Korea 25,593	Argentina 3,863	Saudi Arabia 1,491*	Tunisia 1,016*
Australia 20,603	Spain 22,910	Norway 4,777	India 22,481	Chile 1,979*		
New Zealand 3,472	Netherlands 15,508	Ukraine 1,727	Taiwan 14,809			
	Sweden 9,473	Serbia 1,269*	Singapore 4,543			
	Poland 7,564	Croatia 1,289*	Thailand 2,304*			
	Belgium 7,484		Malaysia 2,092*			
	Denmark 6,071		Pakistan 1,268*			
	Austria 5,103					
	Finland 4,878					
	Portugal 4,621*					
	Greece 4,534					
	Czech Rep. 4,127					
	Ireland 3,186					
	Hungary 2,289					
	Romania 1,626*					
	Slovenia 1,239*					

Source: Adapted from National Science Foundation (2014) data.
* = countries that have entered the one thousand papers group since 1997.

middle-income countries lift the imagined possibilities of tertiary education, further encouraging participation. The growth of tertiary participation, improvements in institutional quality, and the expansion of scientific capacity all feed into one another.

Developments in East Asia and Singapore

In the last fifty years, and especially the two decades since 1995, the most striking developments in the economy, higher education, and science have occurred in East Asia and Singapore, in systems that share a common Sinic heritage in classical Chinese civilization. These nations include Korea and Japan, where early state formation and notions of ethical conduct and educational self-formation were closely affected by Tang China, and later by neo-Confucianism in the Song dynasty and thereafter. These nations have all risen from widespread poverty to become economic powerhouses in which average incomes have risen rapidly and student learning achievement—both as measured by comparative international tests and by the rate of educational participation—is more deeply and broadly distributed than in other countries, facilitating (though not guaranteeing) social mobility. More recently, except in Japan where it happened in the 1970s and 1980s, these nations have become increasingly strong in science and technology, including published science.

There are significant political and cultural differences between China, Taiwan, Japan, Korea, Vietnam, and Singapore, but they have much in common in the configuration of their school, higher education, and science systems. With the exception of Vietnam, these countries have also shared in the takeoff of tertiary educational participation, research science, and "world-class" universities in national trajectories that are striking similar to one another, although not simultaneous—for example, Japan's modern takeoff in higher education and science preceded the other countries by twenty to thirty years. Before looking at these developments in more detail, it is helpful to identify the common cultural elements. All share the Sinic tradition of a strong comprehensive state, responsible for social order, economic prosperity, and national culture. All share the Confucian heritage in education, strong commitment in families, and schooling to self-cultivation through learning. All have also been continually affected by their encounter with Western modernization, beginning in the imperial period. The American research university continues to influence the evolution of science and institutional design. Because of the influence of Western modernization, it is more accurate to describe these higher education systems with the term "post-Confucian" rather than "Confucian."

Political Culture and Educational Culture

The Sinic state tradition is different from that of the limited liberal state that prevails in the English-speaking world. The Sinic state originated in the Qin and Han dynasties 2,200 years ago. The Qin and Han states were responsible for social harmonization and common systems such as language and measurement, while day-to-day management of the rural economy was devolved to the local level. Compared with Europe, the state was stronger vis-à-vis the towns (city-states played a minor role in East Asia) and the occupational and social sectors. East Asian politics has always been supreme vis-à-vis the economy and civil society (Gernet 1996). Government enjoys great prestige. While dissent does occur, the ongoing antistatism that is a feature of Western polities is not part of Sinic political cultures. The responsibilities of government are comprehensive rather than ubiquitous. Government does not administer everything, but it intervenes decisively when necessary in a manner that Western states use only in wartime. All else being equal, there is a high level of consent for focused government intervention. In their modern form, the East Asian states are also highly sophisticated. In contrast with many Western countries, many of the best and brightest graduates seek positions in government— not in business or in other professions. All of these attributes equip Sinic governments to focus effectively on lifting national effort and achievement in education and science, when they choose to do so.

The role of the comprehensive Sinic state is not driven by direct public intervention in the economy to the extent manifest in parts of Western Europe and the English-speaking world, despite the fact that a more limited notion of the state prevails in the West. The Sinic state asserts itself more through moral authority, consent, and political control than via taxing and spending. In 2012 government consumption spending as a proportion of GDP was 7% in Macau, 9% in Hong Kong SAR, 10% in Singapore, 12% in Taiwan, 14% in China, 16% in South Korea, and 20% in Japan, compared with 22% in the United Kingdom (World Bank 2014).

Second, it is difficult to overestimate the importance of Confucian educational culture. These are human societies more profoundly and more universally committed to education than any other. While self-cultivation through learning had origins in the Han selection of officials and the advanced court culture of the Tang, it first became massified in the Song dynasty one thousand years ago. At that time, there was widespread development of both state and private academies focused primarily on the preparation of officials in the educated arts (Hayhoe et al. 2011). The mass examination became established as the medium for focusing educational aspiration and effort and a principal technology of social selection. Massification of the Confucian ethic brought educational aspirations to an ever-growing number of families, which spread literacy. In these families, self-cultivation became installed as a self-reproducing reciprocal norm of family conduct: education became part of the duty of the parent to the child almost from the moment of birth, and part of the duty of the child to the parent. These beliefs are now near universal in East Asia. It is widely believed that success in education is a function of hard work rather than talent (Chua 2011).

Many East Asian families invest as much in education as European or American families invest in housing. The commitment to learning extends not only to middle-class families but to all families. When poor households acquire surplus income, often the first move is to spend it on the children's formal schooling or "shadow schooling"—the various forms of private tutoring and private classes outside school hours that make up an important component of student learning in East Asia. Levin (2011) estimated that total household expenditure on "shadow schooling" in South Korea was equivalent to 3% of national GDP, as much as many nations spend on formal schooling (see also Bray 2007).

One of the effects of the near universalization of the Confucian educational ethic is to weaken socioeconomic status as a determinant of educational aspirations and outcomes. As will be discussed in the following section, the size of the undereducated layer is smaller than in most other societies, even though incomes and wealth are not distributed more equally. Further, the tendency to participate in higher education is less sensitive to socioeconomic position than in many other countries (Wu and Haiyan 2014). On the whole, post-Confucian families are more prepared to invest privately than elsewhere and less likely to be deterred from educational participation by poverty, though for families in extreme poverty, as in much of rural China, tertiary education is still out of reach at this stage. Compared to states in Europe and the English-speaking world, the Sinic state does not have to allocate as many resources to the subsidization of participation in order to secure social inclusion.

Post-Confucian Tertiary Participation

The East Asian nations are all moving or have moved from medium levels of tertiary participation to high participation and, in the case of Taiwan and Korea, have achieved or exceeded North American and European levels of participation. South Korea is the global leader in tertiary participation with a GTER that exceeds 100%, due to near-universal participation of the age cohort combined with some mature age participation. The GTER also exceeds 85% in Taiwan and has reached 60% in Macau SAR, Hong Kong SAR, and Japan (UNESCO 2014). In Taiwan, participation is over 80% in the vocational high school/vocational university strand and at 90% in the academic high school/ academic university strand. In Japan, recent increases in the participation rate have been hastened by a demographic downturn in the school leaver age group, which has encouraged low-demand colleges in the large private sector to take on students that in the past would have been considered insufficiently prepared for degree-level tertiary studies. Hong Kong SAR and Singapore have shifted away from the nonuniversal systems inherited from imperial Britain, with much of the recent educational growth in those two global cities taking place in subdegree institutions and lower-status private sector institutions.

In China, the GTER was only 4% in 1990. It then began to climb at an accelerating rate, reaching 24% in 2011, not far below the world average of 30% and trending toward the official target of 40% in 2020. That would bring China close to the present OECD average. The universal trend to a high-participation tertiary system is apparent in China as everywhere else. The fact that present manifestations of the trend appear uneven between nations reflects differing historical starting points. Likewise, within China participation is still uneven by region. There are pronounced differences between the city and the countryside, and the children of migrant workers in the cities participate at lower rates (and often in less favored institutions) than those families that enjoy residency rights. There is growing research concerning these inequalities, which are associated also with patterns of income inequality and regional differences in national political power (e.g., Cheng 2009; Knight 2013; Li and Yang 2013; Wang 2011).

One of the conditions of the trend toward universal participation in East Asia and Singapore is the relatively high level of student learning achievement across the whole secondary school age group. This pattern of distribution of student learning achievement can be gleaned from the OECD (2014) Program for International Student Assessment (PISA). In the 2012 PISA assessment in mathematics, the East Asian nations were notable for high average scores and a high proportion of students who achieved in the top PISA group (levels 5 and 6). These systems were also noticeable for the relatively low proportion of their students in the lowest achievement group, level 1. Whereas in the OECD as a whole 23.1% of fifteen-year-olds were at level 1, the proportion was only

Table 11.2   Achievement of fifteen-year-olds in mathematics, post-Confucian systems compared with selected other countries, PISA 2012

School system	Position in PISA table for mathematics (*n* = 65)	Mean score in PISA mathematics	Proportion of all students in the top PISA group (Levels 5–6) (%)	Proportion of all students in the bottom PISA group (Level 1) (%)
OECD average	—	494	12.6	23.1
Shanghai, China	1	613	55.4	3.8
Singapore	2	573	40.0	8.3
Hong Kong China SAR	3	561	33.7	8.5
Taiwan	4	560	37.2	12.8
South Korea	5	554	30.9	9.1
Macau China SAR	6	538	24.3	10.8
Japan	7	536	23.7	11.1
Switzerland	9	531	21.4	12.4
Germany	16	514	17.5	17.7
Vietnam	17	511	13.3	14.2
United Kingdom	26	494	11.8	21.8
Russia	34	482	7.8	24.0
United States	36	481	8.8	25.8

Source: OECD (2014).

3.8% in Shanghai, 8.3% in Singapore, 8.5% in Hong Kong, 9.1% in South Korea, 11.1% in Japan, 12.8% in Taiwan, and 14.2% in Vietnam (see table 11.2) (World Bank 2014). This pattern provides a strong, egalitarian platform for near-universal tertiary participation and also suggests that the potential productivity of East Asian workforces is relatively high.

Science and Science Universities

In East, Southeast, and South Asia together—Asia minus the Middle East and former Soviet Central Asia—investment in R&D was $492 billion in 2011, 34% of the global total, more than the $453 billion spent in the United States and Canada and much higher than the $345 billion spent in Europe/United Kingdom. The post-Confucian countries alone spent $448 billion on R&D. East Asia has become the third great region for research and industrial innovation alongside North America and Western Europe/United Kingdom. It is important to remember that the achievement is recent. Three decades ago, all of the post-Confucian systems except Japan were minor players in research. A little over a decade ago, China was the world's tenth largest investor in R&D. It is now second. At present rates of increase, China's investment will exceed that of the United States in the next decade. Between 2001 and 2011, China's R&D rose by 18.1% per year after adjusting for inflation. By 2011, China was spending 1.84% of GDP on R&D, higher than the United Kingdom (1.77%); South Korea invested 4.03% of GDP, second only to Israel. South Korea's total spending at $59.9 billion was fifth highest, well ahead of France and the United Kingdom (National Science Foundation [NSF] 2014). Yet three decades ago, in 1985, China was very poor with a per capita income of $814 (World Bank 2014). Only two decades ago, twelve European countries published more science than South Korea—now there are just three (NSF 2014).

Although most R&D investment in East Asia takes the form of industry innovation, the ramping up of research has led to a dramatic growth in scientific output in universities and the state academies and laboratories. China, the world's twelfth-largest producer of science and quantitative social science in 1995, was second in 2011 with 89,894 journal papers. Since 2001, China's annual output of papers had grown by an average of 15.6% per year. South Korea reached 25,593 papers in 2011 after growing 8.8 % per year in the prior decade. There had also been rapid growth in Taiwan and Singapore. In Japan, which established its science system in the 1970s and 1980s, the annual number of journal papers was falling, but the nation still produced the third-largest number of papers (NSF 2014).

In terms of publication and citation counts, the leading post-Confucian universities are not the equals of those in North America and Europe, but the gap is beginning to close. At this stage, journal paper output in China is especially concentrated in engineering, physics, chemistry, and computing, the disciplines that feed construction, urbanization, transport and communications systems, and energy. In chemistry, China produced 17% of all world papers in 2012 compared to 16% in the United States. The United States had twice as many papers in the top 1% by citation rate, while ten years ago China had almost no top 1% papers. In computing, China published 13% of all journal papers in 2012 but 17% of the world's top 1% papers that year. However, China is weaker than the United States and Europe in biological sciences, medicine, and psychology (NSF 2014). In the number of papers published in *Nature* in 2012, Japan ranked fourth in the world and China sixth. The United States published 2,236 articles, the United Kingdom 677, Germany 594, Japan 398,

France 383, and China 303, less than Harvard University alone in the United States (368 articles). South Korea was the fourteenth nation with 112 articles in 2012. However, China's contribution to the *Nature* publishing index more than doubled between 2008 and 2012 (Nature 2014).

As the improvement in academic publishing suggests, national governments in East Asia and Singapore have placed a high priority on developing a layer of leading universities, or "world-class universities" (WCUs). The objective is to establish concentrations of research capacity and university status comparable to those of North America and Europe. This objective has been pursued through selective investment, performance targets, international benchmarking (a feature of all post-Confucian systems and especially of Singapore and China), and programs of reform in university governance and management designed to install business-like models with strategic leadership, as in many other countries. WCU policy builds on pregiven national hierarchies, like the Imperial universities established prior to World War II in Japan, Peking University (1898) in China, and Seoul National University (1946), which was the first national university in Korea. There are also more recent foundations, such as the Hong Kong University of Science and Technology (HKUST), which opened in 1991 (Postiglione 2011). Would-be WCUs are supported by special funding, such as the 985 program in China and Brain 21 in Korea (Shin 2009).

The Shanghai Jiao Tong University Academic Ranking of World Universities (ARWU), which uses the Thomson-Reuters Web of Science data set, is dominated by the United States (eighty-five of the top two hundred universities) and the rest of the Anglosphere (thirty-three) (ARWU 2014). Most of the other top two hundred research universities are from Western Europe. Asia has just eighteen of the top two hundred universities, including nine from Japan, the National University of Singapore, Seoul National, National Taiwan (the highest-ranked Chinese university), and Tsinghua, Peking, Fudan, Shanghai Jiao Tong and Zhejiang in China, and the Chinese University in Hong Kong. There are no top two hundred Asian universities from outside the post-Confucian group. Between 2005 and 2013, the number of top five hundred universities in mainland China jumped from eight to twenty-eight (ARWU 2014). Hong Kong has five more. There is a time lag between investments in science capacity and a better rank. Present improvements in the ranking of East Asian universities reflect the investments of five to ten years ago. Further improvement is already in the pipeline. It is likely that in fifteen years, there will be many more universities from China, Korea, and Taiwan in the world top two hundred.

Higher Education and Economic Growth: Which Came First?

As table 11.3 shows, the East Asian city systems in Singapore, Hong Kong SAR, and Macau SAR now enjoy per capita incomes at the U.S. level or more, while Japan, Taiwan, and South Korea have per capita incomes at Western European levels. China is becoming a middle-income country, albeit with regional dispari- ties as noted: per capita incomes in Shanghai, Beijing, and parts of coastal East- ern China are much higher than in the country as a whole. Table 11.3 also shows that East Asia was not always wealthy. Whereas Singapore, Hong Kong, and Ma- cau were relatively advantaged in 1980—in Singapore and Hong Kong per capita incomes were already half the level of the United States—there has been excep- tional income growth in China, South Korea, and, to a lesser extent, Taiwan. Did the growth of education and science precede the economic takeoff? Can we discern the possibility that investment in tertiary education helped to lift these nations from poverty? Or did the growth in per capita incomes precede growth in participation in tertiary education? Or were they simultaneous?

Table 11.3   Gross national income (GNI) per capita (1980 and 2012) and population (2014) of post-Confucian nations/systems

Nation/system	Population (millions) 2014	GNI PPP per capita 1980 (US$)	GNI PPP per capita 2012 (US$)	Change in GNI per capita 1980–2012 (1980 = 1.00)
Macau SAR	0.6	10,700	68,000	6.36
Singapore	5.4	6,920	60,110	8.69
Hong Kong SAR	7.2	6,730	52,190	7.75
Taiwan	23.4	3,601	38,462	10.68
Japan	127.1	8,610	36,750	4.27
South Korea	50.2	2,360	30,180	12.79
China	1,364	250	9,040	36.16
Vietnam	89.7	N/A	3,620	N/A
India	1,243	430	3,820	8.88
United States	317.9	12,550	52,610	4.19

Source: Adapted from World Bank (2014); UN Department of Economic and Social Affairs for population estimates; Central Intelligence Agency (2014) for Taiwan economic data for 2013. Historical Taiwan data from International Monetary Fund.
   Note: PPP = purchasing power parity; N/A = data not available. Taiwan GDP *not* GNI per capita 1980 and 2012. Macau GNI per capita 1982 and 2011 *not* 1980 and 2012. South Korea, Vietnam, Hong Kong, Singapore, and Macau population 2013. India and the United States are not post-Confucian nations but have been included for comparison purposes.

Figures 11.2 and 11.3 explore two concurrent trends in both South Korea (figure 11.2) and China (figure 11.3): per capita gross national product (GNP) and the GTER in education. To facilitate the comparison of the trends, in each figure the two graphs cross at the midpoint in time, which is 1997. In both countries in the second half of the time series, the trend of expansion of tertiary participation becomes stronger in comparison to the expansion of income per head. This suggests that in these two cases, a certain level of economic development preceded—and may have been a necessary condition of— the takeoff in educational participation at the tertiary level. These data do not support the idea that building tertiary education is necessary to lift a nation out of severe poverty, as was the case in China before the 1980s. Clearly, economic growth occurred before educational growth.

In particular, the first half of the time series in figures 11.2 and 11.3 demonstrate that the development of mass tertiary education lags behind the economic takeoff that happened in both countries. The data in figures 11.2 and 11.3 do not preclude the possibility that improvements in the quantity and quality of schooling—as distinct from tertiary education—were conditions of the move out of poverty. However, in China the Gross Secondary Enrollment Ratio (GSER) in 1992 (43.2) was slightly lower than in 1982 (43.7), and there was a substantial dip in the GSER during the 1980s while economic growth first took off, with a low point of 30.9 in 1984 (UNECSO 2014). The GSER starts rising consistently at a rapid rate of 3%–5% per year only in the mid-2000s, concurrent with the trend in the GTER, after twenty years of accelerated economic growth. So in China, without looking at further examples, the lifting of educational participation at both secondary and tertiary levels lags well behind the pattern of economic growth.

In the second half of the time series, rapidly rising tertiary participation seems to be associated with economic growth and even moves ahead of it. It may even be that the tendency of increasing participation in tertiary education is necessary (though presumably, not sufficient) to an economy characterized by urbanization and a growing role for advanced manufacturing and technologically intensive services. It is also equally possible that a rising standard of living in both countries enabled a major lift in the level of educational aspirations (i.e., participation in tertiary education again followed and was enabled by, rather than led, economic growth). Overall, the data in figures 11.2 and 11.3 fit better with the assumption that economic growth drives or facilitates growth in educational participation than the assumption that educational participation

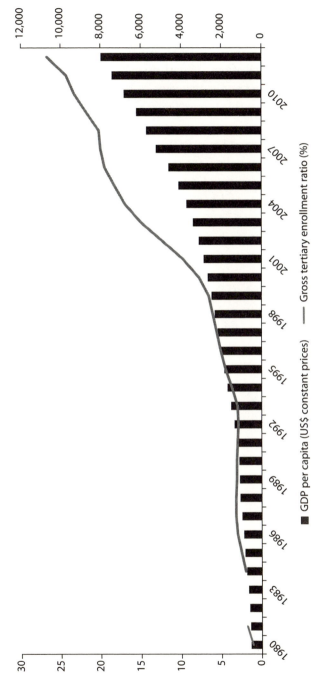

Figure 11.3. Trends in per capita GDP (PPP, constant prices) and in gross tertiary enrollment ratio (%), China, 1980 to 2012 (Constant 2005 USD) (Sources: UNESCO 2014; World Bank 2014)

■ GDP per capita (US$ constant prices) ── Gross tertiary enrollment ratio (%)

drives or facilitates economic growth, though the data also suggest that the growth/education relation may not be a constant but may change as national wealth rises. It is also possible that the two trends, economic growth and growth in tertiary participation, are both associated with a common process of social development and not instrumentally related on a one-to-one basis; that is, both trends have a third cause or are the function of a complex set of causes.

There are also differences between the two cases that caution against too ready a move to general laws about the relationship between economic growth, the transition from poverty, and educational participation. In Korea, the GTER begins the time period at 20%, and though GDP per head increases faster than educational participation during most of the 1990s, participation never stops rising until it reaches the point in the late 2000s when it cannot increase much further. In China, tertiary participation starts the time series at a very low level, less than 2%, and there is very slow change during the economic growth of the 1980s. From 1999 onward, there is a remarkably accelerated takeoff in the GTER. Tertiary participation trends upward much more rapidly than the change in GDP per capita, though the latter increased at a very rapid rate by world standards. This turning point in the late 1990s was a function of state policy. The Chinese government decided to grow tertiary education and invest in the necessary resources. Supply and demand for tertiary education trended sharply up from that time. This highlights the capacity of states in the Sinic tradition to drive rapid change and secure popular consent in doing so.

Figure 11.4 graphs the trend in total GDP against the trend in the total output of scientific papers. As with tertiary educational participation in China, the pattern is again one of a long period of economic growth followed by a sudden lurch upward, this time in research outputs. As with tertiary participation, this trend can be traced to deliberate government policies, in this case to step up R&D and "world-class" science universities. It is plausible to assume that it is impossible for a developing economy to invest in scientific infrastructure at scale until it reaches a certain level of national resources. The movement to world science follows rather than leads the move out of poverty. No doubt the point where science-building is possible is a case-by-case matter, contextually variable. The case of China shows that it is possible for a lower middle-income country to build science. It is not something that is the preserve only of wealthy countries—though it helps to have China's scale.

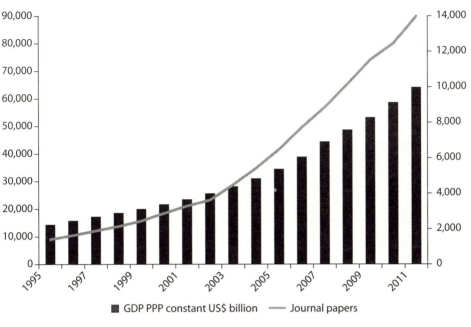

Figure 11.4. Trends in GDP ($US billion, PPP, constant prices) and in number of journal papers in science and social science, China, 1995 to 2012

The Outlier: Vietnam

The Confucian legacy is as widespread among families in Vietnam as in other post-Confucian countries. Universal examinations of the Chinese type have long been used for student social selection. There is a broad normative commitment to self-cultivation and schooling and respect for the teaching profession. Families invested, despite the low level of national income per capita, $3,620 in 2012 in purchasing power parity terms (see table 11.3). There is a strong pattern of household investment through private tutoring and foreign tertiary institutions, and since 1986 part-cost fees have been charged in public education. Schooling in Vietnam is successful. Remarkably, fifteen-year-olds perform better in all three PISA disciplines than their counterparts in the United Kingdom and the United States, though the English-speaking countries have ten to fifteen times the per capita income of Vietnam. Yet tertiary participation is relatively low, the quality of education is continually questioned, the state of research science is very weak, and Vietnam has no prospects of achieving "world-class" universities, despite talk of this in official circles.

Why is this? Of the elements present in the successful post-Confucian systems—strong steering by a state with comprehensive responsibility, targeted system-building supported by focused state investment, Confucian educational ethic in the family, examinations, rapidly growing participation underpinned by state-financed infrastructure and household spending, and accelerated research outputs—only the Confucian ethic is clearly present in Vietnam. The nation has the necessary educational culture but lacks the political culture. The present generation of leaders was partly educated in Russia in the late-Soviet period when Vietnam was part of the Soviet sphere. Political culture in the party-state often seems more Soviet than post-Confucian—subject to arbitrary officialdom and widespread corruption, with incoherent policies and targets more nominal than real. But even if state culture resembled that of Singapore or Taiwan, the nation would lack the resources needed to finance science or adequate university infrastructure, or to pay its state officials, educators, and researchers well enough to ensure that they can focus on their main responsibilities. Vietnam has only 40% of the per-capita income of China. Nevertheless, the Vietnamese state has shown a formidable military capacity, its national role remains strong, the next generation of officials will be more broadly educated, China on the northern border will concentrate national attention on the need to modernize, and economic growth is running at over 5% per annum. It may be only a matter of time before tertiary education in Vietnam takes off.

Conclusion: Post-Confucian Poverty and Higher Education

The post-Confucian countries have four common features that facilitated the takeoff in higher education: the comprehensive Sinic state, Confucian educational cultivation in the home, an effective targeted response to Western modernization under state leadership, and economic growth sufficient to pay for educational infrastructure and research. Statistically, economic growth has preceded rather than followed the development of higher education and science, at least in the first phases of development. Investment and modernization in higher education and science were not integral to the initial economic takeoff out of poverty, though they may play a more generative role at later stages.

Seriously poor countries cannot finance good-quality higher education and science. Aspirations to develop "world-class" universities are more widespread than the capacity to fulfill those aspirations. The development of relatively expensive higher education always rests on the economic growth essential to finance both government and private investment. Tertiary participation also rests on the growth of middle-class families, which demand educational opportunities for their children and are able to share some of the cost.

The post-Confucian systems have combined high participation and high performance, with both a large group of high achievers and a relatively high "floor" of performance in the lower-achieving groups. There is no apparent trade-off between breadth and depth of student learning; and, interestingly, the level of participation in tertiary education seems to be less sensitive to socioeconomic indicators than is the case in Western Europe and North America. This reflects the near-universal socialization into Confucian self-cultivation. This provides an excellent platform for building on the earlier stage of economic growth and breaking through the middle-income ceiling that seems to have affected some nations.

In one respect, educational capacity may have contributed to the initial climb out of poverty in East Asia and Singapore. That is the universal and self-reproducing character of Confucian educational ethic in the home, and the associated normative commitment to schooling, which were already part of those countries, even prior to state educational interventions to harness that same Confucian ethic. The case of Vietnam shows today that these factors were at play in the post-Confucian systems at earlier stages of economic development, though schooling was then underresourced. When accelerated growth began in Japan in the 1950s and Korea in the 1980s, the levels of secondary and tertiary participation were already relatively high for a struggling economy. This was not the case in China, but in that country the intrinsic strength and broad-based distribution of the Confucian ethic was apparent in the extremely rapid take-up of tertiary education from the late 1990s onward as well as the rather exceptional performance of the Shanghai region in PISA.[2]

It also might be argued that these countries were able to draw on their cultural strength in education so as to boost productivity in the transitions from agriculture to manufacturing and then to advanced manufacturing and services, at which point higher levels of tertiary participation came into play, halfway through the evolution out of widespread poverty. But this narrative requires further tests through statistical analysis and case studies.

Is the East Asian Miracle Transferrable?

What are the lessons of the East Asian miracle in higher education and science for nation-building states in Sub-Saharan Africa and South and Central Asia?

Can this model be transferred successfully? And can it inform poverty reduction strategies elsewhere? Policy transfer and strategy transfer are a fraught business. Though all modern societies are sufficiently like one another to open up the possibility of transfer, policies and their success or failure are inescapably context bound. It is apparent that in East Asia and Singapore, the Sinic state and political culture, and the powerful tradition of Confucian educational cultivation in the home, have been essential elements. Perhaps the last is especially important as Sinic state intervention rests on it. Arguably, even if highly effective state machinery emerged in, say, central Africa, it would still face the mammoth job of installing, in popular culture, values and behaviors parallel to those that are reproduced down the generations in China or Korea. Neither Sinic political culture nor post-Confucian educational and social culture is likely to transfer readily. A focused state intervention of the Sinic kind outside the post-Confucian systems is most likely to be effective in nations where there is a broad-based commitment to education, such as Israel or parts of Western Europe. India might be one such nation, but there the lacuna is a focused national state capability.

In other words, there are limits to the potential for transfer of East Asian programs and achievements in upper-secondary and tertiary education to other nations with different cultural roots. Yet the post-Confucian example points to the crucial importance of the family as an incubator for social values in education, and in poverty reduction strategy, the universal need to build educational/social aspirations and motivation on a broad basis. Once these aspirations become near universal, as in East Asia, there is less socioeconomic discrimination in rates of participation; and as soon as economic growth advances and both state and people have the scope to invest, the opportunity to advance learning is taken.

While governments and public-spirited citizens elsewhere cannot replicate the thousand years of engagement in mass education that underpins East Asian dynamism, everywhere government, public agencies and institutions (including the leading universities), and philanthropy have key leadership roles in fostering social inclusion and learning achievement, as well as building institutions and systems that lift the horizon of possibility. For emerging states, the hard question to get right is that of timing—at which point in the journey out of widespread poverty should a government attempt to accelerate the growth of participation in higher education and the rise of science, hoping to utilize the new capacity in the upward spiral of economic development? Premature talk about "world-class" universities in Vietnam and the Central Asian republics might suggest that some governments are not getting their timing right. Here it is not a matter of lifting participation in secondary education prior to lifting that in higher education. Emerging opportunities in higher education can help to lift aspiration and performance earlier, in the school years. As happened in China, it seems best to move at both levels of education simultaneously, once the necessary material threshold has been achieved and family aspirations are established.

NOTES

1. The data on participation that are used in this chapter refer to "tertiary" education rather than "higher education" (i.e., in addition to degree programs in higher education, they encompass two-year subdegree programs). However, the main argument here is about higher education, including universities with substantial activity in research science. Generally, the trend of expansion of higher education has moved in proportion to the expansion of tertiary education, though the two trends are not always correlated in every country.

2. Even if Shanghai is a privileged part of China and not representative of the whole country, and even if Shanghai's PISA performance is artificially boosted by the omission of internal migrant families from the tests (as alleged), the learning achievement of the fifteen-year-olds included in the test is exceptionally strong.

REFERENCES

Academic Ranking of World Universities (ARWU). 2014. *Academic Ranking of World Universities 2013*. http://www.shanghairanking.com/ARWU2013.html.
Altbach, Phillip. 2011. "The Past, Present and Future of the Research University." In *The Road to Academic Excellence: The Making of World-Class Research Universities*, edited by Phillip Altbach and Jamil Salmi, 11–32. Washington, DC: World Bank.
Bray, Mark. 2007. *The Shadow Education System: Private Tutoring and Its Implications for Planners*. Paris: UNESCO Institute for Educational Planning. http://unesdoc.unesco .org/images/0011/001184/118486e.pdf.
Central Intelligence Agency (CIA). 2014. *World Factbook: Taiwan*. http://www.cia.gov /library/publications/the-world-factbook/geos/tw.html.
Cheng, Henan. 2009. "Inequality in Basic Education in China: A Comprehensive Review." *International Journal of Educational Policies* 3 (2): 81–106.
Chua, Amy. 2011. *Battle Hymn of the Tiger Mother*. New York: Penguin Books.
Freeman, Brigid, Simon Marginson, and Russell Tytler. 2014. *The Age of STEM: Educational Policy and Practice across the World in Science, Technology, Engineering and Mathematics*. New York: Routledge.
Gernet, Jacques. 1996. *A History of Chinese Civilization*. 2nd edition. Cambridge: Cambridge University Press.
Hayhoe, Ruth, Jun Li, Jing Lin, and Qiang Zha, eds. 2011. *Portraits of 21st Century Chinese Universities: In the Move to Mass Higher Education*. New York: Springer.

International Monetary Fund. 2014. *World Economic Outlook (WEO) Database, April.* http://www.imf.org/external/pubs/ft/weo/2014/01/weodata/index.aspx.

Knight, John. 2013. "Inequality in China: An Overview." *The World Bank Research Observer* 29:1–19.

Levin, H. 2011. Personal conversation with author.

Li, Mei, and Rui Yang. 2013. "Interrogating Institutionalized Establishments: Urban-Rural Inequalities in China's Higher Education." *Asia Pacific Educational Review* 14 (3): 315–23.

National Science Foundation (NSF). 2014. *Science and Engineering Indicators 2014.* http://www.nsf.gov/statistics/seind14/.

Nature. 2014. *Nature Publishing Index.* http://www.natureasia.com/en/publishing-index/.

Organisation for Economic Co-operation and Development (OECD). 2014. *PISA 2012 Results in Focus: What 15-Year-Olds Know and What They Can Do with What They Know.* Paris: OECD.

Postiglione, Gerard, A. 2011. "The Rise of Research Universities: The Hong Kong University of Science and Technology." In *The Road to Academic Excellence: The Making of World-Class Research Universities*, edited by Phillip G. Altbach and Jamil Salmi, 63–100. Washington, DC: World Bank.

Shin, Jung Cheol. 2009. "Building World-Class Research University: The Brain Korean 21 Project." *Higher Education* 58: 669–88.

United Nations Department of Economic and Social Affairs. 2014. *World Population Policy Database.* http://www.un.org/en/development/desa/population/.

United Nations Educational, Scientific and Cultural Organization (UNESCO). 2014. *Educational Statistics.* UNESCO Institute for Statistics. http://www.uis.unesco.org /Pages/default.aspx.

Vasconcelos, Álvaro de, ed. 2012. *Global Trends 2030: Citizens in an Interconnected and Polycentric World.* Paris: European Union Institute for Security Studies.

Wang, Li. 2011. "Social Exclusion and Inequality in Higher Education in China: A Capability Perspective." *International Journal of Educational Development* 31 (3): 277–86.

World Bank. 2014. *Data and Statistics.* http://data.worldbank.org.

Wu, Ching-Ling, and Bai Haiyan. 2014. *From Early Aspirations to Actual Attainment: The Effects of Economic Status and Educational Expectations on University Pursuit.* Unpublished draft paper. Nantou: National Chi Nan University.

Conclusion

Education, Poverty, and Public Policy

EDWARD P. ST. JOHN AND PHILLIP J. BOWMAN

When analyzing the relationship between education and poverty in the United States, it is important to recognize changes in income inequality. From World War II through about 1980, the trajectory was toward greater income equality, followed by a sustained period of growing income inequality (Piketty 2014). Economic research informed policy remedies to inequality, including a major emphasis on federal student financial aid programs for low-income students and social welfare programs (e.g., Blank 2011; Danziger and Weinberg 1986; Hansen and Weisbrod 1967). After 1980, U.S. policy shifted toward market theories based on Milton Friedman's *Capitalism and Freedom* ([1962] 2002).[1] There were radical changes in education and finance policies, but the consequences of the shift in the trajectory of policy are routinely overlooked in social science and educational research (St. John 2013a). While we agree with Jeannie Oakes's argument (this volume) that social scientists should emphasize social justice in their research and advocacy, we also recognize the need for better public policy.

The authors in this volume have examined the relationship between poverty and educational inequality from different vantages. Authors considered global challenges to local remedies to inequality, correlations between income inequality and achievement, and intervention methods; they also provided diverse perspectives on American Indians and how they have been harmed by Eurocentric conceptions of educational uplift. In combination, the chapters illuminate both causes and potential remedies for educational inequality due to poverty. When he requested this concluding chapter, William Tierney emphasized the importance of reflecting on the volume using a policy perspective. Our challenge was to construct and communicate understandings from this diverse set of critiques while also addressing policy issues underlying proposed remedies.

As a conclusion, we undertake this task in four steps. First, we place the problem of education and poverty into the context of the new and old trajectories of government policy, considering links between globalization of national economies and changes in educational systems. Second, we discuss the importance of integrating social, economic, and educational perspectives when addressing the challenge of reducing income inequality through education reform. Third, given this background, we reconsider the linkages between public policy and inequality in educational opportunity. Finally, we take a "look forward" at the challenges national governments and education agencies face as they attempt to address the challenge of inequality. In addition to discussing the contributions of the authors in this volume to these topics, as is the tradition of writing conclusions to edited volumes, we draw on our recent efforts to encourage reflection on policy trajectories, globalization, and social justice, including several recent and forthcoming volumes (e.g., Bowman and Ebreo, forthcoming; Bowman and St. John 2011; Chen, Li, and St. John, forthcoming; Felder and St. John 2014; Meyer, St. John, Chankseliani et al. 2013; Powers and St. John 2013; St. John, Daun-Barnett, and Moronski-Chapman 2012; St. John, Kim, and Yang 2013).

Poverty and Educational Opportunity

The preceding chapters highlight a set of interrelated underlying problems regarding the links between poverty and educational inequality: (1) the diversity in national, state, and regional contexts for educational and income inequality (policy context); (2) how the mechanisms used to promote equality and expand and equalize educational opportunity have changed over time (change in policy trajectories); and (3) how social theory can better inform the understanding of contexts and policy trajectories in replicating class and uplifting populations (social forces). It is crucial that we understand these three issues before we reconsider the roles of policy contexts and social forces when crafting policy remedies to educational inequality.

Diversity of Policy Contexts

Economic globalization has substantially altered the contexts within nations for addressing income and educational inequality (Friedman 2006; Sassan 1998). It is important to recognize that the engagement of nations in the global economy for the production of goods, services to individuals and businesses, and telecommunications technologies since the end of the Cold War has not only been accompanied by the increased wealth of engaged nations but also by increased income inequality within them (Friedman 2005; Stiglitz 2006, 2012). Within the United States, this growing income inequality further complicates efforts to understand links between education and poverty. For example, in recent decades, educational attainment has increased along with the poverty rates (Friedman 2005; Stiglitz 2012). Attempts to rethink how the global economy influences education inequality must take into account the array of national contexts affected by globalization. In addition, globalization has not affected all nations equally; developing nations continue to face challenges related to access to basic (elementary and secondary) education, while developed nations face growing inequality in opportunities for low-income students to attend college. We briefly review the arguments about policy trajectories made by the authors in this volume before discussing the framing we used to analyze the issues raised. It is crucial that educational reformers and policy advocates recognize how trajectories of policies within nations have shaped responses to neoliberal rationales for accountability and neoconservative advocacy for market remedies.

Arguments about Remedies

In this volume, East Asian (chapter 11) and Western European (chapter 8) nations emerge as models that can inform policy development, but, as these authors note, it is important to consider cultural differences across nations. Broad and sweeping generalizations about education, inequality, and development should be understood within patterns of influence over time. There is a long history of borrowing educational forms across nations, a pattern influenced by postcolonial development (Clark 1978, 1998) during the Cold War and its legacy (Kerr 1978; Stiglitz 2002); since the breakdown of the Soviet Union, internationalization has taken a different form than in the colonial and postcolonial periods (Friedman 2005; Moyn 2010; St. John 2013a; Stiglitz 2012). Our first step in interpreting these and other arguments advanced here is to place them in an evolving global context. Specifically, it is important to consider the changes in the global trajectory of education and finance policies in relation to national contexts.

First, access to basic education continues to be a challenge in underdeveloped nations, as Reimers appropriately argues in chapter 2. The Organisation for Economic Co-operation and Development (OECD) has long promoted this basic right through a number of global initiatives. At the very least, education to the level necessary to support a family represents a basic right for all in the global period, a standard still denied to the poor, especially women, in many developing nations (Nussbaum 2011). The idea that education is a human right is especially important as we consider massive transitions in college opportunities and how they came about within and across nations. In the United States, the basic human right to elementary and secondary education is being redefined to include college preparatory education for all rather than a few (chapter 7). A growing number of other scholars, educators, young people, and ordinary citizens have responded to the persistent educational inequalities facing African Americans, Latinos, American Indians, and the poor with demands for high-quality education as both a human and "constitutional" right (Perry et al. 2010; see also chapter 4).

Second, Simon Marginson's chapter (chapter 11) places nations' initiatives to expand access into context. His comparison of college enrollment rates in 1995 and 2011 across regions of the world using OECD data clearly demonstrates three groupings of nations, which have also been documented in social research: the tradition of advanced education for the social and economic *elite*, including developing nations with limited basic education; expansion of *mass* access as part of economic development, illustrated by rapidly developing nations (e.g., China and other Sino nations); and *universal* preparation for higher education, as illustrated by nations working toward universal college access for high school graduates (e.g., Western Europe and the United States). These patterns not only illustrate the stages of higher education access framed by Martin Trow (1974) but also provide a frame for discussing international differences in educational opportunity and attainment. As we ponder the problems of migrating concepts and strategies across nations, Marginson reminds us that we need to consider the role of culture.

Third, it is necessary to think critically about policy mechanisms within the trajectories of nations. For example, Marginson introduces PISA and uses this resource for comparison; however, we need to critically consider the limitations of PISA because of its potential influence on policy. The use of PISA data allows for troubling comparisons between wealthy and poor nations and cities (Meyer and Benavot 2013). For example, the right to an education in China is limited by where parents were born, which means immigrants often do not have access to local education (Rong and Chen 2013). We must be careful how we interpret data on Chinese cities that do not include low-income immigrants in their schools and, therefore, their tests.

Finally, Heath (chapter 10) raises more basic questions about the social contexts of learning in early childhood that have implications for basic research. She argues that children who live in poverty have fewer opportunities for play as well as engaging in social groups that support learning and partaking in other early social and co-experiences that influence brain development, socialization, and caring for others. She posits that museums and other cultural centers can and should be part of the outreach to children in poverty. We agree that cultural and social organizations of all types share social responsibility for finding remedies to poverty, but our analyses in the following text focus on arguments about educational systems.

We also recognize that Heath's arguments relate to basic social research on formation of capital, neurological research on brain development, and social-biology as an evolutionary force, issues we have previously discussed as they relate to the importance of reframing basic questions in the disciplines. We have argued that diversity in graduate students is needed within the disciplines and professional fields to extend the boundaries addressed in research on basic fields (St. John and Bowman 2014). In the following section, we explore how our theoretical and applied scholarship on strengths-based indicators in the selection of students for graduate school and developing interventions that support academic capital formation are among the mechanisms necessary to ensure these deeper conceptual issues are addressed.

Policy Trajectories

We consider the role of trajectories in policies within the context of national economic development, and we reconsider whether achievement tests can be used as a comparative indicator of educational quality. We argue that it is necessary to consider the problems with simplifying these measures in policy advocacy and exercise caution when interpreting measures of quality, access, and equity in relation to human rights and fairness within and across nations (Meyer, St. John, Jalava, et al. 2013). We also consider differences in contexts within developed and developing nations when comparing and analyzing policy, paying particular attention to the long-term trajectories toward expanding educational opportunity (access) and how they might increase or decrease inequality (equity). In many nations, we observe expanding access *and* increasing inequality (Goastellec 2010; Meyer, St. John, Jalava, et al. 2013). The older policy trajectories toward equity in many developed nations were disrupted by global economic competition. Many researchers have noted that inequality in educational opportunity has frequently been associated with expansion of market models as well as the movement toward universal access to higher education (Altbach 2010; Slaughter and Leslie 1997; Slaughter and Rhoades 2009; St. John 2003, 2006).

Of course there are some exceptions to the global shift toward inequality. In particular, the European Union (EU) has made efforts to decrease inequality through the Bologna Process and the Lisbon Agenda, initiatives that seek to unify and standardize European higher education (Lydon and Morgan 2013), but there are substantial differences in the ways individual European nations have constructed educational and financial policies for institutions and students (Meyer, St. John, Jalava, et al. 2013). In fact, there are substantial variations across nations in the EU in college access, the portion of college costs paid by students and their families, and the structures of educational systems, all of which are forces that can increase inequality in educational opportunity. It is important to take into account the variation within developed nations, even within European nations, when crafting arguments about borrowing educational strategies across nations (e.g., chapter 1). It is also imperative to consider how educational strategies across nations are increasingly influenced by the growing cultural diversity within nations, communities, and organizations (e.g., Janssens et al. 2010).

We also consider the legacies of the Cold War—and implicit Soviet and capitalist frameworks—when analyzing how nations develop competitive economic and educational strategies as they engage in the global economy. The U.S. model of liberalism took on distinct form in this nation after World War II, especially with the expansion of educational opportunity through the GI Bill (St. John 2013b); in addition, the American model of national governance had a substantial influence on reconstruction in Europe. Indeed, the EU commitment to promoting educational equity may have roots in the U.S. tradition of public investment in education, a path Northern European nations have lately followed better than the United States.

During the Cold War, Western scholars like Clark Kerr (1978) noted that there were advantages to the Soviet system with regard to central planning for education. The legacy of central control has made it easier for some former Soviet nations to regulate where students attend school and what they specialize in, a pattern especially evident in China (Ciupak 2013). There is also a legacy of corruption from the Soviet system, especially in European nations that had been part of the USSR (Chankseliani 2013).

Western nations face challenges as a result of their histories as well. For example, the freedom to choose educational and career pathways has been an important social value in the West, especially in the United States, with students having the opportunity to choose career or collegiate preparation as well as a standard diploma. Unfortunately, these different paths often led to the tracking of students; there were serious problems with the intersection of tracking in schools and racial segregation (Oakes 1985; chapter 7). The structure of education systems, especially the pathways open for advanced education in relation to vocational careers, is now at the center of debates. Looking again at the United States, starting in the 1980s the national policy trajectory moved away from the tradition of having vocational education available in high school toward a system of requiring college readiness for all.

More recently, there has been a renewed emphasis on linkages between careers and education (e.g., Commission on the Skills of the American Workforce 2007), and community colleges have started to focus on college transfer as a top priority rather than education for a career. In the United States, there has been a movement to reintegrate career and technical content into the college preparatory high school curriculum required for all. Strategies that link college preparatory and career education are viewed as one possible remedy to inequality, especially in urban schools (chapter 7; chapter 9). In Western Europe, technological universities are largely a separate stream of education opportunity than universities, a pattern consistent with the history of retaining diverse pathways through secondary education (Jalava 2013).

There are good reasons to raise questions about the notion that improvements in skills-based, college preparatory education will reduce income inequality. In *Capital in the Twenty-First Century*, Thomas Piketty (2014) argued that this new skills-based dispute has "a certain tautological quality . . . [because] one can 'explain' any distortion of the wage hierarchy as a result of supposed technological change" (314). In the most comprehensive analysis of causes in income inequality within developing nations, Piketty illustrates how France and other Western European nations have maintained greater income equality than the United States since 1980, despite gains in math education and SAT math scores in the United States (St. John, Daun-Barnett, and Moronski-Chapman 2012).

The underlying question raised is: *How can the U.S. educational system improve the link between education and employment in a nation with labor markets that differ radically from those of the mid-twentieth century?* Even with severe income inequality, individuals can make income gains when they have degrees that are in demand in the labor market. Both social and demographic issues are intertwined with the relationships among education, employment opportunities, and income inequality. The claim that a higher level of education—or even linking career readiness to college preparation—is a universal remedy to income inequality is a specious argument at best.

Changes in Policy Trajectories

Most of the contemporary literature regarding remedies to inequality focuses on disparity in the standards for college and career readiness, including chapters in this volume. In chapter 7, Oakes focused on raising standards and eliminating tracking systems that have historically discriminated against minorities (see also Oakes 1985). This argument has had a substantial impact on state policies to raise high school graduation requirements to college preparatory standards (St. John, Daun-Barnett, and Moronski-Chapman 2012). The movement toward markets developed in parallel had a profound influence on education reform, especially in urban areas, which was also influenced by research-informed advocacy for market approaches to reform, starting with an influential study of New York Schools by Chubb and Moe (1991). In chapter 9, Weis, Cipollone, and Stich compare student experiences with the new standards in a themed academy and a traditional high school, illustrating how students in the academy were more engaged academically.

It may be compelling to leap to the conclusion that market competition coupled with higher standards will raise the quality of schools serving students from poor neighborhoods. But we need to consider the evidence of changes in access and equity outcomes: neither the standards-driven nor market strategies have worked (Ravitch 2010). Realistically, however, whether we are proponents of either standards or markets for addressing inequality, contemporary advocates for students in urban areas must work within these mechanisms.

The overall arc toward educational equity peaked decades ago because of changes in public funding in states (United States) and nation states (internationally). In their analysis of differences in student achievement in biology across regions within the state of Missouri, Hogrebe and Tate (chapter 6) demonstrate how local differences in race and income correlate with student achievement. From this and many other studies of educational outcomes, it is clear that a uniform standard does not affect all groups in the same way, which means it is essential to consider social forces along with policy mechanisms when rethinking remedies to educational inequality. Abedi (chapter 3) and Oakes (chapter 7) agree with Hogrebe and Tate in recognizing the need to consider the role of local resources when examining the relationship between family income and educational outcomes.

Integrating Social Forces into Educational Policy Frameworks

The chapters in this volume contribute to an understanding of the social context of poverty and learning. In addition to arguing that the characteristics of neighborhoods should be considered along with income and other indicators of socioeconomic status (chapter 3; chapter 6), some of the chapters examine how social forces function as mechanisms in uplift and/or reproduction of social class.

In his discussion of social class differences, Leonardo (chapter 5) contrasts Coleman's (1966, 1988) and Marx's (Engels and Marx [1848] 2002) concepts of social class and the way it functions. Of course, Marx represents the origin of contemporary critical theory, while Coleman's concept of social capital represents a crystallization of functionalism in the American tradition. In his most important works, Coleman (1966, 1988) demonstrated how social forces undermine the intent of policy. His discovery of "White flight" after desegregation (Coleman 1966) sent shock waves through education, pointing to problems with court-ordered solutions that are now well documented: public schools in the United States are more segregated now than they were before desegregation started (Kornhaber and Orfield 2001; Orfield and Eaton 1997; Orfield et al. 2007). In his theorizing of social capital, Coleman (1988) identified three functional mechanisms—networks, information, and trust—that reinforce social reproduction in class. Focusing on altering the ways these mechanisms actually work has transformed the theory and practice of college outreach (Tierney, Corwin, and Colyar 2005; Tierney and Venegas 2007).

Two possible alternative pathways toward addressing inequality were raised by authors in this volume. Tierney (chapter 8) recognizes that there are limits to the efficacy of social interventions that promote college preparation, which is the reason he considers adapting the European model. He recognizes that tracking in U.S. schools was intertwined with racism but argues that we should reconsider dual pathways. Others promote thematic high schools, including a chapter by Oakes (chapter 7). In particular, Weis, Cipollone, and Stich (chapter 9) compare school cases to demonstrate how using a focused thematic approach in an urban high school engages low-income students, resulting in higher aspirations. In combination, these authors build a case for integrating career and technical education with higher standards.

We point to differences between Coleman's functionalist reasoning and Marx's analytic method, a distinction not made sufficiently by Leonardo (chapter 5). Recent applications of Marxist analytics reveal how social class can be reproduced across generations and that cultural capital can either reproduce class or contribute to uplift across generations (Bourdieu 1990; McDonough 1997; Winkle-Wagner, Bowman, and St. John 2012). We raise cautions about shifting to alternative mechanisms—like the thematic high schools now widely advocated or borrowing the European system that differentiates career preparation from college preparation—as a requirement for all schools or all students. That approach fails to consider context in which students live and educators work.

In particular, Snipp's analysis of American Indian education in chapter 4 provides additional insights into the social contexts for education, especially for historically oppressed racial/ethnic groups. His chapter explains how self-determination (i.e., tribal control of education systems and content) replaced cultural hegemony and contributed to transforming opportunity for American Indians. Tribal control of education is consonant with the longstanding tradition of local control of schools in the United States, but over the past three decades this tradition has eroded as a consequence of national policies. For American Indian tribes, self-determination in education substantially raised the percentage of students attaining high school diplomas and provided a process for aligning school purpose with the culture of the community, altering the implicit racial and class-based assumptions in the education system.

The representation of American Indians in higher education[2] has improved substantially during this century, actually exceeding the representation of Whites, a probable artifact of development of tribal colleges and student aid programs (St. John et al. 2013). Tribal colleges, along with specially directed scholarship programs like Gates Millennium Scholars (Tippeconnic and Faircloth 2008) and race-based grant programs (St. John, Affolter-Caine, and Chung 2007), may eventually increase retention. It is important to continue the agenda of transforming cultural barriers within mainstream higher education (Tierney 1992, 2000) and the development and expansion of tribal colleges that provide a basis for improving degree completion.

Snipp also discusses the link between high school completion and economic well-being. He questions whether high school diplomas will be sufficient to ensure a way out of poverty for American Indians. This issue may relate directly to education linking to employment, which brings us back to the possibility of reintegrating employment-related themes into U.S. high schools and the role of globalization. Snipp's chapter raises the issue of culture and engagement—concepts aligned with educational self-determination and the resulting shift away from the old model of "civilizing" American Indians and eradicating their tribal cultures—as additional forces for change. Finding culturally responsive alternatives to Eurocentric policies remains a major challenge for addressing persistent educational inequalities faced by African Americans and Latinos in segregated K–12 schools and minority-serving post-secondary institutions (e.g., Banks 2004; Gonzalez, Moll, and Amanti 2005; Gutiérrez 2006; Ladson-Billings 1994; Orellana and Bowman 2003; Rowley and Bowman 2009; Yosso et al. 2009).

Previously, we have proposed theories and methods for integrating explicit consideration of social forces into schools and colleges as well as state and national policy. St. John has argued that cultural capital—culturally situated knowledge about navigation of college and careers—is an essential part of uplift along with economic and social capital, leading to the theory of academic capital formation (ACF) (St. John 2013a; St. John, Hu, and Fisher 2010; Winkle-Wagner, Bowman, and St. John 2012). Bowman (2006, 2011) has used social psychological theory to propose and test strengths-based indicators that can inform mentoring, admissions screening, testing for admissions, and social support in college. More recently, he and his graduate students have partnered with Educational Testing Service (ETS) to develop new approaches to test graduate programs to identify students' navigational and social strengths (Bowman and Ebreo, forthcoming; Bowman and St. John 2011; St. John and Bowman, 2014). While it is not easy to reconstruct policy to explicitly consider the role of social and cultural forces, it may be necessary if we are to contend with the inequalities inherent in the current market system of education.

Reconstructing Frames for Analysis of Policy Trajectories

There is little reason to doubt that scholarship influences public finance of education. Thus far, we have noted that economic research influenced education programs after WWII, research on tracking influenced changes in graduation requirements, and research on school choice influenced the development of market strategies like charter schools. What is important and new is the argument that social research should be used to inform advocacy for social justice (chapter 7).

The Shift toward Using Policy Research for Advocacy

In the prior liberal trajectory after World War II, when the United States cre-ated the mass middle class, grand social theories informed systemic thinking about policy. The theoretical frame used in liberal-minded research from the 1950s through the 1970s was that both the social and private good should be considered when examining the role of government (e.g., Becker 1975; Blau and Duncan 1967). While progress was made (St. John 2013a), policy remedies de-veloped during this period did not remedy inequality, especially in inner cities (e.g., Jencks 1972). Interestingly, neoconservatives captured and utilized the in-equality rationale in arguments for market models (Jencks and Peterson 1991).

In recent decades, a neorational model has been adopted in U.S. education policy analysis, with research on social characteristics and educational experi-ences being used to discern significant relationships (e.g., correlation between completing algebra in high school and college success) and provide rationales for new policies (e.g., requiring algebra in middle school), followed by analyses using causal statistical methods, or other sophisticated methods, to determine effects. Subsequent research has not confirmed the untested hypotheses embed-ded in the policy rationales. For example, there had been no prior research linking state policies on algebra with the intended outcomes, and, in fact, re-search on implementation of the algebra requirements have shown no significant effect on outcomes related to test scores, high school completion, or college en-rollment rates (Allensworth et al. 2009; Daun-Barnett 2008; Daun-Barnett and St. John 2012). At a minimum, policymakers and researchers should use a better-informed approach when crafting policy recommendations.

It is important to distinguish research from advocacy (St. John 2013a). Research has been used to advocate for market reforms rationalized as being efficient and innovative. If we use research studies and reviews to consider equity along with other outcomes, as we have advocated thus far, we have a better basis for generat-ing research that is actionable in the sense that it can inform interventions to promote fairness and attempt to overcome barriers to equality; however, sound re-search must maintain an objective stance about evidence in relation to outcomes.

Framing the Comparison of Policy Trajectories

Our review and analysis of chapters in this volume and other related research projects focus on three elements in the critical analysis of policy aimed at re-ducing inequality in educational outcomes:

1. Policy Trajectories in Context: How engagement in the global economy, including shifts in employment opportunities, influences policies and outcomes within situated contexts (nations and states).
2. Links between Policies and Outcomes: The relationship between changes in underlying policy mechanisms and outcomes, including the growing inequality in educational outcomes.
3. Social Forces and Cultural Forces in Cross-Generation Uplift: How local cultures influence the ways underlying policy mechanisms correspond with changes in outcomes and how social and cultural forces interact with patterns of uplift and reproduction.

Whether policy analysts and researchers use functional assumptions (e.g., neoliberal, rational analytics) or critical social frames (e.g., neo-Marxism analytics), we argue that there are benefits to taking these three steps before leaping to policy solutions. Not only is there consonance between focusing on the role of social forces in educational outcomes, as Leonardo (chapter 5) argues, but the central question is similar in either case: Will a specific policy change reinforce patterns of inequality or will it change them?

Public Policy and Inequality in Educational Opportunity

Motivated by engagement in the global economy, most nations have expanded access to higher education in the past two decades (chapter 11), but this has been accompanied by increasing inequality in wealth and access to high-quality institutions (Meyer, St. John, Jalava, et al. 2013). Using the chapters in this volume as a starting point, we examine this problem from a comparative global perspective before drilling further into the role of policy in remedying inequality within U.S. education systems.

Adding an Emphasis on Social Justice to Research on Access and Inequality

Based on the set of studies of national systems conducted in this and other recent volumes (e.g., Meyer, St. John, Jalava, et al. 2013; St. John, Kim, and Yang 2013), table 12.1 summarizes challenges among developing nations (Group I), rapidly developing nations (Group II), formerly communist nations (Group III), and developed nations (Group IV); we examine evidence from recent case studies of two or three nations in each group. Given the complexity of China, it is in two groups: China-A is part of Group II because of its accelerated

Table 12.1 Global framework applied to access and inequality developments and challenges across nations

	Status of educational access	Policy and financial challenges
	Group I: Developing nations	
A. South Africa (Nieuwenhuis and Sehoole 2013; Meyer, St. John, Jalava, et al. 2013; Somers et al. 2013)	• Expanding access in K–12 and higher education • Extreme inequality in education of Blacks compared to Whites	• Expanding education for Africans as strategy for fairness and economic development • Use of affirmative action in historically White universities
B. Colombia (Uribe 2013)	• Expanding educational opportunity, especially vocational-technical • Decline in state funding and increased tuition	• Greater gains in access for low-income than high-income families • Regional inequalities in access to universities due to tuition
C. Chile (Espinoza and González 2013)	• Expansion of private universities and rise in student costs • Oversupply of professionals	• Student protest movement (in 27 of 60 universities) • Modest government response but continuation of model
	Group II: Rapidly developing nations	
A. China-A (Marginson, this volume; Ciupak 2013; Rong and Chen 2013)	• Rapid movement to mass higher education following economic uplift • Extreme inequality in educational opportunity (urban–rural divide) • One-child policy influences family investment in children	• Substantial government investment in education, especially engineering and science (E&S) • Concentration on E&S education (highly constrained choice for many in peasants and rural students) • Pending revision of admissions testing
B. South Korea (Heath, this volume; Marginson, this volume; Kim and Kim 2013)	• Government policies promote quality basic education for all • Comprehensive state control (decentralized party control) • Deep infusion of communist party into academic governance	• Emphasis on STEM education across the system • Privatization of postsecondary education with high loans • Government-enforced fairness policy • Government constrains tuition in public colleges

C. Brazil (Somers et al. 2013; Meyer, St. John, Jalava, et al. 2013; Ritter dos Santos, in press)	• Strong government support for commercialization of research • Use of affirmative action as a strategy for achieving fairness

Group III: Formerly Soviet nations

A. Georgia (Chankseliani 2013)	• Legacy of Russian model of central control • Strong evidence of corruption • Middle class funds private options for college preparation • Extremes in inequality perpetuated within the system
B. China-B (Marginson, this volume; Chen, Li, and St. John, forthcoming)	• Emphasis on capitalism rather than democracy in transition • Legacy of Soviet system evident • Reinvesting in traditional models • Low actualization of policies on participatory governance • Tasking by government primary mechanism for change (and opportunity to improve fairness)

Group IV: Developed nations

A. Western Europe (Lydon and Morgan 2013; Tierney, this volume)	• Highest global rates of college enrollment (universal access) • High tax rates and substantial investment in education • Strong cultural traditions in education and universities • Strong European tradition, accelerated after World War II (Marshall Plan) • Public finance of educational opportunities • High taxation and shared benefits of economic development

(continued)

Table 12.1 (continued)

	Status of educational access	Policy and financial challenges
	Group IV: Developed nations (continued)	
1. Germany (Kroth 2013; Meyer, St. John, Jalava, et al. 2013)	• Slowed educational progress after consolidation of East and West Germany • Strong commitment to both traditional and technical universities	• Evidence of declining enrollment as artifact of loans • Class-based pattern of college choice
2. Finland (Jalava 2013; Meyer, St. John, Jalava, et al. 2013)	• Substantial funding of institutions and students • Emphasizing growth of technical higher education • Quality challenges in traditional universities	• Concern about declining quality of colleges • Class-based pattern of educational choice
B. United States (multiple chapters in this volume; St. John et al. 2013)	• History of K–12 for all in most states since late nineteenth century • College grant aid expanded in 1950s (GI Bill) and 1965–80 (federal need-based grants) • Federal K–12 programs focused on raising high school graduation standards • Market models in K–12 (charters), especially in urban areas • High tuition and loans in higher education due to changes in state and federal financing of higher education	• Led the world in education and science attainment from World War II until early 1980s • Decline in high school graduation rates after 1980s (especially in urban areas) • Improved SAT math scores and participations rates (1990–2010) • Increased inequality in access to four-year colleges • College encouragement programs • High tuition, high loan approach related to low tuition and high grants

educational and economic development, and China-B is part of Group III because vestiges of the old communist system constrain equity in opportunity.

Middle Eastern nations were not explicitly discussed by the authors in this volume, but the brief period of antigovernment protest in 2011, known as the Arab Spring, raised interesting questions about human rights and aspirations for them within these nations. For example, Stiglitz (2012) argued that the Arab Spring and the "99%" protests in the United States harkened a new period of global transformational change; certainly, there was also evidence of protest about educational costs in the United States and Latin America during this period (Meyer, St. John, Jalava, et al., 2013). Further, since there has been recent rapid expansion of higher education in some of the Arab nations, with some seeking to develop globally competitive universities (Wildavsky 2009), there may be reason to speculate about movement toward greater rights in these nations. We are mindful of the very substantial differences in human rights in Islamic nations compared to nations that have developed with the secular tradition of Western Europe; as John Rawls (1999b) noted, we should not judge human rights in the Middle East through the same lens we use for social democratic societies. In addition, Benjamin Friedman (2005) noted that human rights have remained extremely limited in oil-rich nations like Saudi Arabia. So we expect actual ground-level change toward greater democracy with an emphasis on human rights will be gradual in the Middle East, rather than sudden. Since none of the chapters in this volume explicitly examined these nations, we do not speculate further about the trajectory toward educational and human rights in the Middle East.

Developing Nations

As Reimers argues in chapter 2, access to basic education remains a challenge in most developing nations, with those with the greatest poverty having the least access (Oduaran and Bhola 2006; Sen 2009). It is apparent that the reasons for inequality vary across developing nations and are influenced by regional patterns and national legacies, as illustrated by three nations:

- Colombia had high privatization, typical of Pacific region countries, but funded student grants to expand access for low-income students (Uribe 2013);
- Chile also had substantial privatization but had excessive student debt and widespread student protest with only modest changes (Espinoza and González 2013); and

- South Africa went through a democratic transformation, including the use of grants and affirmative action to expand college access for Blacks, but systemic inequalities in basic education impeded progress (Nieuwenhuis and Sehoole 2013).

Rapidly Developing Nations

The rapidly developing nations illustrate a relationship between economic development and education through coordinated policy across sectors. Marginson (chapter 11) demonstrates that South Korea and China-A are experiencing rapid economic development and expansion of educational opportunity. Both have strong national control of education and industry and expanded access but have not overcome inequality. South Korea regulates tuition charges by private colleges (Kim and Kim 2013) and has systemic education policies promoting fairness in basic education. Its use of privatization and government cost control result in low costs, and could lessen inequality; however, there is substantial evidence that wealthier families learn how to navigate through policy mechanisms promoting fairness, including lottery schemes for allocating access to high-quality elementary and secondary schools, to maintain advantages for their children. Thus, while Marginson's argument that there is a strong cultural foundation for expanding educational opportunity is correct, there are persistent and troublesome patterns of inequality.

China-A is often portrayed as making progress in access and economic development, but inequality remains. Like South Korea, China's strong governmental control of education systems and both national and state strategies for investment in scientific research accelerate quality improvement in traditional indicators like scientific publications and test scores (see chapter 11). With the legacy of the one-child policy in China, parents have additional incentives to invest in their child as a means of maintaining or improving their status, because in Chinese culture, children are expected to provide for their parents in old age (Chen, Li, and St. John, forthcoming). The values and culture in China undoubtedly contribute to educational success, but state control has helped.

Brazil is another nation often noted as an exemplar of rapid economic development. Through investments in commercialization and science (e.g., alternative energy), the country has made rapid economic progress (Ritter dos Santos, forthcoming). Brazil has also taken steps toward overcoming its legacy of slavery and segregated education (Somers et al. 2013). With privatized higher education, Brazil uses student grants and affirmative action in admissions to lessen its historic inequality but has not yet overcome its deeply embedded legacy.

Post-Soviet Nations

Rapid globalization post–Cold War has obfuscated the legacy of the centralized education and economic planning central to the Soviet model. As Marginson illustrates in chapter 11, there have been substantial gains in access in Eastern Europe, a region that includes many former Soviet states with mixed success on economic progress. To understand inequality in education in former Soviet countries, the China-B and Georgia cases provide insight.

In the rush to perestroika (Gorbachev 1987), the Soviet system turned to capitalism and democracy, but neither economic nor social democratic change has been easy. In many of the Eastern European nations, the economic transition was based on providing extremely low-cost labor for clothing manufacturing and other industries, the petty side of global capitalism (Smart and Smart 2005). Education was viewed as a way out of poverty. The universities and basic education systems in these countries started to create pathways to better education, but the Georgia case (Chankseliani 2013) illustrated how corruption complicated this transition. Many avenues into advanced education, including buying paths around meritocratic admissions, favored the middle class.

After the Tiananmen Square protests of 1989, China chose to pursue capitalism but remained a communist state. The nation moved toward economic and educational opportunity, but the change came through adaptation of the party structure, which was hierarchical and community based. Today, colleges and other educational systems often have a party secretary as well as a president. Many orders for change come through this system, constraining local democratic change. Change advocates in China who are committed to social justice face complicated choices about how to work within the system, and there are very few opportunities to change the system from outside of it, even in the private sector. For example, the party plays a role in negotiating agreements with global corporations and western universities.

The China-B case illustrates the underlying inequality related to the old Soviet system. Specifically, the right to a basic education is situated in the parents' home community, so rural families have limited access to basic education when they migrate to cities for employment, leading to savage inequalities in basic education access (Rong and Chen 2013). Since so many immigrants from rural to urban areas are excluded from basic education, there are many good reasons to question the meaning of test scores from PISA. In addition, pending changes in admissions testing will further complicate any move toward greater fairness in educational opportunity.

Recognition of the underlying forces behind changes in the Soviet system in China and the former Soviet countries helps us understand how strategies evolve. The former Soviet nations have a rhetorical and philosophical commitment to local democracy (e.g., Engels and Marx [1848] 2002) and actually some success in building infrastructure though centralized educational planning; however, these older mechanisms of control had local elements that were adapted in China-B but broke down in post-Soviet Georgia. Regardless of the structure of social control, there is evidence in both nations that families with economic resources frequently use them to support education for their children, and, like most nations engaged in the global economy, wealth disparities are growing.

Developed Nations

Developed nations in Western Europe and North America have entered a period of nearly universal access to higher education. Northern Western Europe has made the greatest progress and, as Tierney argues in chapter 8, the United States could probably learn from the European model.

Northern European nations were assisted in rebuilding after World War II with support from the Marshall Plan. They adopted democratic constitutions and systems of taxation that supported the development of educational and social infrastructure, similar to the ethos of public investment in the United States after World War II (e.g., GI Bill, mortgages backed by the Veterans Administration; St. John 2013b). The U.S. trajectory through multiple presidential administrations was of increased state and federal investment in both basic and higher education, establishing a new global progressive standard that included equity and expansion of opportunity (St. John 2003, 2006). While this changed in the 1980s due to a myopic focus on college preparation and a decline in student need-based grants because of reductions in state and federal taxes, Northern European nations moved toward greater social equity, even after the breakup of the Soviet Union.

In addition to leading the world in access, Western Europe nations have established new avenues for intellectual exchange, especially through the Bologna Process. For example, it appears that Chinese scholars are engaged in publishing with scholars across networks as part of the transformation of the scholarly community (Clements 2013). Interestingly, networks of trust are evolving across nations and within disciplinary areas that simultaneously constrain and expand exchange (Lydon and Morgan 2013). It may be easier for graduate students to take advantage of learning opportunities across nations within Europe than it is within the United States.

Still, there are substantial, growing inequalities within European nations, as evident in Finland (Jalava 2013) and Germany (Kroth 2013). These highly progressive nations have systems for access to technical higher education and universities that often reinforce class reproduction despite government generosity to students from low-income families through assessment tests that essentially sort students, a mandatory process that was never fully developed in the United States, although there was tracking within comprehensive high schools and urban educational systems (Oakes 1985; chapter 7). Finland and Germany have followed different pathways to investment in higher education: Germany maintains a stronger resource commitment to their universities than Finland, where there are more concerns about quality (Meyer, St. John, Jalava, et al. 2013).

Compared to the Northern European standards, the United States has fallen behind (chapter 11; chapter 8). Based on analyses of trends in policies and outcomes, multivariate studies, and case studies, there has been a convergence of: (1) changes in K–12 policy, emphasizing college preparation for all with no real funding for these reforms in most states; and (2) cuts in per-student funding of undergraduates in public colleges, leading to higher tuition and a shift to loans as a primary mechanism for financing low- and middle-income college students (St. John 1994, 2003, 2006).

Diversity in Opportunity within the United States

A major undertaking in this volume has been the examination of links between poverty and educational outcomes, including arguments based on basic research examining this linkage (e.g., chapters 2 and 3), applied policy scholarship (e.g., chapters 4 and 11), and critical essays (e.g., chapters 7 and 8). Among these new contributions, chapter 4 gives us the most cause to reflect on prior critical scholarship on U.S. policy. Snipp provides a policy perspective situated in the perspective of native peoples, including American Indians and Mexicans. He illustrates the substantial differences in the histories of these groups and their inclusion, exclusion, and representation in U.S. education.

Trajectory of Educational Policy Change in the United States after the Cold War

There is evidence that the trajectory of educational and public finance policies changed more substantially in the United States than in Western Europe after the Cold War. Economists have argued that the end of the Cold War was evidence that capitalism had won the battle against communism, fueling the neoconservative argument for market models and less public funding. While many scholars have critically examined the neoliberal rationales for transforming education through the use of standards, testing, and accountability (e.g., Henry et al. 2001; Meyer and Benavot 2013), it is essential to consider more fully how both neoconservative and neoliberal rationales influenced the trajectory of educational policy if we are to build a better understanding of how to move forward.

The trajectories of education and public finance policies in the mid-1970s compared to the mid-2010s are outlined in table 12.2. Four policy mechanisms are examined: funding of schools and colleges, supplemental programs for underrepresented groups, market mechanisms and regulation, and testing and accountability.

The reconstructed trajectory of federal and state education policy decreased emphasis on supplemental education and direct government regulation of educational practices in K–12. While federal programs were retained, Title I shifted from supplemental education for high-need students within high-poverty schools to school-wide programs, and special education students were mainstreamed (i.e., moved to regular classrooms) to the extent possible. Urban schools have been subjected to successive waves of reform models, creating trade-offs between improving achievement test scores and retaining low performers in their grades (St. John et al. 2006; Wong 2012). The mainstreaming of students diagnosed as having special learning needs complicates the comparison of test scores across periods. The shift away from federal regulation of educational practices was accompanied by an increased emphasis on testing and curriculum alignment, replacing one form of control with another.

The idea that regulation of K–12 education actually decreased at the local level is highly suspect because of the ways state and local administrations responded to the new accountability regime. Urban districts used their centralized regulatory processes to seize greater control of curriculum and instruction through accountability. The fact that unions had to negotiate with

Policy and funding mechanisms	Patterns in mid-1970s: Progressive reform trajectory (1880–1980)	Patterns in mid-2010s: Post–Cold War reform trajectory
Direct funding of schools and colleges	• Formulas based on adequacy, excellence, and fairness • State and local funding for K–12 subject to litigation (e.g., cases in Texas and California) • Higher education funding often based on master plans and peer studies	• Per-student funding in public schools and charter schools (less emphasis on adequacy and fairness in K–12 in urban schools) • Decline of formula funding in state budgeting for higher education; new pattern of substitution of tuition for declining state revenues
Market mechanisms	• K–12: Middle income families exercised *school choice* by moving to suburbs • Higher education: Need-based grants for low-income students; loans generally available	• Charter schools compete for resources with public schools with money following students • High-loan, high-tuition outcome of changes in financing policies at state and federal levels
Regulatory controls	K–12 • Federal regulation of K–12 practices for ESEA programs • State and local regulation of schools	K–12 • Federal emphasis on standards (Common Core) • District control of curriculum to align with standards in public schools • Greater freedom to adapt education programs in charter schools

Continued

Table 12.2 (Continued)

	Patterns in mid-1970s: Progressive reform trajectory (1880–1980)	Patterns in mid-2010s: Post–Cold War reform trajectory
Policy and funding mechanisms	Higher education • State coordination (often includes approval of new programs, especially in public colleges) • Controls on spending	Higher education • Low-cost community colleges (most courses taught by part-time faculty) • Revenue-based budget models increase flexibility (especially in research universities)
Testing and accountability	• Tests used as part of tracking within K–12 schools • State testing systems used to monitor quality • Tests used for admission to most four-year colleges	• K–12: Tests used in accountability (aligned curriculum and tests) • Higher education has fended off most attempts at federal regulation through Title IV (student aid programs)
Outcomes	• Tracking limited college choices for many high school graduates • Strong employment options for vocational graduation in industrial economy • College enrollment rates nearly equal across racial and ethnic groups (contributions of HBCUs and outreach to minority enrollment)	• Decline in the industrial economy alters employment opportunities for vocational graduates • After a decline, recent improvement in high school graduation rates • Mixed results on achievement (improved SAT/ACT math scores but not SAT/ACT English; decline on NAEP; poor international comparisons) • Increased inequality in enrollment in four-year colleges (by income and race)

districts rather than schools reinforced the rigidity. The result was too often more constraints on teachers and teaching methods.

The new trajectory also increased emphasis on markets and testing in K–12 education, but it is difficult to untangle the consequences of these strategies. In contrast, both the average level of funding and increases in funding were associated with improved outcomes controlling for other factors. The evidence regarding achievement outcomes is mixed, especially for standardized tests. Across the states, there was a decline in high school graduation rates following implementation of higher graduation requirements, although there have been recent gains (St. John, Daun-Barnett, and Moronski-Chapman 2012).

In higher education, the shift away from formula funding and need-based grants had serious consequences. Rising tuition and debt have complicated efforts to make sense of the consequences of three decades of K–12 reform. The increased sorting of students, with higher numbers of low-income students entering two-year colleges, is especially problematic.

Along with labor force inequality, historical and sociopolitical factors that impact educational policies also promote poverty. We used Snipp's analyses as a starting point (see table 12.3) for examining how the change in trajectories of U.S. educational policy have influenced three groups: emigrant peoples, including Europeans (Group 1); African Americans, many of whom were brought to this continent originally as slaves before the Civil War (Group 2); and native peoples, differentiating between American Indians and Mexican Americans (Groups 3a and 3b). Of course, a brief review of this type cannot give full and fair treatment to literature related to all of these groups.[3] We use our understandings of the research literature on poverty, race, and educational opportunity along with our review of these chapters to consider inequality within the four groups and how the new inequality and post–Cold War policy trajectory have affected each of these groups.

It is appropriate to consider the origins of these groups, a point Snipp drives home in his analysis. It is clear that the early British colonists were immigrants, while American Indians were native to the continent and Mexican Americans were native to the Southwestern United States before American rebellions and wars in the region. African Americans originally came to the new world as slaves and have historically faced segregation, racism, and policy mechanisms that increased inequality.

Table 12.3 Access and inequality for groups within the United States population

U.S. population groups	Access and inequality	Policy and finance challenges
Immigrant populations (European, as well as Asian, after World War II)	• Shift from supplemental education to education for all advantaged middle class • Suburban schools (first "schools of choice" after desegregation) had stronger base for shift to higher standards than urban or rural schools • Inequality in funding continues to advantage middle-class schools	• College representation improved in public four-year colleges following improved college preparation • Large debt burden for many graduates • Underemployment for most undergraduates (millennial generation) • College graduation rates rise • Income comparison to underrepresented minorities
African Americans	• *Legacy of racial isolation:* slavery; denied education opportunity before 1954; desegregation attempted (after *Brown* in 1954) and higher education (after *Adams* in 1977) • Underfunding of schools • Decline in pull-out programs that provided supplemental education in favor of school-wide reforms	• Schools and colleges more segregated than before desegregation • Essentially equal opportunity for college enrollment in the middle 1970s, but gap reopened 1980–2000 • Under match in college quality for many low-income, minority high school graduates • Growing overrepresentation in two-year and for-profit colleges • Extreme loan debt for African Americans
Native populations	*American Indians* • BIA schools introduce American culture (complex patterns of racial identity); • Self-determination expands educational opportunity *Mexican Americans* • Segregated schools (California) • New immigrants denied fair access (especially to college) • Variable responses to Dream initiative for illegal immigrants (in-state tuition and state grants) across states	*American Indians* • Higher college enrollment rates (as percentage of population) than Whites (may be artifact of census race/ethnic reporting) • Lower college degree attainment than other groups • Education not well aligned with economic development in tribal areas *Mexican Americans* • More extreme underrepresentation than Whites, Asians, and American Indians • Some modest, recent signs of progress but resistance in some states

Source: Adapted from St. John, Daun-Barnett, and Moronski-Chapman (2013); informed by Snipp (this volume).

Immigrant Populations (Mostly European and Asian)

An examination of the history of educational opportunity across groups since 1980 shows substantial gains in rates of high school graduation, college going, and enrollment in four-year colleges for Asian Americans, while Whites have maintained their status (St. John, Daun-Barnett, and Moronski-Chapman 2012). Interestingly, post–World War II, despite the internment of Japanese Americans in camps during the war and the fact that mainland China became a communist state, Asian Americans overall benefited from the "American Dream." While some recent immigrant groups remain underrepresented in higher education, especially Hmong Americans, it is apparent that even they do not experience severe prejudice but instead face the challenge of building support for cross-generation uplift (Lee 2014; Lee and St. John 2012).

Even though Whites maintain their status compared to other groups, the rising net cost of college and debt burden in the context of the new economy that has driven down wages have caused problems for growing numbers of middle- and low-income Whites. In particular, the high debt burden and under-employment of college graduates has meant that many low- and middle-income Whites delay marriage, home ownership, and other benefits of the middle class, themes that were emphasized in the 99% movement this decade, causing Stiglitz (2012) to speculate about whether citizen revolt would change policy; Meyer (2013) has also considered whether student revolts in Chile and California might yield radical changes in the global trajectory.

African Americans

To understand the achievement gaps for African Americans, it is necessary to look at urban schools because of the high proportion of African Americans in many of the largest cities in the United States. Unfortunately, successive waves of reforms have failed to address the challenges in urban schools (Mirón and St. John 2003; Payne 2008).

The historical problems in urban education are intertwined with a sequence of events prior to the post–Cold War reform trajectory: the migration of African Americans to the north for better jobs starting in the 1930s resulted in de jure segregation, followed by migration of middle-class urban Whites to suburbs after desegregation orders (Orfield 1988, 1992). It is hard to overlook the implicit White self-protectionist attitude underlying reforms in the post–Cold War period; these reforms redirected federal and state funds to favor wealthier school districts by directing resources toward the good of all students rather than students with special needs or programs to meet the most critical challenges.

As Mark Hogrebe and William Tate demonstrate in their study of Missouri school reform (chapter 6), structural inequality is not seen just in urban areas. They found that after controlling for poverty, the concentration of African Americans also influences achievement of equality regardless of whether the district is urban, rural, or suburban. To correct this, they recommend an approach tailored to the learning needs of students within local communities, not a new practice but one that is too seldom used. It is time to rethink how education policy can be honed to accelerate learning in schools serving low-income African Americans, an approach that has been successful for American Indians in tribal areas (chapter 4).

There was a strong tradition of African American education before desegregation (Anderson 1988; Du Bois 1973; Siddle Walker 1996; Siddle Walker and Snarey 2004; Woodson 1933). To be sure, African American education in the twentieth century was profoundly shaped by the "accommodationist" policies negotiated by Booker T. Washington for both the South and the North (Anderson 1988; Washington 1901). However, W. E. B. Du Bois (1973) advanced a more progressive tradition of educational uplift across generations that also advocates for struggle against racial barriers within educational and social systems. Similar to Snipp, both W. E. B. Du Bois (1973) and Carter G. Woodson (1933) critiqued Eurocentric educational policies that indoctrinated African Americans to become dependent and settle for inferior places in the greater society rather than empowering them for uplift and self-determination.

Anderson's (1988) award-winning book, *The Education of Blacks in the South*, traces the strong African American commitment to education as the pivotal pathway to both economic mobility and community uplift across the generations, from ex-slaves in the 1860s through the depression era in the 1930s. Despite evolving race-related barriers, a growing body of scholarship documents the powerful effects of a strong African American commitment to cross-generation uplift (e.g., Ladson-Billings 1994; Rowley and Bowman 2009; Tripp 1987), the encouragement of which has emerged as a core component of exemplary interventions to reduce educational inequalities and promote talent development in science, technology, engineering, and mathematics (STEM) fields (e.g., Hrabowski, Maton, and Greif 1998; Hrabowski et al. 2002; Martin 2000; Moses and Cobb 2001).

When we compare trends in outcomes for African Americans compared to Whites, we see a troubling picture (St. John, Daun-Barnett, and Moronski-Chapman 2012). Growing numbers of college-prepared African Americans graduate from high school and enroll in two-year rather than four-year colleges. This is referred to as an "under-matching" problem (Bowen, Chingos, and McPherson 2009), leading to a new generation of research that considers whether information on student aid can influence students to consider applying to four-year colleges (Hoxby and Avery 2012; Hoxby and Turner 2012). While there is reason to question whether information will make a difference, it is evident from research on several initiatives (e.g., Gates Millennium Scholars, Washington State Achievers, and Carolina Covenant©) that guaranteed student aid coupled with student support services can attract and retain African Americans in elite colleges (St. John, Hu, and Fisher 2010; St. John, Ort, and Williford 2012).

Native Populations

The fact that Snipp combined Mexican Americans with American Indians in his critique of policy was especially revealing. In particular, it is crucial to note how gains in K–12 high school graduation followed self-determination in education on reservations.[4] The analysis on national trends provides evidence that American Indians enroll in college at a higher rate than Whites, something attributed to tribal colleges and race-conscious student aid (St. John, Affolter-Caine, and Chung 2007), but access alone is not sufficient. Snipp discusses employment and college graduation rates as intertwined problems. While the legalization of gambling and development of casinos on reservations has improved the financial well-being of some tribal communities, gambling is not the type of economic development that provides jobs for college graduates, a problem shared by the states of Mississippi and Louisiana and other locales with casinos. But the economic challenges in rural tribal areas are fundamentally different than poverty in New Orleans and the Mississippi Gulf Coast. On reservations, self-determination in education has not been a catalyst for new economic development. Economic challenges can be found in many other parts of the country (Dalton, Bigelow, and St. John 2012), but most of the rest of rural America has not experienced the hegemony, prejudice, and violence that has plagued American Indians.

Looking Forward

The link between poverty and educational inequality has been durable over time, as the chapters in this volume demonstrate, but it is not a static relationship. At present, the increasing income inequality within nations engaged in the global economy, and more of the U.S. population entering poverty, comes as access to education expands. However, the correlation between college access and inequality does not mean education causes inequality, nor the reverse. We argue that it is important to consider the pivotal role of policy in both access and inequality as well as how the role of policy has changed as part of the global transition. Our aim in this conclusion has been to focus explicitly on the role of policy in reducing education inequality. As a final step, we look forward in a speculative way to possible strategies to reduce inequality. Responding to Jeannie Oakes's argument, we consider the roles of researchers and social justice advocates in redefining educational rights, providing social support for uplift across generations, and adapting policy mechanisms to achieve these aims.

Promoting Rights to Education

The international progress on human rights in recent decades provides a potential balancing mechanism with pursuit of market efficiencies, providing a consensus that such rights can be constructed within nations. Across nations, it is increasingly evident from international trends that a redefinition of education rights is underway as part of the global economic transition. Thus, redefining the meaning of rights necessarily precedes debate over fairness in access to these rights, consonant with John Rawls's (1999a) lexical order.

Right to Basic Education

The education rights debate is more than rhetorical in that it involves fundamental changes in the relationship between education and work. We agree with Nussbaum's (2011) argument that basic education should include the humanities and her earlier argument that women—and indeed, we argue, all citizens—should have the right to an education that enables them to support their families (Nussbaum 1999). In the United States, this definition has shifted from a basic high school education to which all students are supposed to have access (college *or* vocation ready) to a standard of students being both college *and* career ready. At this time, most other nations have maintained traditional and career tracks, providing two pathways; it is appropriate to consider the progression and possible future of the U.S. model.

The shift in the definition of basic educational rights in the United States necessitates a transformation of the role of high schools. This change is underway but has not progressed well in many instances, especially in urban and rural systems that serve high concentrations of low-income students. The government is obligated to provide an education that meets the standards for *all*, not just a few. An example of how this has failed is math education: the methods of instruction once thought to be most effective did not fit the learning needs of many low-income students (e.g., Martin 2000; Moses and Cobb 2001).

Perhaps research informing policymakers and practitioners about approaches that can be used by schools and in classrooms can help them reach the goal of college- and career-ready education for more, if not all, students. For example, Weis, Cipollone, and Stich (chapter 9) found that thematic schools may be more engaging for low-income urban students than schools that simply implement the new standards. Hogrebe and Tate (chapter 6) demonstrate the limitations of one-size-fits-all biology education and argue for a differentiated approach. Thematic schools provide a more strategic means for aligning high school curriculum with career readiness, but this approach can alter content in advanced math, social sciences, and other areas, further undermining a tight alignment of standards and curriculum content and their appropriate delivery to all students. But we should not confuse college readiness with the reduction of poverty or possibly gains in college opportunity if there is not adequate financial aid.

Equal Educational Opportunity and Wealth Inequality

Fairness in access to advanced education—collegiate and other postsecondary—becomes even more crucial when an increasing number of careers require degrees. In theory, alignment of college preparatory courses with career content can help students prepare for college, but this approach pushes family decisions about education and career pathways into middle schools; this may be difficult for some families because not all have an adequate level of college and career knowledge. Further, even when students graduate from high school ready for college, the high-tuition and high-loan collegiate marketplace can severely constrain college choices for low- and middle-income students who do not qualify for generous merit scholarships.

Fairness in access to college is an especially important topic for research informing policy and practice. Along with inequalities in both K–12 and higher education, funding inequality is a major issue. Political advocacy for fair funding can be informed by high-quality studies that analyze the impact of different funding practices on educational outcomes; however, since the one goal is to improve college success as measured by the percentage of students who complete college, it is crucial to also build understanding of the social forces that support educational attainment.

We are cautious about claiming that the goal of education reform is to reduce wealth inequality or redistribute wealth because, as Piketty (2014) clearly demonstrates, the trajectory to wealth inequality in the United States after 1980 was undeterred by gains in educational quality or attainment. Indeed, thirty years of reforms with at least modest effect (St. John et al. 2013) illustrate that education improvement—raising standards and related test scores—can co-vary with increases in wealth inequality. So it is simply fallacious to further suggest that improvement in education will reduce income inequality in the nation unless there are fairer and just economic policies, as there is in Scandinavia and continental Western Europe (Piketty 2014).

Social Support for Educational Uplift

Universal college preparation and college/postsecondary enrollment have become widely accepted and advocated goals in many developed nations, including the United States. Moving forward, we anticipate two very complex and interrelated issues will confront educators and families engaged in this massive shift in expectations: (1) forces that maintain family culture (e.g., reinforce working-class values) must transform to promote cross-generation uplift and (2) the development of diverse social forces for uplift must become integral to create better educational pathways to professional careers.

Social Forces Supporting Uplift

The aims of increasing college preparation, access, and success to a universal standard not only redefine education as a right of citizenship but also may alter the patterns of cultural maintenance in families. Our studies of education intervention programs for low-income students in middle schools, high schools, and colleges confirm the importance of mentoring and other social support. Mentoring and related social support reinforce the development of higher education and career goals and also provide students with new information that they share with their families. Easing family concerns about college costs is integral to promote student and family willingness to engage in the extracurricular programs provided by these interventions (St. John, Hu, and Fisher 2010; Winkle-Wagner, Bowman, and St. John 2012).

The transition to obtaining some education beyond high school (e.g., technical postsecondary education) is easier for many working-class families to consider than the excessive borrowing that would be needed to pay for four-year degrees to enter teaching, nursing, or other middle-class professions; another barrier is that these professions often pay less than technical positions. Studies of patterns of postsecondary enrollment in developed nations with high levels of access illustrate that most students from poor and working-class families end up attending technical/technician programs rather than four-year colleges.

It may be difficult to integrate understanding of advanced educational pathways in families with deep cultural patterns of class reproduction. Building this understanding can be facilitated by mentoring from professionals with backgrounds similar to their mentee students who are facing the challenges of uplift or mentoring by adults who understand students with diverse backgrounds (Dalton, Bigelow, and St. John 2012; Harper et al. 2012; Lee and St. John 2012; Turner 2012). When parents aspire for a better life for their children *and* they can envision this as a realistic possibility, uplift is easier to actualize.

Building Students' Strengths in Advanced Education

With the growing number of college-qualified high school graduates and the under matching in enrollment (i.e., students choosing lower-quality colleges for which they are qualified), it is past time to rethink the exclusive use of merit-aware indicators in admissions to include other measures such as strengths-based indicators. While class rank has worked as a selection mechanism to support diversity at the University of Texas (Tienda and Niu 2006; Tienda, Alon, and Niu 2008), there is still a great need to holistically recognize students' strengths in admission to advanced programs.

Based on decades of research, the Educational Testing Service (ETS) has developed the Personal Potential Index (ETS® PPI), an innovative noncognitive assessment system to promote more diversity, equity, and fairness in graduate and professional school admissions (Burris et al. 2011; Kyllonen 2005, 2008; Walpole et al. 2002). In addition to test scores, using measures of skills related to knowledge, integrity, resilience, communication, teamwork, and organization can yield diversity among students who meet the basic academic

Table 12.4   Summary of major social indicators for assessment
systems and social support

ETS PPI	Sedlacek–NCQ	Bowman–SAS
Knowledge/integrity	Long-term goals Positive self-concept Knowledge in a field	Path-goal motivation Academic self-efficacy Career-related efficacy
Resilience/communication	Realistic self-appraisal Handling the system	Resilient problem-solving Diversity commitment
Teamwork/organization	A strong support person Leadership experience Community involvement	Perceived social support Leadership commitment Service commitment

Source: Adapted from St. John and Bowman (2014).

qualifications for admission to graduate and professional programs. The ETS®PPI is consistent with two evidence-based approaches to promote greater diversity and equity in admissions: William Sedlacek's (2004) noncognitive variables, already widely adapted for innovative holistic assessment in college admissions, and Bowman's (2011) strengths-based assessment system (SAS), a related approach grounded in social psychological theory and research (see table 12.4). These approaches can give admissions committee members a wide range of resources to improve diversity in undergraduate, graduate, and professional programs (Bowman and St. John 2011; St. John and Bowman 2014).

The SAS approach helps clarify similarities and differences in the operation of noncognitive strengths toward successful intervention outcomes across underrepresented students from diverse backgrounds, based on race, gender, and income (Bowman 2006, 2011). In work currently underway with support from the National Institutes of Health, three cross-cultural propositions are being explored: (1) diverse underrepresented students bring both universal (etic) and group-specific (emic) cultural strengths to pipeline intervention settings, (2) both etic and emic cultural strengths can enhance intervention efficacy and benefits for underrepresented students, and (3) both etic and emic cultural strengths can *buffer* the adverse effects of systematic barriers that often *impede* intervention efficacy and reduce benefits for underrepresented students.

Researchers can play a substantial role in the development of new practices and policies to ensure fairness in admission and college support. For example, Bowman involved researchers from ETS and ACT, as well as independent researchers including William Sedlacek, in the exchange of ideas for research leading to the development of SAS (Bowman and St. John 2011). Basic research is needed to further validate SAS, and additional actionable intervention research is needed to inform the development of innovative practices and new policies.

Adapting Policy Mechanisms

Changes in education policy aimed at reducing poverty and promoting opportunity have been more rapid in some regions of the world than others. Western Europe remains the icon for directly promoting expansion of college access, while Korea, the United States, and other Pacific region countries have used market mechanisms to indirectly expand access, unfortunately accelerating inequality in wealth, education, and living standards.

Changing Policy Mechanisms within the Global Trajectory

There are diverse patterns of policy within nations engaged in the global economy. There is also a long history of borrowing systemic forms of education across diverse educational systems, evident from English and Spanish colonization in the Americas forward through Cold War development of a cross-national Soviet approach to educational planning and institutional development. The post–Cold War development of market models and accountability schemes has been a global phenomenon affecting various nations in different ways.

Within the context of globalizing loan schemes, testing, and other neoliberal policy mechanisms, it is especially interesting how patterns of resistance and adaptation have evolved. For example, South Korea not only ranks high on college access but has also used government control on tuition and other forms of social and economic control to achieve this expansion of access at low public cost (Kim and Kim 2013; St. John, Kim, and Yang 2013). In contrast, Northern European nations have high access, but have maintained a high government investment in institutions and students (Kroth 2013; Meyer, St. John, Jalava, et al. 2013). The argument has been made that the United States should look to the Western European model (chapter 8; Lydon and Morgan 2013), but before considering adapting this model, we need to ponder how the American liberal model of funding was adapted in Western Europe after World War II, discussed earlier in the chapter. We must also consider that critiques of accountability and market models have been more strenuous in Europe than in the United States (Meyer, St. John, Jalava, et al. 2013), while the U.S. literature focuses more on how to make new market-driven accountability systems work, perhaps a necessity given the extensive investment in change.

This volume has raised questions about how nations can learn from one another. As Marginson demonstrates in chapter 11, understanding cultural context is vitally important when assessing the feasibility of borrowing systemic strategies. In addition, Snipp (chapter 4) illuminates the role of self-determination among marginalized racial/ethnic groups as a significant force within the U.S. education system. As we have demonstrated in our thought experiments, we think these perspectives can be valuable for researchers who engage in comparing strategies and systems and considering what features can be adapted.

In this chapter, we have also focused on a set of policy mechanisms (funding, supplemental programs, regulation, testing, and accountability) to illustrate how the trajectories of policies have changed as part of globalization. Further research can add substantially to the collective understanding of how these new mechanisms have been rationalized as a means of expanding access, improving fairness, reducing inequality, improving quality, and improving efficiency; researchers must also uncover how well these policies have achieved these goals. While we provide an initial illustration of this type of reasoning, the empirical research base for such comparisons is still limited.

It is also important to periodically reconsider the purposes of education and how well various systems achieve them (Meyer 2013). Our argument has been that fairness and equity have lagged in recent decades, and we agree with Jeannie Oakes's argument that more social and educational researchers should tackle the problem of conducting research to inform adaptive change.

State and Local Change

Given the trajectories of policy within nations engaged in the global economy, including the widespread use of testing linked to accountability and market mechanisms rationalized based on false efficiencies, it is important to consider how institutions adapt to new policy regimes. In addition to global cross-national adaptations, it is crucial to build an understanding of local and institutional adaptive change in education. For example, one of the principles behind the multilevel standards movement has been that schools could have flexibility in the ways they organized to reach the new standards (Finn 1990; Ravitch 2010). However, implementation of standards in public schools has tended to reduce local flexibility because of the need to align tests and curriculum with standards. In this volume, several authors focused on standards-related adaptive changes in schools: Oakes addressed the context of urban school reform; Weiss et al. illustrated the role of school comparisons; and Hogrebe and Tate argued for a differentiated approach to teaching biology, an advanced science often required for high school graduation.

While we hope for reduction in income inequality and poverty in the United States, these social conditions have little to do with education policy per se. Certainly, we encourage rethinking of economic policies in the United States so we, like most of the nations in Western Europe, can enjoy greater fairness. However, we do not expect education reform per se to solve this problem, nor should self-respecting educational scholars use such tautological and unsound reasoning. Instead, we hope for more thoughtful dialogue and action about U.S. economic policies in relation to wealth distribution and fairness in life opportunities.

Conclusion

For several decades, there have been many claims of a looming education crisis. Indeed, the process of claiming crisis to advocate for new policies has been widely used since the publication of Earl F. Cheit's (1971) *New Depression in Higher Education* by the Carnegie Foundation. In K–12 education, this approach has been widely used since the publication of *A Nation at Risk* (U.S. Department of Education 1983). Indeed, conjecture about crises has become a common tool in the political arsenal of neoliberal and neoconservative reformers. To step past this crisis orientation, it is important to gain perspective on the trajectory of change. Perhaps the claims about crises in education are related to false hopes that education can solve economic problems created by faulty public finance policies. Instead of looking for a magic solution, it is time to begin the serious business of solving educational problems created by grand solutions that may have been well intended but were seldom well conceived.

This volume has concentrated on the role of education in reducing poverty and inequality in the twenty-first century. The authors have stepped back from the common pattern of claiming crisis to examine underlying causes and possible remedies. Our review placed this research into a historical perspective that considers the role of social, economic, and educational polices in the post–World War II period through the period of acceleration of the global economy since the end of the Cold War. Six concluding themes have emerged from our comparative analyses.

First, there is no simple solution to inequality, although some nations have made greater progress since the end of the Cold War than others. Nations that adhered to an old liberal model of investing in institutions and students (e.g., Norway and Germany) and nations with strong central control (e.g., China and South Korea) have made more substantial gains in educational attainment than the United States, which has more completely adopted the neoliberal policies of accountability coupled with market mechanisms within polycentric governing systems. All of these systems are deeply situated within national cultures, which hopefully reinforce the efficacy of the policy mechanisms used.

Second, in the United States the idea that capitalism had beat communism during the Cold War was used to rationalize new market and accountability strategies for education. If we contrast Western Europe and the United States, it would be easy to conclude that Western Europe's resistance to neoliberal market reforms accelerated success, but the South Korea case defies this simple explanation. In addition, it appears that both Western Europe and South Korea had strong cultural alignment with education strategies used to accelerate the transition to universal access.

Third, the challenge in accelerating access to education in the United States has been influenced by the shift from a high school system with both college preparatory and vocational tracks to a system that emphasized both college and career readiness. College readiness was consistently defined as completing a college preparatory curriculum, while the older vocational tracks gave way to higher-order conceptions of professions that required college (e.g., health, engineering, and science). This new standard represented a cultural shift for many working-class Americans and was implemented during a postindustrial period when older factory jobs were in decline and increasing levels of debt were necessary for the typical student to graduate from college. Driven by global forces, these new policy patterns were not congruent with the working-class cultural traditions of many American families, especially in urban and rural areas that were hard hit by economic dislocation.

Fourth, the history of racial discrimination in the United States has further undermined attempts to implement higher standards in areas with historical working-class cultures. The older methods of vocational and college preparatory tracks were intertwined with racial discrimination (e.g., segregated schools, reservation schools, and differentiated vocational and preparatory high schools in cities). With the explicit focus on high standards, the new public school model was set up for failure because many schools lacked the history, culture, and resources for success. In addition, greater attention should have been paid to the social and culture contexts of educational uplift in both urban and rural areas that faced the greatest challenges when attempting to transform schools to meet the new standards.

Fifth, a community resource hypothesis posits that the formation of social and cultural capital for family and community uplift, along with the new STEM-based rationale for human capital, may be necessary to accelerate the pace of reform in urban communities in the twenty-first century. We refer to interventions that facilitate the development of human, social, and cultural capital to support cross-generation uplift as *academic capital formation*. While a few of the chapters in this volume illuminate the need for a differentiated approach to reform of public and charter schools, we also looked at evidence from other research to explore the community resources hypothesis for uplifting marginalized populations. While a growing number of studies provide some support for this hypothesis, future research needs to provide more definitive empirical evidence. We especially encourage researchers to work with social justice advocates in local schools and community-based organizations to build a better knowledge base related to the pivotal roles of family, social, cultural, and human resources in cross-generational educational uplift.

Sixth, after many decades the field of noncognitive measures of student strengths is beginning to mature, with a better theoretical ground and more empirical evidence generated by national testing organizations. The systematic assessment of students' diverse strengths provides information that can be used in both holistic admissions and cradle-to-career pipeline interventions. Viable strengths-based assessment systems provide opportunities for researchers to examine the efficacy of educational interventions to support the development of the social-psychological strengths that are necessary for student success in both college and careers, especially given the diversifying population.

We suspect that academic capital formation is one of the mechanisms through which students develop the skills needed for social and career navigation and success, but this hypothesis needs to be further validated by more rigorous strengths-based intervention research. Multilevel strengths-based research also needs to clarify the role of educators and community organizations as vital resources in efforts to improve mentoring, social support, and family knowledge of educational and career pathways as part of the academic capital formation process.

The Northern European model of public finance should be further studied, but the implicit tracking in the European systems of education is unlikely to be a successful model for the United States. The coordination of policies evident in South Korea and China is noteworthy, but since American educational systems are highly polycentric in governance, it would be difficult to more tightly align policies. Indeed, given the roles of local discretion and adaptation built into the system in the United States, tight alignment of policy and regulation does not appear to be a workable solution to inequality; instead, the implementation of common standards and tight accountability has been accompanied by increased inequality. In addition, the loan-based scheme of college finance creates legitimate concerns about college affordability, work burden, and lifelong indebtedness. Certainly, there is a lot for the United States to learn from international comparisons, but it is important to pay attention to the ways social, financial, and cultural matters influence educational inequality.

NOTES

1. For example, in contracted research on a project for the U.S. Department of Education, St. John was asked to use Milton Friedman's book as a guiding framework for a paper on economic returns from federal investment in student financial aid (St. John and Masten 1990). Although the report documented the substantial tax revenue returns from federal spending on need-based student aid in the 1970s, federal policy began to emphasize loans rather than grants (Hearn and Holdsworth 2004).

2. Measured by the ratio of the percentage of college full-time equivalent students (FTEs) enrolled in a state compared to the percentage of the group in the state's population (St. John, Daun-Barnett, and Moronski-Chapman 2012).

3. In a recent e-mail, Michael Olivas reminded me that I had overlooked the substantial literature on Mexican Americans in a new book, *Public Policy and Higher Education*, which I published with Nate Daun-Barnett and Karen Moronski-Chapman. In particular, I had underemphasized the historical struggle of Mexican Americans in the California case.

4. Given his comprehensive treatment of these developments, we refer readers back to his chapter if they want to know more about American Indian K–12 education.

REFERENCES

Allensworth, Elaine, Takako Nomi, Nicholas Montgomery, and Valerie E. Lee. 2009. "College Preparatory Curriculum for All: Academic Consequences of Requiring Algebra and English I for Ninth Graders in Chicago." *Educational Evaluation and Policy Analysis* 31 (4): 367–91.
Altbach, Philip G. 2010. "Preface." In *Understanding Inequalities in, through, and by Higher Education*, edited by Gaële Goastellec, vii–ix. Boston: Sense Publishers.

Anderson, James D. 1988. *The Education of Blacks in the South, 1860–1935.* Chapel Hill: University of North Carolina Press.

Banks, James A. 2004. *Handbook of Research on Multicultural Education.* 2nd edition. San Francisco: Jossey Bass.

Becker, Gary S. 1975. *Human Capital: A Theoretical and Empirical Analysis, with Special Consideration of Education.* 2nd edition. New York: National Bureau of Economic Research.

Blank, Rebecca M. 2011. *Changing Inequality.* Berkeley: University of California Press.

Blau, Peter M., and Otis D. Duncan. 1967. *The American Occupational Structure.* New York: Wiley.

Bourdieu, Pierre. 1990. *Reproduction in Education, Society, and Culture.* London: Sage.

Bowen, William G., Matthew M. Chingos, and Michael S. McPherson. 2009. *Crossing the Finish Line: Completing College at America's Public Universities.* Princeton, NJ: Princeton University Press.

Bowman, Phillip J. 2006. "Role Strain and Adaptation Issues in the Strength-Based Model: Diversity, Multilevel, and Life-Span Considerations." *Counseling Psychologist* 34 (1): 118–33.

———. 2011. "Diversity and Merit in Higher Education: Challenges and Opportunities for the 21st Century." In *Diversity, Merit, and Higher Education: Toward a Comprehensive Agenda for the Twenty-First Century, Readings on Equal Education, Volume 25,* edited by Phillip J. Bowman and Edward P. St. John, 17–36. New York: AMS Press.

Bowman, Phillip J., and Angela Ebreo. Forthcoming. "Rethinking Stem Pipeline Interventions: A Strengths-Based Agenda for the 21st Century." In *Readings on Equal Education, Volume 28,* edited by Phillip J. Bowman and Edward P. St. John. New York: AMS Press.

Bowman, Phillip J., and Edward P. St. John. 2011. "Diversity, Merit, and Higher Education: Toward a Comprehensive Agenda for the Twenty-First Century." In *Diversity, Merit, and Higher Education: Toward a Comprehensive Agenda for the Twenty-First Century Readings on Equal Education, Volume 25,* edited by Phillip J. Bowman and Edward P. St. John. New York: AMS Press.

Burris, Jeremy, Carolyn MacCann, Patrick C. Kyllonen, and Richard D. Roberts. 2011. "Noncognitive Constructs in K–16: Assessments, Interventions, Educational and Policy Implications." In *Diversity, Merit, and Higher Education: Toward a Comprehensive Agenda for the Twenty-First Century, Reading on Equal Education, Volume 25,* edited by Phillip J. Bowman and Edward P. St. John, 233–74. New York: AMS Press.

Chankseliani, Maria. 2013. "Higher Education Access in Post-Soviet Georgia: Overcoming a Legacy of Corruption." In *Fairness in Access to Higher Education in a Global Perspective: Reconciling Excellence, Efficiency, and Justice,* edited by Heintz-Dieter Meyer, Edward P. St. John, Maria Chankseliani, and Lina Uribe, 171–88. Rotterdam, The Netherlands: Sense Publications.

Cheit, Earl F. 1971. *The New Depression in Higher Education.* New York: McGraw-Hill.

Chen, Wang, Xu Li, and Edward P. St. John. Forthcoming. *Globalization and Social Justice: U.S. and Chinese Perspectives.* New York: AMS Press.

Chubb, John E., and Terry M. Moe. 1991. "Schools in a Marketplace: Chubb and Moe Argue Their Bold Proposal." *The School Administrator* 48 (1): 18, 20, 22, 25.

Ciupak, Yan Z. 2013. "On the Nexus of Local and Global: Educational Choice in China during the Era of Globalization." In *Issues in Globalization and Social Justice: Comparative Studies in International Higher Education, Volume 3.* New York: AMS Press.

Clark, Burton R. 1978. "Concepts, Models, and Perspectives." In *Academic Power: Patterns of Authority in Seven National Systems of Higher Education,* edited by John H. Van de Graff, 164–90. New York: Praeger.

———. 1998. *Creating Entrepreneurial Universities: Organizational Pathways to Transformation*. Oxford: Pergamon Press.

Clements, Margaret M. 2013. "The Global Invisible College: Knowledge Networks and Academic Patenting." In *Higher Education, Commercialization, and University-Business Relationships in Comparative Context: Issues in Globalization and Social Justice; Comparative Studies in International Higher Education, Volume 2*, edited by Joshua Powers and Edward P. St. John, 89–112. New York: AMS Press.

Coleman, James S. 1966. *Equality of Education Opportunity Study*. ICPR 3689-v 3. Ann Arbor, MI: Inter-University Consortium for Political and Social Research.

———. 1988. "Social Capital in the Creation of Human Capital." *American Journal of Sociology* 94:S95–S120.

Commission on the Skills of the American Workforce. 2007. *Tough Choices, Tough Times: The Report of the New Commission on Skills of the American Workforce*. Washington, DC: National Center on Education and the Economy.

Dalton, Rick, Victoria Bigelow, and Edward P. St. John. 2012. "College for Every Student: A Model for Postsecondary Encouragement in Rural Schools." In *Expanding Postsecondary Opportunity for Underrepresented Students: Theory and Practice of Academic Capital Formation Readings on Equal Education, Volume 26*, edited by Rachelle Winkle-Wagner, Phillip J. Bowman, and Edward P. St. John, 181–204. New York: AMS Press.

Danziger, Sheldon H., and Daniel Weinberg. 1986. *Fighting Poverty: What Works and What Doesn't*. Cambridge, MA: Harvard University Press.

Daun-Barnett, Nathan J. 2008. "Preparation and Access: A Multi-level Analysis of State Policy Influences on the Academic Antecedents to College Enrollment." PhD diss., University of Michigan.

Daun-Barnett, Nathan J., and Edward P. St. John. 2012. "Constrained Curriculum in High Schools: The Changing Math Standards and Student Achievement, High School Graduation and College Continuation." *Education Policy Analysis Archives* 20 (5): 1–25.

Du Bois, W. E. B. 1973. *The Education of Black People: Ten Critiques, 1906–1960*. New York: Monthly Review Press.

Engels, Friedrich, and Karl Marx. [1848] 2002. *The Communist Manifesto*. London: Penguin Classics.

Espinoza, Oscar, and Luis E. González. 2013. "Causes and Consequences of the Student Protests in Chile." In *Fairness in Access to Higher Education in a Global Perspective: Reconciling Excellence, Efficiency, and Justice*, edited by Heintz-Dieter Meyer, Edward P. St. John, Maria Chankseliani, and Lina Uribe, 239–58. Rotterdam, The Netherlands: Sense Publications.

Felder, Pamela F., and Edward P. St. John, eds. 2014. *Supporting Graduate Students in the 21st Century: Implications for Policy and Practice. Readings on Equal Education, Volume 27*. New York: AMS Press.

Finn, Chester E., Jr. 1990. "Why We Need Choice." In *Choice in Education: Potential and Problems*, edited by William L. Boyd and Herbert J. Walberg, 3–20. Berkeley, CA: McCutchan Publishing Corporation.

Friedman, Benjamin M. 2005. *The Moral Consequence of Economic Growth*. New York: Vintage.

Friedman, Milton. [1962] 2002. *Capitalism and Freedom*. Chicago: University of Chicago Press.

Friedman, Thomas L. 2006. *The World Is Flat: A Brief History of the 21st Century*. New York: Farrar, Straus & Giroux.

Goastellec, Gaële, ed. 2010. *Understanding Inequalities In, Through, and By Higher Education*. Boston: Sense Publishers.

Gonzalez, Norma, Luis C. Moll, and Cathy Amanti. 2005. *Funds of Knowledge: Theorizing Practices in Households, Communities, and Classrooms*. Mahwah, NJ: Erlbaum.

Gorbachev, Mikhail S. 1987. *Perestroika: New Thinking for Our Country and the World*. San Francisco: HarperCollins.

Gutiérrez, Kris D. 2006. *Culture Matters: Rethinking Educational Equity*. New York: Carnegie Foundation.

Hansen, W. Lee, and Burton A. Weisbrod. 1967. *An Income Net Worth Approach to Measuring Economic Welfare*. Madison: Institute for Research on Poverty, University of Wisconsin.

Harper, Shaun R., Collin D. Williams, David Pérez II, and Demetri L. Morgan. 2012. "His Experience: Toward a Phenomenological Understanding of Academic Capital Formation among Black and Latino Male Students." In *Expanding Postsecondary Opportunity for Underrepresented Students: Theory and Practice of Academic Capital Formation, Readings on Equal Education, Volume 26*, edited by Rachelle Winkle-Wagner, Phillip J. Bowman, and Edward P. St. John, 65–88. New York: AMS Press.

Hearn, James C., and Janet M. Holdsworth. 2004. "Federal Student Aid: The Shift from Grants to Loans." In *Public Funding of Higher Education: Changing Contexts and New Rationales*, edited by Edward P. St. John and Michael D. Parsons, 40–59. Baltimore: Johns Hopkins University Press.

Henry, M., Bob Lingard, Fazal Rizvi, and S. Taylor. 2001. *The OECD, Globalization and Education Policy*. Amsterdam: Pergamon Press.

Hoxby, Caroline M., and Christopher Avery. 2012. *The Missing One-Offs: The Hidden Supply of High-Achieving, Low Income Students*. Working Paper 18586. Cambridge, MA: National Bureau of Economic Research.

Hoxby, Caroline, and Sarah Turner. 2012. *Expanding College Opportunities for Low-Income, High-Achieving Students*. NBER Working Paper 18728. Stanford, CA: Stanford Institute for Economic Policy Research.

Hrabowski, Freeman A., Kenneth I. Maton, Monica L. Greene, and Geoffrey L. Greif. 2002. *Overcoming the Odds: Raising Academically Successful African-American Young Women*. New York: Oxford University Press.

Hrabowski, Freeman A., Kenneth I. Maton, and Geoffrey L. Greif. 1998. *Beating the Odds: Raising Academically Successful African-American Males*. New York: Oxford University Press.

Jalava, Marja. 2013. "The Finnish Model of Higher Education Access: Does Egalitarianism Square with Excellence?" In *Fairness in Access to Higher Education in a Global Perspective: Reconciling Excellence, Efficiency, and Justice*, edited by Heintz-Dieter Meyer, Edward P. St. John, Maria Chankseliani, and Lina Uribe, 79–94. Rotterdam, The Netherlands: Sense Publications.

Janssens, Maddy, Myriam Bechtoldt, Arie de Ruijter, Dino Pinelli, Giovanni Prarolo, and Vanja M. K. Stenius. 2010. *Sustainability of Cultural Diversity: Nations, Cities, and Organizations*. Cheltenham, UK: Edward Elger.

Jencks, Christopher. 1972. *Inequality: A Reassessment of the Effect of Family and Schooling in America*. New York: Basic Books.

Jencks, Christopher, and Paul E. Peterson, eds. 1991. *The Urban Underclass*. Washington, DC: Brookings Institution.

Kerr, Clark. 1978. *12 Systems of Higher Education: 6 Decisive Issues*. New York: International Council for Educational Development.

Kim, Jiyun, and Hee S. Kim. 2013. "Globalization and Access to Higher Education in Korea." In *Fairness in Access to Higher Education in a Global Perspective: Reconciling Excellence, Efficiency, and Justice,* edited by Heintz-Dieter Meyer, Edward P. St. John, Maria Chankseliani, and Lina Uribe, 129–52. Rotterdam, The Netherlands: Sense Publications.

Kornhaber, Mindy, and Gary Orfield. 2001. *Raising Standards or Raising Barriers? Inequality and High Stakes Testing in Public Education.* New York: Century Foundation Press.

Kroth, Anna J. 2013. "The Effects of College Cost and Financial Aid in Germany: Why Are Students Sensitive to College Costs in a Low-Cost/High-Aid System?" In *Fairness in Access to Higher Education in a Global Perspective: Reconciling Excellence, Efficiency, and Justice,* edited by Heintz-Dieter Meyer, Edward P. St. John, Maria Chankseliani, and Lina Uribe, 153–70. Rotterdam, The Netherlands: Sense Publications.

Kyllonen, Patrick C. 2005. *The Case for Noncognitive Assessments (R&D Connection No. 4).* Princeton, NJ: Educational Testing Services.

———. 2008. *The Research behind the ETS Personal Potential Index.* Princeton, NJ: Educational Testing Services.

Ladson-Billings, Gloria. 1994. *The Dreamkeepers: Successful Teachers of African American Children.* San Francisco: Jossey Bass.

Lee, Malisa. 2014. "Hmong Americans' Predisposition to College: A Qualitative Study." PhD diss., University of Michigan.

Lee, Malisa, and Edward P. St. John. 2012. "Academic Capital Formation among Hmong Students: An Exploratory Study of the Role of Ethnic Identify in College Transitions." In *Expanding Postsecondary Opportunity for Underrepresented Students: Theory and Practice of Academic Capital Formation, Readings on Equal Education, Volume 26,* edited by Rachelle Winkle-Wagner, Phillip J. Bowman, and Edward P. St. John, 89–116. New York: AMS Press.

Lydon, Julie, and Bob Morgan. 2013. "The Bologna Process and the Lisbon Agenda: Implications for European Higher Education." In *Higher Education, Commercialization, and University-Business Relationships in Comparative Context. Issues in Globalization and Social Justice: Comparative Studies in International Higher Education, Volume 2,* edited by Joshua B. Powers and Edward P. St. John, 145–66. New York: AMS Press.

Martin, Danny B. 2000. *Mathematics Success and Failure among African-American Youth: Roles of Sociohistorical Context, Community Forces, School Influence and Individual Agency.* London: Lawrence Erlbaum.

McDonough, Patricia M. 1997. *Choosing Colleges: How Social Class and Schools Structure Opportunity.* Albany: State University of New York Press.

Meyer, Heintz-Dieter. 2013. "Reasoning about Fairness in Access to Higher Education: Common Sense, Normative, and Institutional Perspectives." In *Fairness in Access to Higher Education in a Global Perspective: Reconciling Excellence, Efficiency, and Justice,* edited by Heintz-Dieter Meyer, Edward P. St. John, Maria Chankseliani, and Lina Uribe, 15–40. Rotterdam, The Netherlands: Sense Publications.

Meyer, Heintz-Dieter, and Aaron Benavot. 2013. *PISA, Power, and Policy: The Emergence of Global Educational Governance.* Oxford: Symposium Books.

Meyer, Heintz-Dieter, Edward P. St. John, Maria Chankseliani, and Lina Uribe, eds. 2013. *Fairness in Access to Higher Education in a Global Perspective: Reconciling Excellence, Efficiency, and Justice.* Rotterdam, The Netherlands: Sense Publications.

Meyer, Heintz-Dieter, Edward P. St. John, Marja Jalava, Anna J. Kroth, and Patricia Somers. 2013. "Fairness in Access to Higher Education: Towards a Global Public

Debate." In *Fairness in Access to Higher Education in a Global Perspective: Reconciling Excellence, Efficiency, and Justice*, edited by Heintz-Dieter Meyer, Edward P. St. John, Maria Chankseliani, and Lina Uribe, 277–88. Rotterdam, The Netherlands: Sense Publications.

Mirón, Louis F., and Edward P. St. John. 2003. "Implications of the New Global Context for Urban Reform." In *Reinterpreting Urban School Reform: Have Urban Schools Failed, or Has the Reform Movement Failed Urban Schools?*, edited by Louis F. Mirón and Edward P. St. John, 299–326. Albany: State University of New York Press.

Moses, Robert P., and Charles E. Cobb. 2001. *Radical Equations: Math Literacy and Civil Rights*. Boston: Beacon Press.

Moyn, Samuel. 2010. *The Last Utopia: Human Rights in History*. Cambridge, MA: Harvard University Press.

Nieuwenhuis, Jan, and Chika Sehoole. 2013. "The Quest for Access, Equity and Social Justice in Higher Education in South Africa." In *Fairness in Access to Higher Education in a Global Perspective: Reconciling Excellence, Efficiency, and Justice*, edited by Heintz-Dieter Meyer, Edward P. St. John, Maria Chankseliani, and Lina Uribe, 189–202. Rotterdam, The Netherlands: Sense Publications.

Nussbaum, Martha C. 1999. *Sex and Social Justice*. Oxford: Oxford University Press.

———. 2011. *Creating Capabilities: The Human Development Approach*. Cambridge, MA: Belcamp Press.

Oakes, Jeannie. 1985. *Keeping Track: How Schools Structure Inequality*. New Haven, CT: Yale University Press.

Oduaran, Akpovire, and Harbans S. Bhola, eds. 2006. *Widening Access to Education as Social Justice: Essays in Honor of Michael Omolewa*. New York: Springer.

Orellana, Marjorie F., and Phillip J. Bowman. 2003. "Cultural Diversity Issues in Learning and Development: Conceptual, Methodological and Strategic Considerations." *Educational Researcher* 32 (5): 26–33.

Orfield, Gary. 1988. "Exclusion of the Majority: Shrinking College Access and Public Policy in Metropolitan Los Angeles." *Urban Review* 20 (3): 147–63.

———. 1992. "Money, Equity, and College Access." *Harvard Educational Review* 62:337–72.

Orfield, Gary, and Susan E. Eaton. 1997. *Dismantling Desegregation: The Quiet Reversal of Brown v. Board of Education*. New York: Free Press.

Orfield, Gary, Patricia Marin, Stella M. Flores, and Liliana M. Garces. 2007. *Charting the Future of College Affirmative Action: Legal Victories, Continuing Attacks, and New Research*. Los Angeles: Civil Rights Project, UCLA School of Education.

Payne, Charles M. 2008. *So Much Reform, So Little Change: The Persistence of Failure in Urban Schools*. Cambridge, MA: Harvard Education Press.

Perry, Theresa, Robert P. Moses, Joan T. Wynne, Ernesto Cortes Jr., and Lisa Delpit. 2010. *Quality Education as a Constitutional Right: Creating a Grassroots Movement to Transform Public Schools*. Boston: Beacon Press.

Piketty, Thomas. 2014. *Capital in the 21st Century*. New York: Belknap Press.

Powers, Joshua B., and Edward P. St. John, eds. 2013. *Higher Education, Commercialization, and University-Business Relationships in Comparative Context. Issues in Globalization and Social Justice: Comparative Studies in International Higher Education, Volume 2*. New York: AMS Press.

Ravitch, Diane. 2010. *The Death and Life of the Great American School System: How Testing and Choices Are Undermining Education*. New York: Basic Books.

Rawls, John. 1999a. *A Theory of Justice*. Cambridge, MA: Harvard University Press.

———. 1999b. *The Laws of Peoples*. Cambridge, MA: Harvard University Press.

Ritter dos Santos, Marli E. Forthcoming. "University Technology Transfer in Brazil."
    In *Higher Education, Commercialization, and University-Business Relationships in
    Comparative Context, Issues in Globalization and Social Justice, Volume 2*, edited by
    Joshua B. Powers and Edward P. St. John. New York: AMS Press.
Rong, Liying, and Rong Chen. 2013. "Educational Development in China: Policy and
    Access." In Privatization and Inequality: Comparative Studies of College Access,
    Education Policy, and Public Finance, Globalization and Social Justice, Volume 1, edited
    by Edward P. St. John, Jiyun Kim, and Lijing Yang, 105–37. New York: AMS Press.
Rowley, Larry L., and Phillip J. Bowman. 2009. "Risk, Protection, and Achievement
    Disparities among African American Males: Cross-Generation Theory, Research
    and Comprehensive Intervention." *Journal of Negro Education* 78 (3): 305–20.
Sassan, Saskia. 1998. *Globalization and Its Discontents: Essays on the New Mobility of People
    and Money*. New York: The New Press.
Sedlacek, William E. 2004. *Beyond the Big Test: Noncognitive Assessment in Higher
    Education*. San Francisco: Jossey-Bass.
Sen, Amartya. 2009. *The Idea of Justice*. Cambridge, MA: Belknap.
Siddle Walker, Vanessa. 1996. *Their Highest Potential: An African American School
    Community in the Segregated South*. Chapel Hill: University of North Carolina Press.
Siddle Walker, Vanessa, and John Snarey, eds. 2004. *Race-ing Moral Formation: African
    American Perspectives on Care and Justice*. New York: Teachers College Press.
Slaughter, Sheila E., and Larry L. Leslie. 1997. *Academic Capitalism: Politics, Policies, and
    the Entrepreneurial University*. Baltimore: Johns Hopkins University Press.
Slaughter, Sheila E., and Gary Rhoades. 2009. *Academic Capitalism and the New Economy:
    Markets, State, and Higher Education*. Baltimore: Johns Hopkins University Press.
Smart, Alan, and Josephine Smart. 2005. "Introduction." In *Petty Capitalists and
    Globalization: Flexibility, Entrepreneurship, and Economic Development*, edited by Alan
    Smart and Josephine Smart, 1–22. Albany: State University of New York Press.
Somers, Patricia A., Marilia Morosini, Miriam S. Pan, and James E. Cofer. 2013.
    "Brazil's Radical Approach to Expanding Access." In *Fairness in Access to Higher
    Education in a Global Perspective: Reconciling Excellence, Efficiency, and Justice*, edited by
    Heintz-Dieter Meyer, Edward P. St. John, Maria Chankseliani, and Lina Uribe,
    15–40. Rotterdam, The Netherlands: Sense Publications.
Stiglitz, Joseph E. 2002. *Globalization and Its Discontents*. New York: W. W. Norton.
———. 2006. *Making Globalization Work*. New York: W. W. Norton.
———. 2012. *The Price of Inequality: How Today's Divided Society Endangers Our Future*.
    New York: W. W. Norton.
St. John, Edward P. 1994. *Prices, Productivity and Investment: Assessing Financial Strategies in
    Higher Education*. ASHE/ERIC Higher Education Report No. 3. Washington, DC:
    George Washington University, School of Education and Human Development.
———. 2003. *Refinancing the College Dream: Access, Equal Opportunity, and Justice for
    Taxpayers*. Baltimore: Johns Hopkins University Press.
———, ed. 2006. *Public Policy and Equal Educational Opportunity: School Reforms,
    Postsecondary Encouragement, and State Policies on Postsecondary Education, Readings on
    equal education, Volume 21*. New York: AMS Press.
———. 2013a. *Research, Actionable Knowledge, and Social Change: Reclaiming Social
    Responsibility through Research Partnerships*. Sterling, VA: Stylus.
———. 2013b. "The Legacy of the GI Bill: Equal Opportunity in U.S. Higher Educa-
    tion after WWII." In *Fairness in Access to Higher Education in a Global Perspective:
    Reconciling Excellence, Efficiency, and Justice*, edited by Heintz-Dieter Meyer, Edward P.

St. John, Maria Chankseliani, and Lina Uribe, 57–76. Rotterdam, The Netherlands: Sense Publications.

St. John, Edward P., Brittany Affolter-Caine, and Anna S. Chung. 2007. "Race-Conscious Student Financial Aid: Constructing an Agenda for Research, Litigation, and Policy Development." In *Charting the Future of College Affirmative Action: Legal Victories, Continuing Attacks, and New Research*, edited by Gary Orfield, Patricia Marin, Stella M. Flores, and Liliana M. Garces, 173–204. Los Angeles: Civil Rights Project, UCLA School of Education.

St. John, Edward P., and Phillip J. Bowman. 2014. "Race Neutrality and Diversity in Graduate and Professional Education." In *Supporting Graduate Students in the 21st Century: Implications for Policy and Practice, Readings on Equal Education, Volume 27*, edited by Pamela F. Felder and Edward P. St. John, 3–37. New York: AMS Press.

St. John, Edward P., Nathan J. Daun-Barnett, and Karen M. Moronski-Chapman. 2012. *Public Policy and Higher Education: Reframing Strategies for Preparation, Access, and Success.* New York: Routledge.

St. John, Edward P., Carol-Anne Hossler, Glenda Droogsma Musoba, Choong-Geun Chung, and Ada B. Simmons. 2006. "Comprehensive School Reform: Intervention Designs, Teacher Practices, and Classroom Outcomes." In *Public Policy and Equal Educational Opportunity: School Reforms, Postsecondary Encouragement, and State Policies on Postsecondary Education, Readings on Equal Education, Volume 21*, 127–63. New York: AMS Press.

St. John, Edward P., Shouping Hu, and Amy S. Fisher. 2010. *Breaking through the Access Barrier: Academic Capital Formation Informing Public Policy.* New York: Routledge.

St. John, Edward P., Jiyung Kim, and Lijing Yang, eds. 2013. *Privatization and Inequality: Comparative Studies of College Access, Education Policy, and Public Finance. Globalization and Social Justice, Volume 1.* New York: AMS Press.

St. John, Edward P., and Charles L. Masten. 1990. "Return on the Federal Investment in Student Financial Aid: An Assessment of the High School Class of 1972." *Journal of Student Financial Aid* 20 (3): 4–23.

St. John, Edward P., Shirley Ort, and Lynn Williford. 2012. "Carolina Covenant: Reducing the Retention Gap." In *Expanding Postsecondary Opportunity for Underrepresented Students: Theory and Practice of Academic Capital Formation, Readings on Equal Education, Volume 26*, edited by Rachelle Winkle-Wagner, Phillip J. Bowman, and Edward P. St. John, 235–54. New York: AMS Press.

Tienda, Marta, Sigal Alon, and Sunny X. Niu. 2008. *Affirmative Action and the Texas Top 10 Percent Admission Law: Balancing Equity and Access to Higher Education.* theop .princeton.edu/reports/wp/AffirmativeAction_TopTen.pdf.

Tienda, Marta, and Sunny Niu. 2006. "Capitalizing on Segregation, Pretending Neutrality: College Admissions and the Texas Top 10% Law." *American Law and Economics Review* 8:312–46.

Tierney, William G. 1992. "An Anthropological Analysis of Student Participation in College." *Journal of Higher Education* 63 (6): 603–18.

———. 2000. "Power, Identity, and the Dilemma of College Student Departure." In *Reworking the Student Departure Puzzle*, edited by John M. Braxton, 213–34. Nashville, TN: Vanderbilt University Press.

Tierney, William G., Zoë B. Corwin, and Julia E. Colyar, eds. 2005. *Preparing for College: Nine Elements of Effective Outreach.* Albany: State University of New York Press.

Tierney, William G., and Kristan Venegas. 2007. "The Cultural Ecology of Financial Aid Decision Making." In *Confronting Educational Inequality: Reframing, Building*

Understanding, and Making Change, Readings on Equal Education, Volume 22, edited by
Edward St. John, 1–36. New York: AMS Press.

Tippeconnic, John W., and Susan C. Faircloth. 2008. "Socioeconomic and Cultural
Characteristics of High-Achieving and Low-Income American Indian and Alaska
Native College Students: The First Two Years of the Gates Millennium Scholars
Program." In *Resources, Assets, and Strengths among Success Diverse Students: Under-
standing the Contributions of the Gates Millennium Scholars Program, Readings on Equal
Education, Volume 23*, edited by William T. Trent and Edward St. John, 107–42.
New York: AMS Press.

Tripp, Luke S. 1987. *Black Student Activists: Transition to Middle Class Professionals.*
London: University Press of America.

Trow, Martin. 1974. *Problems in the Transition from Elite to Mass Higher Education.*
New York: McGraw-Hill.

Turner, Caroline S. V. 2012. "Mentoring Latinas/os in Higher Education: Intentional
Cultivation of Talent." In *Expanding Postsecondary Opportunity for Underrepresented
Students: Theory and Practice of Academic Capital Formation, Readings on Equal
Education, Volume 26*, edited by Rachelle Winkle-Wagner, Phillip J. Bowman, and
Edward P. St. John, 89–116. New York: AMS Press.

Uribe, Lina. 2013. "Access Policy and Social Justice in Higher Education: The Colom-
bian Case." In *Fairness in Access to Higher Education in a Global Perspective: Reconciling
Excellence, Efficiency, and Justice*, edited by Heintz-Dieter Meyer, Edward P. St. John,
Maria Chankseliani, and Lina Uribe, 111–28. Rotterdam, The Netherlands: Sense
Publications.

U.S. Department of Education. 1983. *A Nation at Risk.* Washington, DC: Author.

Walpole, Mary B., Nancy W. Burton, Kamau Kanyi, and Altamese Jackenthal. 2002.
Selecting Successful Graduate Students In-Depth Interviews with GRE Users. Princeton,
NJ: Educational Testing Services.

Washington, Booker T. 1901. *Up from Slavery.* New York: Dover Press.

Wildavsky, Ben, 2009. *The Great Brain Drain: How Global Universities Are Reshaping the
World.* Princeton, NJ: Princeton University Press

Winkle-Wagner, Rachelle, Phillip J. Bowman, and Edward P. St. John, eds. 2012.
*Expanding Postsecondary Opportunity for Underrepresented Students: Theory and Practice
of Academic Capital Formation, Readings on Equal Education, Volume 26.* New York:
AMS Press.

Wong, Kenneth K. 2012. "Federal Title I as a Reform Strategy in Urban Schools." In
*Reinterpreting Urban School Reform: Have Urban Schools Failed, or Has the Reform
Movement Failed Urban Schools?*, edited by Louis F. Mirón and Edward P. St. John,
55–76. Albany: State University of New York Press.

Woodson, Carter G. 1933. *The Mis-Education of the Negro.* New York: SoHo Books.

Yosso, Tara J., William A. Smith, Miguel Ceja, and Daniel G. Solórzano. 2009.
"Critical Race Theory, Racial Microaggressions, and Campus Racial Climate for
Latina/o Undergraduates." *Harvard Educational Review* 79 (4): 659–90.

Contributors

Jamal Abedi is a professor of educational measurement at the University of California, Davis. Dr. Abedi's research interests include studies in the areas of psychometrics and test and scale development. His recent works include studies on the validity of assessments, accommodations, and classification for English language learners (ELLs). Dr. Abedi serves on assessment advisory boards for a number of states and assessment consortia as an expert in testing ELLs. He is the recipient of the 2003 American Educational Research Association National Professional Service Award, the 2008 California Educational Research Association Lifetime Achievement Award, the 2013 National Association of Test Directors Outstanding Contribution to Educational Assessment Award, and the 2014 University of California, Davis, Distinguished Scholarly Public Service Award. He holds a master's degree in psychology and a PhD in psychometrics from Vanderbilt University.

Phillip J. Bowman is a professor of higher education and director of the Diversity Research and Policy Program at the University of Michigan. Dr. Bowman is also a faculty associate at the UM Institute for Social Research and National Poverty Center, and was founding director of the National Center for Institutional Diversity. As a theoretical and applied social psychologist, his scholarly work bridges strengths-based theory with policy-relevant research to address achievement gaps, health disparities, family poverty, and other complex policy challenges facing African Americans and other racial/ethnic populations. Other interests include innovative research methods training and mentoring for diverse postdoctoral, graduate, and undergraduate scholars. Dr. Bowman's research has been supported by several federal, state, and foundation sources, and he is an active national and international lecturer on pressing diversity, higher education, and public policy issues.

Kristin Cipollone is a lecturer in the Department of Sociology at Buffalo State College and associate director of the College Success Center at International

Prep, a public high school in Buffalo, NY. Her research focuses on social class, inequality, social reproduction, and the transition from high school to postsecondary education. She is the coauthor of the recently released book *Class Warfare: Class, Race, and College Admissions in Top-Tier Secondary Schools* (University of Chicago Press).

Shirley Brice Heath is a learning research scientist and professor of English, dramatic literature, and linguistics at Stanford University. She carries out her primary research in nonschool learning environments with youth living in underresourced neighborhoods in various parts of the world. With museums, theaters, and science studios, she establishes design experiments that involve cross-age community members in projects, performances, and art exhibitions. She is the author of more than two hundred articles and a dozen books.

Mark C. Hogrebe is an educational researcher in the Department of Education at Washington University in St. Louis. He compiles data and conducts research on K–12 attainment and other education indicators. Dr. Hogrebe received his PhD in educational psychology from the University of Georgia and has taught courses in applied statistics, research methods, tests and measurement, and GIS for educational researchers. His interests include research and evaluation methodologies in applied settings, education in STEM fields, and using GIS to give geospatial perspective to social science data.

Zeus Leonardo is a professor of education, affiliated faculty of the Critical Theory Designated Emphasis, and part of the Educational Disparities Group in the Haas Institute for a Fair and Inclusive Society at the University of California, Berkeley. He has produced several dozen articles and book chapters on critical educational theory, particularly around issues of race and class politics. His articles have appeared in the journals *Educational Researcher, Teachers College Record*, and *Discourse*. He is the author of *Race Frameworks: A Multidimensional Theory of Racism and Education* (Teachers College), *Education and Racism: A Primer on Issues and Dilemmas* (with W. Norton Grubb; Routledge), and *Race, Whiteness, and Education* (Routledge). He has received several recognitions, including the Early Career Award from AERA's Division G, the American Educational Studies Association's R. Freeman Butts Endowed Lecture in 2011, and the Barbara Powell Humanities Lecture at the University of Regina in 2014. He has delivered keynote lectures domestically and internationally, including in England, Sweden, Australia, and Canada.

Simon Marginson is a professor of international higher education at the Institute of Education in London and joint editor-in-chief of *Higher Education*. He is a member of Academia Europaea, a fellow of both the Academy of Social Sciences Australia and the Society for Research into Higher Education in the United Kingdom, and was the 2014 Clark Kerr Lecturer in Higher Education at the University of California. His recent scholarly works include jointly and sole-authored books and papers on higher education and globalization, international education and cross-border students, intercultural learning, university rankings, STEM policies and programs, universities and science in East Asia, and higher education in Vietnam.

Jeannie Oakes is Presidential Professor Emeritus in Educational Equity at the University of California, Los Angeles. Her scholarship examines the effect of social policies on the education of low-income students of color and investigates equity-minded reform. Among Oakes's numerous books, articles, and chapters, *Keeping Track: How Schools Structure Inequality* was named one of the twentieth century's "most influential" education books, and *Becoming Good American Schools: The Struggle for Civic Virtue in Education Reform* won the American Educational Research Association's (AERA) Outstanding Book Award. She is currently president-elect of AERA.

Fernando M. Reimers is the Ford Foundation Professor of the Practice of International Education at the Harvard Graduate School of Education. He directs the Global Education Innovation Initiative, a cross-national research project examining how various nations define and support the skills that youth need to thrive in the twenty-first century. He is also director of the International Education Policy Master's Program, which educates system-level leaders who are advancing educational inclusion globally. His research and teaching focus on the relationship between education policy, leadership, and educational innovation and improvement to support children and youth. He has also studied the effects of policies and programs that advance educational opportunities for disadvantaged groups. He is a member of the U.S. Commission for UNESCO and has worked with policymakers in the United States, Asia, Latin America, and the Middle East. He is also a fellow of the International Academy of Education and serves on the boards of several educational organizations.

C. Matthew Snipp is the Burnet C. and Mildred Finley Wohlford Professor of Humanities and Sciences in the Department of Sociology at Stanford University. He is also director of the Institute for Research in the Social Science's Secure Data Center and formerly directed Stanford's Center for the Comparative Study of Race and Ethnicity (CCSRE). Snipp has published three books and over seventy articles and book chapters on demography, economic development, poverty, and unemployment. His current research and writing deal with the methodology of racial measurement, changes in the social and economic well-being of American ethnic minorities, and American Indian education. Snipp holds a PhD in sociology from the University of Wisconsin–Madison. His tribal descent is Oklahoma Cherokee and Choctaw.

Edward P. St. John, the Algo D. Henderson Collegiate Professor of Higher Education at the University of Michigan's Center for the Study of Higher and Postsecondary Education, is concerned with education for a just society, an interest that stems from three decades of research on educational policy and practice. He is a fellow of the American Educational Research Association and has received awards for leadership and research from the Association for the Study of Higher Education. St. John is series editor for Globalization and Social Justice, a book series with AMS Press addressing comparative issues in higher education. He serves as series coeditor for both *Readings on Equal Education*, an annual volume focusing on initiatives seeking to reduce inequalities in K–12 and higher education, and *Core Issues in Higher Education*, topical texts for professors and graduate students with an interest in the field. St. John's current research projects focus on strengthening pathways between high schools and college for underrepresented students. His recent books include *Public Policy and Higher Education* (Routledge) and *Research, Actionable Knowledge and Social Change* (Stylus).

Amy E. Stich is a visiting assistant professor at Northern Illinois University. Her research focuses on social class and inequality of access, opportunity, and outcome in higher education. Her first book published in 2012 is titled *Access to Inequality: Reconsidering Class, Knowledge and Capital in Higher Education* (Lexington). Her current research explores the structure and social consequences of postsecondary tracking and will be included in a 2015 volume with Routledge, coedited by Stich, on the working class and higher education.

William F. Tate IV is the Edward Mallinckrodt Distinguished University Professor in Arts & Sciences, dean of the Graduate School of Arts & Sciences, and vice provost for Graduate Education at Washington University in St. Louis. He is an urbanist and social scientist interested in the application of epidemiological and geospatial models to explain the social determinants of science, technology, engineering, and mathematics attainment and related developmental outcomes. He is a past president and fellow of the American Educational Research Association (AERA) and also served as an editor of the Association's *American Educational Research Journal.*

William G. Tierney is a university professor and the Wilbur-Kieffer Professor of Higher Education at the Rossier School of Education and codirector of the Pullias Center for Higher Education at the University of Southern California (USC). A former president of the USC Academic Senate, he has chaired both the PhD program for the USC Rossier School of Education and the University Committee on Academic Review. Tierney is committed to informing policies and practices related to educational equity. He is involved in projects pertaining to the problems of remediation to ensure that high school students are college ready, interactive web-enhanced computer games for preparing low-income youth for college, and a project investigating how to improve strategic decision making in higher education. His recent publications include: *The Impact of Culture on Organizational Decision-Making* (Stylus), *Trust and the Public Good: Examining the Cultural Conditions of Academic Work* (Peter Lang), and *Understanding the Rise of For-Profit Colleges and Universities* (Johns Hopkins University). Tierney earned a master's degree from Harvard University and holds a PhD from Stanford University in administration and policy analysis. Tierney has been president of ASHE, president and vice president of AERA, and is a fellow of AERA.

Lois Weis is the State University of New York Distinguished Professor of Sociology of Education at the University at Buffalo, State University of New York. She has written extensively about the current predicament of White, African American, and Latino/a working-class and poor youth and young adults, and the complex role gender and race play in their lives in light of contemporary dynamics associated with the global knowledge economy, new patterns of emigration, and the movement of cultural and economic capital across national boundaries. She is the author and editor of numerous books and articles relating to race, class, gender, education, and the economy.

Weis's most recent volumes include *Class Warfare: Class, Race, and College Admissions in Top-Tier Secondary Schools* (with Kristin Cipollone and Heather Jenkins, University of Chicago) and *Education and Social Class: Global Perspectives* (edited with Nadine Dolby, Routledge). Her articles appear in a wide variety of journals, including *American Educational Research Journal, Review of Educational Research, Harvard Educational Review Teachers College Record, Signs, Anthropology and Education Quarterly,* and *British Journal of Sociology of Education,* among others. Weis is a winner of the Outstanding Book Award from the Gustavus Meyers Center for the Study of Bigotry and Human Rights in North America. She is a member of the National Academy of Education (NAEd), an Honorary Fellow of the American Educational Research Association (AERA), past president of the American Educational Studies Association, and past editor of *American Educational Research Journal.* Her research has been generously funded by the Spencer Foundation, Carnegie Foundation, NSF, and Association for Institutional Research (AIR).

Index

Page numbers in *italics* indicate figures and tables.